Public Administration and Legislatures

John A. Worthley

Public Administration and Legislatures

Examination and Exploration

Nelson-Hall
nh Chicago

030695

Library of Congress Cataloging in Publication Data
Worthley, John A
    Public administration and legislatures.

    Bibliography: p.
    Includes index.
    1. Legislative bodies.   2.   Public administration.
I. Title.
JF514.W67   350'.00372   75-23150
ISBN 0-88229-233-1

Manufactured in the United States of America

Contents

Preface

This is a study of a field with a past. It is also a sermon expounding conversion. It reviews and analyzes the thought and activity of the public administration field from the perspective of its treatment of legislatures.

The goals of the study are to raise the consciousness of public administrationists concerning the past drift of our field and to develop foundations enabling us to pursue new directions and make greater contributions. It is thus hoped that the work will be useful to students and practitioners, and to legislators as well as public administrationists.

A word on tenor: A consciousness-raising function can entail overstress, and indeed my intent was to marshall all the evidence possible in order to make the point not merely manifest but mired. The presentation of the record may thus seem as opportunistic as it is comprehensive; and without doubt my bent was to indulge in fulsomeness as much as necessary to clarify an absonance.

James J. Heaphey has for several years pioneered the application of public administration perspectives to legislatures. It was he who suggested to me that a study of this type be undertaken. Because I have benefited so much from his efforts, it is a pleasure to cite Heaphey as possessing a rare combination of uncommon qualities. He is an innovative thinker; he freely shares his ideas with others; and he translates his thoughts into pragmatic projects. This volume would not have been conceived but for those attributes. It would not have been born but for the support of the Comparative Development Studies Center of State University of New York at Albany, which Heaphey heads.

Once the effort began, I was fortunate to have around me incisive, interested, and generous people to pick me up when my vision and verve failed. It is a pleasure to praise them: Abdo Baaklini, Walter Balk, Ed Crane, Lester Hawkins, Lenore Heaphey, Richard Nunez, and Harry Smith, as well as the many public administrationists and legislative practitioners who responded to my requests for advice.

My family and other friends made little contribution to the intellectual substance of the study. Instead, they have given me, all my life, those transcendent things that in the last analysis are the source of any achievement: encouragement to persevere when the end is distant, confidence that the effort will be efficacious, and joy to delight in the frivolous, including a neat insight or a pleasing phrase. I say these things here because, unless they see it in print, they won't believe me when I tell them that this effort is fundamentally due to their inspiration.

Introduction

Public administration as a recognized field and an identified profession in the United States has developed so rapidly, and with such diverse characteristics, that a broad perspective of its activity—of what it is, where it has been, and where it is going—has often been elusive. As is typical of fledglings, the field has perhaps tended more to leap toward challenging and unexplored horizons and react to urgencies than to reflect on the past and deliberate the future.

Examinations of the development of American public administration are not unknown but, with few exceptions, are either cursory[1] or focused on a particular aspect or interpretation of the field.[2] There have been significant analyses of the influences and forces that affected the development of the field.[3] There have been studies characterizing the focus of different periods in the development of public administration.[4] And there have been efforts to identify trends.[5] But all these studies have, implicitly if not explicitly, considered the field primarily within the scope of the executive bureaucracy. There is no comprehensive examination of the activity and perspective of the public administration field regarding the entire spectrum of government—that is, the legislature and the judiciary as well as the executive. There are thus some striking gaps in our knowledge of where the field has been and why, and some uncertainty about where it is and where it should be going.

This study probes one of those gaps and attempts to provide a framework for studying one area in which public administration might develop. That gap is the involvement of the field in legislative administration, in the organization and management of legislatures. The topic is particularly piquant because of the apparent stress placed on government as a whole system by seminal thinkers and early luminaries of the field on the one hand, and the impression of actual, nonsystemic involvement with only a single branch on the other hand; for the field of public administration has an image of identifying almost solely with the executive branch of government. Indeed, the analyses cited earlier evidence such a perspective. The present study asks whether this appearance of near exclusive focus, of neglect of other parts of the government system, is a misconception or an accurate commentary. Did and does public administration intend to assist and improve the whole of government administrative operations, and did and does it instead, inadvertently or otherwise, focus on merely a single part of government to the neglect of the other parts of the system?

This volume seeks some answers with respect to the involvement of public administration with the legislative branch; another study might do the same concerning attention to the judiciary.⁶

BACKGROUND

The Watergate episode underscores the importance of self-examination and consciousness in the public administration field, for public administration is open to charges of negligence. In reflecting on Watergate, James L. Sundquist, one of the most distinguished public administrationists, found cause for taking the field to task: "What did the profession of public administration have to do with that [Watergate]? Quite a bit, I think. The profession has devoted 40 years to aggrandizing presidential power. It has consistently sought—and contributed in no small measure to the consequence—to strengthen the President at the expense of the other elements that make up the government system." ⁷

Sundquist's suggestion is all the more alarming when we realize that many of the most noted writers in the field have reminded us of the importance of other parts of the government system. In his pioneering and provocative essay, usually cited as the beginning of public administration study, Woodrow Wilson stressed a systemic perspective.⁸ In admonishing students of government to give attention to the administering aspect of government, he cautioned not to look merely to the mechanics of bureaus but to all aspects of accomplishing government activity: "Our duty is to supply the best possible life to a federal organization, to systems within systems ...." ⁹ Further, in what can be interpreted as an allusion to legislatures, he said: "Public criticism is altogether indispensable. Let administrative study find the best means for giving public criticism this control."¹⁰

Max Weber, who together with Wilson is frequently

cited as an intellectual framer of the discipline, explicitly wrote that legislative bodies are an indispensable counterweight to a bureaucratic government, that a functioning legislature is needed to secure a steady administration.[11] In 1934 William F. Willoughby, another pioneer in the field, wrote a book entitled *Principles of Legislative Organization and Administration*.[12] Previously he had written a work on administration in the executive branch and one on judicial administration. Clearly, Willoughby considered all branches of government to be within the purview of the field.

Leonard D. White, author of the first textbook on public administration and first editor-in-chief of the *Public Administration Review*, stated in 1945 that "the next major development in the improvement of administration depends on reform of American Legislatures."[13]

Voicing a similar refrain, Marshall Dimock, author of a more recent public administration textbook, affirmed: "A key concern of public administration is how to inject more administrative efficiency into popular assemblies."[14] And in 1948, while criticizing the dichotomy between politics and administration as unreal and illusory, Dwight Waldo commented that "administration can [now] even think about invading the field of politics, the field of policy determination."[15]

It is uncertain what perspective on legislatures prompted the remarks of these respected public administration figures, but for present purposes this is unimportant. Whether they were motivated by a concern to strengthen legislatures, or to make legislatures more responsive to bureaucratic urgings, the salient point is that they all seem to have considered legislative organization as pertinent to the field of public administration.

In view of these statements from within the field,

it is striking that the more evident recent efforts at the organizational improvement of legislatures stem from outside the field of public administration. The Citizens Conference on State Legislatures, a private group funded by foundations, has produced a comprehensive study of legislative institutions.[16] The National Conference of State Legislatures, an organization of legislators and staff, has conducted numerous studies and projects on legislative administration. But what has the field of public administration done in this area? Has public administration, as Sundquist intimates, concentrated on the executive and neglected the legislature? Specifically, what have schools of public administration taught regarding legislatures? What does public administration literature offer on legislative organization? What has the American Society for Public Administration done concerning legislative administration?

Recently, James J. Heaphey, in proposing that legislative improvement be seen as a subfield of public administration, suggested that neither the profession nor the academic discipline has shown concern for legislative administration.[17] This study assesses whether the evidence supports Heaphey and Sundquist's suggestion, or whether they were unfoundedly presumptive. Additionally, the study explores Heaphey's proposal in terms of either expanding what is already being done or beginning what has been neglected.

THE IMPORTANCE OF LEGISLATURES

Motivating this examination and exploration is a considered conviction that legislatures are important in government systems generally, and that they are relevant to a field, such as public administration, that aims at fostering the administration of government. Three bases can be suggested for supporting the contention that legislatures constitute a key component of government: (1) the importance of legislatures to the life of a democracy, (2) the importance of legislatures to efficient and effective government, regardless of political ideology, and (3) the importance of legislatures in the development process.

For Democracy. In democratic systems the legislature developed to ensure representative government—indeed, to distinguish democracy from autocracy. As one American political figure has put it: "If we don't have an effective check on the Executive, through the power of the legislature to consider, scrutinize, and reflect public opinion, then we do not have a [democratic] form of government, we have instead an elected monarch." [18] And, in the words of a noted public administrationist: "One of the hard earned truths that we tend to forget . . . is that representation is the essence of the democratic process. The health of popular government is measured by the efficiency of the popular assembly. . . ." [19]

Charles Adrian is more specific: "The adequacy of the law in meeting social needs . . . cannot be expected to be better than that of the legislative body, for it, in a democracy, is supposed to speak for the people." [20] And under the American democratic system in particular, the Citizens Conference on State Legislatures points out, the concept of checks and balances and of separation of powers requires that there be powers to share by separate, effective bodies. [21] A nearly inexhaustible supply of pithy quotes is available to support the argument. The point is clear: Legislatures are surely important in a democracy. Moreover, in a modern democracy, good management may be an essential ingredient of a viable legislature. As Dimock has said: "What must be guarded against—if popular government is to endure—is the weakening of legislative assemblies due to inefficiency to the point where they virtually abdicate in favor of an executive branch characterized by vitality and efficiency of administration. In a healthy government both branches are strong and both are equal." [22]

For Effective Government. A good case can be argued to the effect that a legislative body is important in the operation of any bureaucratic government, whether it be autocratic, democratic, or of whatever type. Indeed, Weber, in a frequently overlooked part of his writings, argued that without a legislature, government efficiency and effectiveness are jeopardized.[23] In developing his thesis that, within a rational-legal system of authority, bureaucratic organization is essential and the key instrument for effective government, he also observed that bureaucracy alone is not entirely sufficient. Weber regarded legislatures as an "indispensable counterweight" in a bureaucratic government system and, based on analysis of bureaucratic tendencies, as a required element for a steady administration. He viewed government as a *system* in which a bureaucracy was essential but dependent, for proper functioning, on the viability of each other part of the system. A healthy legislative component was thus crucial to the bureaucratic component and vice versa, if the system was to work.

It is this concept of government as a system that is the most compelling argument concerning the importance of legislatures for effective government. The American emphasis on separation of powers and on independent branches of government tends to blur this perspective and produce instead a legislative-executive rivalry in which the relationship is likely to be seen in terms of conflict instead of complementarity. The suggestion here is that such a view is a misconception. As Norton E. Long has remarked: "To meet our needs, we have developed a complex system in which the bureaucracy and the legislature perform complementary and interlocking functions." [24] The Citizens Conference on State Legislatures recognized this when it commented on its work: "We are rediscovering the legislatures not out of filial respect for our forefathers, or a fine regard for our political heritage, but for the most pragmatic of reasons: our . . . system simply will not work well without them, and it is the only system we have." [25] The point was perhaps best expressed by the American Enterprise Institute in its study of Congress: "Congress affects all other institutions and in turn is affected by them. Together they represent the different forces that are part of a general dynamic equilibrium in which no force acts independently of the others." [26]

United States foreign aid programs appear also to be recognizing the utility of a systemic perspective. After years of effort at improving the governing ability of developing countries through assistance to the bureaucracy had met with considerable frustration, the 1967 U.S. Foreign Assistance Act, Title IX, required that attention be given to other components of government systems, including political institutions such as legislatures. [27]

Evidence in support and defense of this perspective is elaborately presented in E. L. Normanton's study, *The Accountability and Audit of Governments*. [28] Normanton investigated the auditing practices of several countries, including the United States, Great Britain, France, Israel, India, and the USSR. He found that audit is essential for bureaucratic accountability and that such accountability is necessary for effective bureaucratic operations. [29] Further, Normanton found that executive audits were inadequate and that legislative audits alone seemed to provide the necessary accountability.[30] His data and analysis form a convincing argument that government must be viewed as a system and that a legislature is a crucial element for effectiveness of that system.

For Development. Although much literature on development has promoted a view that legislatures are ineffective in the process of modernization,[31] increasing empirical evidence supports the suggestion that legislatures might be quite significant in the realization of development goals.[32] Certainly the arguments of Weber and Normanton apply equally to governments concentrating on development efforts.

Based on research in a number of developing countries, the Comparative Development Studies Center of State University of New York at Albany has found that legislatures make significant systemic contributions: "Even the most resolutely executive government can find some of its most persistent structural problems eased through the efforts of an efficiently functioning legislature."[33] Specifically, the Albany Center's work indicates that legislatures serve distributive and adaptive functions of upward information feedback to the regime, of promotion of popular support for development policies, and of absorption of political shocks and societal strains that often accompany development. They are key vehicles for the legitimation of government. In one representative case, the center found a military regime favoring improvement of the legislature because of a conviction that stability is essential for economic growth and that only a functioning legislature can provide that stability.[34]

In Brazil, Lebanon, and Costa Rica indigenous participants in legislative reform have specifically justified legislative improvements on the ground of aiding development. A member of the staff of the Brazilian Congress, in speaking on advances in her country, has expressed the belief that "the legislative institution performs functions . . . such as tension release, socialization, influence, and interest articulation which are essential parts of the social development process of a nation." [35] A Brazilian senator has stated that legislative reform in Brazil is regarded as a means of "attending to the process of development." [36]

Enabling bills for legislative improvement in Lebanon expressed a similar justification.[37] And a Costa Rican legislator has stated that the aim of legislative improvements in his country was the "modernizing of our system and turning it into an efficient legislative chamber so it may help meet what modern needs demand of a developing country like Costa Rica." [38]

These statements by people directly involved in the development process are weighty indicators that legislatures are indeed an important element of national development.

Gerald Caiden's work on administrative reform supports this conclusion.[39] In addition to serving functions of information distribution and promotion of stability, legislatures can play other important roles in bringing about administrative reforms that, according to Caiden, are necessary for development.

In sum, a legislature is an important component of government. It is important for realization of democratic goals, important for overall government effectiveness, and important in development processes.

THE NEEDS OF LEGISLATURES

If, then, legislatures are evidently important on a broad scale, are they in good condition or do they need attention? Are there circumstances that could justify and give urgency to the concern of this study? Is it important to learn what the public administration field has done and could do for legislatures?

First, it should be stressed that though legislatures are properly described as political institutions, they are also administrative organizations. Legislatures have particular managerial and procedural requirements in addition to, or in support of, their political purposes. Willoughby said it well: "One does not at first view the legislative branch as one presenting problems of administration. Examination, however, does show that it does so to a scarcely less extent than do the other two branches. Here too are encountered practical problems of organization, personnel, and procedure, analogous to those presented by the other two branches, and the manner in which they are handled determines to an equal extent the efficiency with which the functions assigned to it are performed." [40] In simplistic terms, whereas executive administration can promote the efficient implementation and maintenance of programs and policies, legislative administration can promote the efficient and effective formulation and audit of programs and policies.

Returning to the system perspective, the administrative aspect of government might be conceptualized as a circle consisting of three arcs—formulation, implementation, and audit/evaluation. Administration is then portrayed as a function of more than just the executive. Emmette S. Redford has recognized this: "In the American polity, administration is not a function solely of the executive branch; it is a continuing function of both the legislative and executive branches, exercised through parallel hierarchies in the two branches interacting with each other." [41]

While executive agencies formulate and propose

many programs, so do legislatures, and increasingly so. Certainly the process of working hundreds of bill drafts through committees and eventually to the full chamber has some imposing administrative aspects. Implementation and maintenance of programs, which admittedly form the greatest part of the administrative system, are largely the task of executive agencies, but even here legislative committees more than occasionally exercise a voice that requires administrative capability. And the audit and evaluation of programs, though often undertaken by executive agencies, are more and more performed by legislatures and are requiring considerable administrative competence.

As a private group of businessmen and educators affirmed: "The quality of management throughout the federal establishment depends heavily upon Congress. The nature of basic legislation, appropriations, and legislative oversight can either impair an agency's effectiveness or make successful operation possible." [42]

The systemic perspective suggests that if we have an administratively excellent implementation component but a poor formulative or evaluative element, then the entire administrative system is and remains inefficient and ineffective no matter how superior our efforts to further improve the already adequate implementation sector. Again, Willoughby made the point: "The manner in which a legislature organizes itself and the rules of procedure that it adopts for the handling of its business determine in no small degree the character of the whole resulting governmental system." [43]

Thus, though the need of administrative competence may be quantitatively greater in the executive bureaucracy, it is not a monopoly of the executive. The political functions of the legislature also require administrative capabilities. Moreover, the administrative needs of legislatures are qualitatively as well as quantitatively increasing. Legislatures are faced with new complexities and demands, yet, in many cases, have only old, simplistic procedural mechanisms for handling them. As a U.S. senator has observed: "The technological advances of the past twenty years have put massive new demands on the legislative machinery. . . . We face the necessity of finding the organizational tools to reach well-considered judgments on major public-policy problems or of suffering the diminution of congressional influence." [44] And, in the words of one report: "As its burdens have grown in range and scope far beyond anything foreseen only a few years ago, a competent and vital Congress is more essential than ever before." [45] Watergate can be seen as a result of "diminution of congressional influence" and, at least partially, as due to a lack of adequate organizational tools within the legislature.

Concerning American state legislatures, Alexander Heard has described their institutional lag as follows: "In their formal qualities, they are largely nineteenth century organizations and they must address themselves to twentieth century problems." [46] Specifically, Heard has found the state legislatures poorly organized and technically ill-equipped, short on adequate staffing and professional help, and burdened with outmoded procedures and committee systems. [47]

According to the comprehensive study in 1971 by the Citizens Conference on State Legislatures, state legislatures are largely unable to tackle the complicated government tasks of the 1970s. [48] They are not capable of developing sound proposals, of analyzing and revising proposals of the executive, or of assessing programs and policies already underway. Certainly many of the needs of these legislatures require political attention, but undeniably many also require administrative assistance.

In pointing out that few institutions in the United States have been as consistently ignored and neglected as state legislatures, John Gardner of Common Cause has noted that in some cases very basic assistance will increase their effectiveness.[49] It will be instructive to discover whether Gardner's indictment of neglect is applicable to the public administration field.

Local legislatures, too, are becoming recognized as in need of assistance. An Urban Institute report affirmed: "In recent years the increased role of local governments and the increased expenditures made by local governments . . . have tremendously upgraded the importance of these councils [local legislatures]. No longer can we be casual in our country about the role these play and neglect them." [50]

In developing countries similar conditions have been found concerning legislatures—new complexities requiring administrative technical assistance. Abdo I. Baaklini's study of the Lebanese Parliament found legislators aware of a shift from mostly general, political, nontechnical issues to a present condition of complexity.[51] In fact, recent reforms in the Lebanese chamber were justified as follows: "It should be noticed that the legal, economic, and cultural matters in this age have reached a high degree of complexity beyond the ability of the individual to comprehend without the necessary help. . . ." [52] Work by the Comparative Development Studies Center in Costa Rica and Brazil also revealed that legislatures were seeking administrative assistance because of a perceived inability to handle the modern complexities of a developing country.[53]

A study of legislative staffing revealed another level of legislative need: As attention is directed toward legislatures and as improvements are attempted, little knowledge exists concerning the impact of proposed reforms. No one really knows whether administrative improvements will do what they intend, or what side effects they could have.[54] Assistance is thus needed in this predictive area as well.

Finally, returning to the system perspective, it should be noted in this context that the condition of the legislature affects the condition of the other parts of the system and of the system as a whole. E. Pendleton Herring was among the first to consider legislative inadequacies in this framework. He wrote: "It is in the legislature that the reconciliations essential to democratic government are expected to take place.... Our legislatures have demonstrated their inadequacy for synthesizing group conflict...." [55] Herring went on to observe that the reconciliation tasks not being performed by the legislature were being shouldered by the bureaucracy. In systemic terms, weakness in the legislature was being coped with by the system through an evolution of the bureaucracy. Herring argued that this was an altogether proper and healthy adjustment in the system, but his conclusion can be forcefully attacked by recalling Max Weber's warning that devolution of functions and power from political organs to the bureaucracy leads to inefficiency and ineffectiveness in government.

An alternative tenable conclusion is that, while needs of the legislature indeed generate needs in the system, many of those needs are best located and resolved at their source—that is, in the legislative component—and that many systemic needs are therefore better described in terms of improving legislative capacity than in terms of unnecessarily broadening the functions of the executive bureaucracy.[56]

A study by the Ohio Legislative Service Commission

has noted: "Because of the more adequate resources available to the executive branch, many functions which were traditionally performed by the legislature are now being performed by the executive." [57] The present study investigates whether the assistance of the public administration field was among those "resources" made available chiefly to the executive.

While it can be argued that Watergate reflects a need for more legislative power over the executive, considerable evidence suggests that the need is rather for better means of operating with the power that already exists. Particularly in the American context legislatures appear to have adequate political and constitutional power to maintain the system. What appears to be lacking is adequate organizational power—that is, sufficient skill to use properly the power that the system envisions, provides, and relies on.

The Relevance of Public Administration

If there then appears to be justification for concern about improving legislatures, is the public administration field a suitable source of assistance? Should there be any logical expectation that public administration would be involved in legislative administration? Would it be useful to know what the field has done for legislatures?

First, public administration appears to have characteristics and resources particularly suited to the needs of legislatures. The goal of the field, at the risk of oversimplification, can be said to be improvement of the efficiency and effectiveness of government. The goal of the profession, in the words of its national organization, is "to improve administration of the public service at all levels of government." [58] Certainly public administration, on the basis of its avowed goals, seems predisposed to involvement with legislative administration.

Additionally, the character of the field appears suited to a relationship with legislatures. Earlier, Herring was criticized for a misdirection of the valid observation that a reconciliation function is performed by the bureaucracy. In that context, Max Weber was cited in support of the argument that it is dangerous to shift a properly legislative function to the bureaucracy. In the present context, Herring's observation, properly directed, leads to a pertinent point. That is, as Herring clarified, there is a reconciliation or "political" function performed by administration. (The point, in contrast to Herring's, is that this function correctly exists in the bureaucracy without usurping it from the legislature. Both parts of the system have a particular and different kind of reconciliation function.) Whereas some pioneer theorists in the field viewed administration as a scientific function based on the value of efficiency,[59] Herring's analysis shows that administration is also a reconciliation activity,[60] that administration is in fact politicized, that a dichotomy between politics and administration is an illusion.

The point of this digression is merely to indicate that the character of the public administration field does not necessarily conflict with the political character of the legislative institution. There would be little immediate danger of public administration's losing an efficiency purity by forming a relationship with a primarily political organ; for, as Herring affirms, administration is already politicized. Moreover, it might be suggested that precisely because public administration does have a political perspective, it may be all the better suited for involvement with legislatures.[61]

Further, with regard to the capacity of the field for assistance in legislative administration, American public administration has significant and appropriate resources. The National Association of Schools of Public

Affairs and Administration lists over one hundred universities with schools, departments, or programs of public administration (see Appendix C). These universities are annually producing hundreds of people educated in public management.

The profession has a thriving national organization, the American Society for Public Administration, which has numerous local chapters spread across the country and a total membership of more than 14,000 consisting of administrators, teachers, researchers, consultants, students, and civic leaders. Additionally, the field publishes a distinguished journal, the *Public Administration Review*, with a readership of over 15,000. The field, further, has abundant academic, organizational, and journalistic resources around the world. This listing alone reveals a wealth of potential assistance for legislatures.[62]

These resources of the field represent expertise in a variety of administrative areas pertinent to modern legislatures. Public administration incorporates knowledge and experience in the problems of organization design, management science, and public finance, as well as in the arts of human relations, organizational behavior, and comparative analysis. Each of these, and particularly the combination of them, is relevant to the functioning of legislatures.

Second, there are some indications that, in its own pragmatic interest, public administration should be concerned with legislatures. Three of the most significant innovations in recent public administration have been program budgeting, productivity designs, and program evaluation. In each of these areas, legislative activity has been viewed as a crucial factor.

In lamenting the failure of planned-program-budgeting (PPB), Allen Schick has written that legislative inability to understand and cope with the new system was a fundamental cause of the demise of the innovation.[63] He has affirmed that "most important is a reformulation of legislative-executive relations that sees the two branches as interdependent."[64] Robert C. Casselman, in analyzing the failure of a similar budgetary system at the state level, echoed the judgment that incapacity in the legislature was a chief cause.[65] Walter Balk has identified legislative understanding and activity as a key element in productivity efforts.[66] And Urban Institute studies of program evaluation indicate that this approach will succeed depending on the capacity of the legislature to act with understanding of the concept.[67] These expressions support the previously argued point that effective government administration requires a systemic perspective.

In the theoretical realm, too, it can be argued that there would be benefits to the field from involvement in legislative administration. The intellectual core of the field has been based largely on a hierarchical-bureaucratic notion of organization that in recent years has been found inadequate for coping with modern vagaries and demands. The basic theoretical core of the likes of Weber, Frederick W. Taylor, and Luther Gulick[68] has been modified through efforts of Elton Mayo, Chris Argyris, Warren Bennis, and others.[69] But dilemmas and problems remain concerning how to incorporate nonhierarchical elements into organization, how to cope with realities of ambiguity. Legislatures in the United States incorporate varying elements of consensuality and nonhierarchy. The experience of legislatures might thus be a valuable resource in the efforts of public administrationists to improve organizations generally.

Finally, as previously indicated, the study will hopefully close a gap in the knowledge that public administration has of itself. It appears that the field has neglected legislatures, but it would be useful to know, if the impression is verified, the extent of the neglect and the causes of it. Then perhaps from that knowledge bridges can be built linking the resources and needs of the public administration field with needs and resources of the legislative component of government. Fritz Morstein-Marx's influential volume made the point that the principal error of reformers is that they approach Congress in isolation from the rest of government when "the basic issues involve the structure of the entire government rather than Congress alone." [70] Can that criticism be altered to say that the principal error of public administrationists is that we have approached administration as isolated in the executive?

The Focus of the Study

In brief, a relationship between legislatures and the field of public administration appears to be a "natural." Legislatures are important to the efficient and effective operation of government, and excellence in government is an avowed goal of public administration. Legislatures are in a turbulent condition and generally require administrative improvement. Public administration does possess resources relevant to the needs of legislatures. In the face of these observations, the present study asks three basic questions: (1) Has this "natural" relationship existed? (2) Is a relationship continuing or developing now? (3) If not, how could a relationship be developed?

In the process of examination and exploration, the literature of the field was thoroughly scrutinized, as were the programs of schools and organizations for public administration. The record is presented in the following chapters. Additionally, numerous public administration scholars, legislators, and legislative staff members (identified in Appendix A) were consulted for further information, insight, and opinion. Their views are incorporated throughout.

The study is limited to legislatures and the field of public administration in the United States, although foreign legislatures are occasionally cited for illustrative purposes. Just as the record of the public administration field relative to Parliament in Great Britain may differ from that of the field in the United States relative to American legislatures, so too the administrative characteristics and needs of legislatures in a presidential system may differ from those of parliaments in a parliamentary system.[71] Thus, this study applies only to American public administration and only to legislatures in the American presidential system of government, although it may be useful in other contexts as well.

Finally, the term "legislative administration" is used both broadly and narrowly depending on one's perspective. Broadly speaking, it includes the management or "housekeeping" of the legislative organization in itself, as well as its staffing concerns, committee procedures, and so forth. The term also includes the functional concerns of legislatures that relate to the overall administrative system of government, such as budgeting, oversight, and program evaluation. Chapter 8 elaborates on these points. Narrowly speaking, the term "legislative administration" is limited to those areas in which the particular skills of public administrationists are germane. It does not include, for example, analysis of voting patterns. As one scholar who was consulted put it: "I interpret 'legislative administration' narrowly. Otherwise it quickly converts into legislative behavior and politics, on which there are political scientists far better qualified than those specializing in public administration." [72] The point is well taken.

Within these parameters, Part 1 examines the record, and Part 2 explores the prospects of relationship.

NOTES FOR THE INTRODUCTION

1. Most textbooks in public administration include an introductory chapter that sketches the history of the field.

2. For example, Herbert Simon, *Administrative Behavior* (New York: Macmillan, 1947) and Anthony Downs, *Inside Bureaucracy* (Boston: Little, Brown, 1967).

3. Dwight Waldo, *The Administrative State* (New York: Ronald, 1948).

4. Keith Henderson, *The Emerging Synthesis in American Public Administration* (New York: Asia House, 1966) and Howard E. McCurdy, *Public Administration: A Bibliography* (Washington, D.C.: American University Press, 1973).

5. Dwight Waldo, "Developments in Public Administration," *Annals of the American Academy* 404 (November 1972): 217–245. Gerald E. Caiden, *The Dynamics of Public Administration* (New York: Holt, Rinehart, and Winston, 1971).

6. In recent years organizational and administrative problems within the judicial branch have become visible, and there appears to be increasing attention to this area by the public administration field. But, as with involvement by public administration with legislatures, there is a knowledge gap on the subject and a study would be useful.

7. James L. Sundquist, "Reflections on Watergate: Lessons for Public Administration," *Public Administration Review* 34, no. 5 (September–October 1974): 453.

8. Woodrow Wilson, "The Study of Administration," *Political Science Quarterly* 2, no. 2 (June 1887): 197–222.

9. Ibid., p. 221.

10. Ibid., p. 215.

11. Reinhard Bendix, *Max Weber: An Intellectual Portrait* (New York: Bantam, 1967), p. 448.

12. William F. Willoughby, *Principles of Legislative Organization and Administration* (Washington, D.C.: Brookings Institution, 1934).

13. *New Horizons in Public Administration* (Birmingham: University of Alabama Press, 1945), pp. 1–4.

14. Ibid., p. 24.

15. Waldo, *The Administrative State,* p. 121.

16. Citizens Conference on State Legislatures, *The Sometime Governments* (New York: Bantam, 1971).

17. James J. Heaphey, "Technical Assistance in the Administration of Legislatures," paper presented at the annual conference of the American Society for Public Administration, New York, March 1972.

18. Howard Samuels, "Legislative Reform: Up from Chaos," position paper issued in 1970.

19. Dimock in *New Horizons,* p. 24.

20. Charles Adrian, *Governing Our Fifty States* (New York: McGraw-Hill, 1967), p. 355.

21. Citizens Conference on State Legislatures, *The Sometime Governments,* p. 71.

22. Marshall E. Dimock and Gladys O. Dimock, *Public Administration* (New York: Holt, Rinehart, and Winston, 1953), p. 64.

23. Bendix, *Max Weber,* pp. 448–449.

24. Norton E. Long, "Bureaucracy and Constitutionalism," *American Political Science Review* 46 (September 1952): 812.

25. Citizens Conference on State Legislatures, *The Sometime Governments,* p. 15.

26. Alfred de Grazia, ed., *Congress: The First Branch of Government* (Washington, D.C.: American Enterprise Institute, 1966), p. 7.

27. Title IX, U.S. Foreign Assistance Act, 1967.

28. E. L. Normanton, *The Accountability and Audit of Governments* (Manchester, England: University Press, 1966).

29. He points out that the United Kingdom has a lower level of accountability than other countries and has a poorer record of administrative performance. Ibid., 'p. 410.

30. Ibid., passim.

31. For example, see Robert A. Packenham, "Legislatures and Political Development" in Allen Kornberg and Lloyd Musolf, eds., *Legislatures in Developmental Perspective* (Dur-

ham, N.C.: Duke University Press, 1970).

32. See Abdo I. Baaklini, *Legislatures and Political Development: Lebanon 1840–1970* (Durham, N.C.: Duke University Press, forthcoming) and John A. Worthley, "Legislatures and Political Development: The Congress of Micronesia," *Western Political Quarterly* 27, no. 4 (December 1973): 675–685.

33. Comparative Development Studies Center, "The Development of Legislatures" (Albany, N.Y., 1972), p. 3.

34. Comparative Development Studies Center, Internal Report, October 13, 1972.

35. Rosinethe M. Soares, "Legislative Reform in Brazil," paper presented at the annual meeting of the National Legislative Conference, Chicago, 1973, p. 5.

36. Statement of Senator Ney Braga, First Secretary of the Brazilian Senate, quoted in Eduardo Pereira, "Legislative Reform in Brazil," paper presented at the annual convention of the Society for International Development, San Jose, Costa Rica, February 1973, p. 9.

37. Abdo I. Baaklini, "Legislative Staffing Patterns in Developing Countries," paper presented at the annual convention of the American Society for Public Administration, Los Angeles, April 1973, p. 6.

38. Deputy Saborio Alvarado in minutes of the ordinary meetings of the Costa Rican National Assembly, no. 52, September 7, 1971.

39. Gerald Caiden, *Administrative Reform* (Chicago: Aldine, 1969), pp. 145–156.

40. Willoughby, *Principles of Legislative Organization and Administration*, p. v.

41. Emmette S. Redford, *Democracy in the Administrative State* (New York: Oxford, 1969), p. 81.

42. Committee for Economic Development, *Making Congress More Effective* (New York: CED, 1970), p. 10.

43. Willoughby, *Principles of Legislative Organization and Administration*, p. 305.

44. Senator A. S. Mike Monroney in Roger H. Davidson, et al., *Congress in Crisis* (New York: Hawthorn, 1969), pp. xi–xii.

45. Committee for Economic Development, *Making Congress More Effective*, p. 9.

46. Alexander Heard, ed., *State Legislatures in American Politics* (Englewood Cliffs, N.J.: Prentice-Hall, 1966), p. 3.

47. Ibid., pp. 1–2.

48. Citizens Conference on State Legislatures, *The Sometime Governments*, pp. 17, 39.

49. John Gardner in *The Sometime Governments*, pp. viii, ix.

50. The Urban Institute, *The Forgotten Men of Government: Local Legislators* (Washington, D.C., 1972), p. 1.

51. Baaklini, "Legislative Staffing Patterns in Developing Countries," pp. 6–7.

52. Ibid., p. 6.

53. Ibid. Also Eduardo Pereira, "Legislative Reform in Brazil."

54. Alan P. Balutis, "Professional Staffing in the New York State Legislature" (Ph.D. diss., State University of New York at Albany, 1973), p. 258.

55. E.. Pendleton Herring, *Public Administration and the Public Interest* (New York: McGraw-Hill, 1936).

56. Of course, there are differences between parliamentary and presidential systems of government and related differences in legislative roles and needs. And perhaps Herring's and Weber's observations are as applicable to political parties as to legislatures. Nevertheless, the point is that where legislatures exist they are important and they need improvement.

57. Ohio Legislative Service Commission, *Legislative Services, Facilities, and Procedures*, Staff Research Report No. 81, December 1966, p. 5.

58. This statement is printed on the back cover of every issue of *Public Administration Review*.

59. Most notably Frederick W. Taylor, *The Principles of Scientific Management* (New York: Harper and Row, 1911) and Luther Gulick and L. Urwick, eds., *Papers on the Science of Administration* (New York: Augustus Kelley, 1937).

60. See also Long, "Bureaucracy and Constitutionalism," pp. 808–818.

61. This opens a sensitive and crucial aspect of the study, and there is no intention of dismissing it here. It will be thoroughly analyzed in the investigation. See Chapters 8 and 9.

62. For example, Balutis, "Professional Staffing in the New York State Legislature," found that more New York State legislative staff were trained in public administration than in any other discipline (pp. 59–60).

63. Allen Schick, "A Death in the Bureaucracy: The Demise of Federal PPB," *Public Administration Review* 33, no. 2 (March–April 1973): 146–156.

64. Allen Schick, "Review and Evaluation Can Focus Light on Legislative Reform," in National Conference of State Legislative Leaders *Annual*, 1971, p. 51.

65. Robert C. Casselman, "Massachusetts Revisited: Chronology of a Failure," *Public Administration Review* 33, no. 2 (March–April 1973): 129–135.

66. Walter Balk, "Decision Constructs and the Politics of Productivity," paper presented at the annual convention of the New York Political Science Association, Albany, March 1973, p. 11.

67. Joseph S. Wholey et al., *Federal Evaluation Policy* (Washington, D.C.: Urban Institute, 1970).

68. Frederick W. Taylor, *Scientific Management* (New York: Harper, 1947); Luther Gulick and L. Urwick, eds., *Papers on the Science of Administration*.

69. Elton Mayo, *Human Problems of Industrial Civilization* (New York: Viking, 1933); Chris Argyris, *Personality and Organization* (New York: Harper, 1957); Warren Bennis, *Changing Organizations* (New York: McGraw-Hill, 1966).

70. Fritz Morstein-Marx, ed., *Elements of Public Administration* (Englewood Cliffs, N.J.: Prentice-Hall, 1959), p. 330.

71. For example, in a parliamentary system, the administration is directly responsible to the leadership of the House, unlike the presidential system. The effect of this and other differences on public administration would make an interesting study.

72. For reasons of confidentiality, the identity of legislators, staff, and scholars quoted from responses to questionnaires and interviews is not cited throughout. A list of all those consulted, however, is found in Appendix A. Questionnaires are reprinted in Appendix B.

PART 1

Examination of the Record

Introduction

Public administration is one of the more conglomerate academic and professional fields. It draws from various disciplines and careers and is more like a network than a nucleus. In academic circles it is sometimes independent, sometimes subsumed within the political science discipline, and sometimes joined with business administration studies. Indeed, the status of a distinct "academic discipline" has by no means been generally conferred on public administration.[1]

Professionally, there is a similar lack of focus. Civil servants normally identify with the profession of public administration, but so do many educators, lawyers, psychologists, writers, businessmen, diplomats, and others. Thus, demarcating precisely what describes public administration is a difficult and risky task. Even referring to it as a distinct discipline or profession can cause considerable disagreement.

Examination of the Record

What is generally recognized is that there exists a "field" of public administration that encompasses numerous individuals and activities and that is institutionalized in certain forms. There are schools that teach public administration. There is a literature generally recognized as comprising public administration works. There are organizations of public administration. It is these institutional manifestations that identify the field of public administration for purposes of this study. Further, the present investigation is limited to those institutionalized manifestations in the United States.

Thus, when examining and exploring in this volume the question of the involvement of public administration with legislatures, "public administration" *is* schools of public administration, texts and journals of public administration, and professional organizations specifically concerned with public administration; and the content and activity of these manifestations constitute the content and activity of the field. Admittedly, these parameters are not comprehensive; surely hundreds of individuals and activities that are excluded by these parameters can legitimately claim to be part of the field. But the enterprises identified are valid and representative and certainly constitute the fundamental core of the field.

It is, then, to these manifestations—the literature, the schools, and the professional organizations—that this study turns for answers to the question of what has been and could be the involvement of American public administration with legislatures. This section examines the record. What has public administration literature offered concerning legislatures? What have schools of public administration taught and researched regarding legislatures? What has the American Society for Public Administration done for legislatures? Was Heaphey right in

[4]

suggesting that the field has neglected legislatures?[2] Did Wendall G. Schaeffer represent the true record when he stated: "For many years those concerned with the improvement of administrative organization and practices in government have concentrated their attention primarily upon the executive branches of national, state, and local jurisdictions"?[3] Was Allen Schick accurate in affirming: "For more years than most of us can remember, the cause of government reform has been dominated by an executive perspective. As a consequence, there has been overwhelming neglect of the essential role of legislative bodies in the maintenance of responsive and effective government"?[4]

THE LITERATURE

Because it is difficult to define comprehensively what encompasses the field of public administration, it is problematical to identify what constitutes the literature of the field. The survey conducted for this examination of the record attempted to be as comprehensive and inclusive as possible, but undoubtedly some important works were overlooked. Nevertheless, the record revealed by the examination remains useful in that it can at least portray the essence of the major writings in the field with regard to legislatures. The purpose is to provide a thoroughly representative picture rather than a pandemic enumeration.

The literature is divided into three categories both for convenience of presentation and for insight on different types: textbooks, periodicals, and books most frequently utilized in the field. Dwight Waldo's contention that public administration as a "self-conscious" field[5] did not begin until the appearance of the textbooks of Leonard D. White and William F. Willoughby in the

1920s is accepted; the literature is examined only as far back as those pioneering twenties.

Charles Hyneman in 1950 found a dearth of literature on the subject of legislative control of administration.[6] Three years later Schaeffer wrote that the public administration literature clearly reflects a preoccupation with the management functions of the executive.[7] And Seymour Scher, in 1963, observed that little had been written about the management of legislatures.[8] The present examination confirms, broadens, and updates these judgments: The public administration literature, with very few exceptions, has consistently and thoroughly neglected legislatures.

THE INSTITUTIONS

The content of the literature might be expected to be a major determinant of the substance of education programs and perhaps, to a lesser extent, of the activity of professional organizations. It might be expected, for example, that if the literature has neglected legislatures, then certainly the schools have not given them much attention. Nevertheless, the record of schools and professional organizations for public administration was studied in terms of involvement with legislatures. Specifically, the curricula and research programs of public administration schools and the activities of the American Society for Public Administration were examined. Not surprisingly, schools and organizations were also found to have neglected legislatures.

NOTES FOR INTRODUCTION TO PART 1

1. See, for example, John C. Honey, "Research in Public Administration," *Public Administration Review* 17, no. 4 (autumn 1957): 239; Dwight Waldo, "Scope of the Theory of Public Administration" in James Charlesworth, ed., *Theory and Practice of Public Administration* (Philadelphia: American Academy, 1968), pp. 1–26; and Vincent Ostrom, *The Intellectual Crisis in American Public Administration* (Birmingham: University of Alabama Press, 1973).

2. James J. Heaphey, "Technical Assistance in the Administration of Legislatures," paper presented at the annual conference of the American Society for Public Administration, New York, March 1972.

3. Wendall G. Schaeffer, "Management in the Judiciary," *Public Administration Review* 13, no. 2 (spring 1953): 89.

4. Allen Schick, "Review and Evaluation Can Focus Light on Legislative Reform," National Conference of State Legislative Leaders *Annual*, 1971.

5. Dwight Waldo, *The Administrative State* (New York: Ronald, 1948), p. 27, footnote 12.

6. Charles Hyneman, *Bureaucracy in a Democracy* (New York: Harper, 1950), p. 73.

7. Schaeffer, "Management in the Judiciary," p. 89.

8. Seymour Scher, "Conditions for Legislative Control," *Journal of Politics* 25, no. 3 (August 1963): 527.

1

Literature: Textbooks

Every available textbook (and major volume of readings) in public administration was examined and analyzed in terms of attention to legislatures. Table 1 lists those included in the study. The major finding is that legislatures are routinely neglected or dismissed. Analysis of the texts yields the following observations.

EXECUTIVE BRANCH ORIENTATION

All textbooks are decidedly oriented toward the executive branch. Most of them specifically identify public administration exclusively with the executive; others merely assume or imply this bent. As Bertram M. Gross expounded: "The major orientation in public administration literature has been toward 'executive agencies.' Judicial and legislative bodies are customarily regarded as being outside the place of public administration and relevant to it only by their interrelations with executive agencies."[1] In many texts legislatures are mentioned chiefly in terms of how to make that branch more compliant with executive visions. Not a single text devotes even one chapter to the administration of legislatures.

TABLE 1
TEXTBOOKS EXAMINED

Year of Publication	Author(s)	Title
1926	White	*Introduction to the Study of Public Administration*
1927	Willoughby	*Principles of Public Administration*
1935	Pfiffner	*Public Administration*
1937	Walker	*Public Administration in the United States*
1939	White	*Introduction to the Study of Public Administration*, 2nd ed.
1946	Pfiffner and Presthus	*Public Administration*, 2nd ed.
1946	Morstein-Marx	*Elements of Public Administration*
1948	White	*Introduction to the Study of Public Administration*, 3rd ed.
1950	Graves	*Public Administration in a Democratic Society*
1950	Simon, Smithburg, and Thompson	*Public Administration*
1952	Stein	*Public Administration and Policy Development*
1952	Lepawsky	*Administration*
1953	Dimock and Dimock	*Public Administration*
1953	Pfiffner and Presthus	*Public Administration*, 3rd ed.
1954	Millett	*Management in the Public Service*
1955	Waldo	*The Study of Public Administration*
1955	White	*Introduction to the Study of Public Administration*, 4th ed.

TABLE 1 (Continued)

Year of Publication	Author(s)	Title
1958	Dimock and Dimock	*Public Administration*, 2nd ed.
1959	Morstein-Marx	*Elements of Public Administration*, 2nd ed.
1960	Pfiffner and Presthus	*Public Administration*, 4th ed.
1963	Corson and Harris	*Public Administration in Modern Society*
1964	Dimock and Dimock	*Public Administration*, 3rd ed.
1965	Nigro	*Modern Public Administration*
1966	Golembiewski	*Public Administration*
1967	Pfiffner and Presthus	*Public Administration*, 5th ed.
1968	Altshuler	*The Politics of the Federal Bureaucracy*
1968	Buechner	*Public Administration*
1969	Dimock and Dimock	*Public Administration*, 4th ed.
1969	Reagan	*The Administration of Public Policy*
1970	Sharkansky	*Public Administration*
1970	Nigro	*Modern Public Administration*, 2nd ed.
1971	Caiden	*The Dynamics of Public Administration*
1972	Bartholomew	*Public Administration*
1972	Golembiewski	*Public Administration*, 2nd ed.
1972	Sharkansky	*Public Administration*, 2nd ed.

Executive Focus

The first text book in the field, that of Leonard White, set this direction.[2] In describing the scope and nature of public administration, White made no reference to legislative bodies. He spoke of structure and organization, of fiscal management and personnel administration, all with hardly any references to legislatures. Subsequent texts followed the lead. W. Brooke Graves began his treatise with the parochial phrase, "The administrative organization of the executive branch." [3] Marshal E. Dimock and Gladys O. Dimock's first edition made the same identification.[4] John D. Millett dealt with the "common problems of management . . . which spread from one agency to another." [5]

Fritz Morstein-Marx's widely used book, in addition to a consistent focus on executive administration, included an entire chapter on "The Chief Executive."[6] There were none on the legislature or the judiciary. White's fourth edition similarly had a chapter entitled "The Chief Executive" and gave no equal time to the other branches of government.[7] Consistently in the texts reviewed, in fact even in chapters such as "Reorganization," which might in most discussions evoke some thoughts on Congress, the focus is still exclusively on the executive branch.[8]

Recent volumes that aim at providing an overview of the field reflect the historical focus on the executive. Golembiewski's highly successful book of readings has the stated intention of providing "depth and breadth for the central subjects treated by the texts." [9] Of fifty-three selections included, one relates to "Administration of Justice," none addresses legislative administration. Indeed, one selection suggests that legislative organizational matters are unimportant: "Congressional-executive patterns of interaction underscore the importance of strategic decision making procedures in the *executive* branch." [10] Harold Stein's casebook testified to the executive focus of the field. After defining the field as the activities of the executive branch, he specifically limited the subject matter of his volume to that area.[11] Unquestionably, as Stein recognized: "In considerable part the study of Public Administration has tended to be both one-sided and fragmentary." [12]

Executive-Legislative Relations

The discussion above is not intended to suggest that legislatures have hardly been mentioned at all in public administration textbooks; for many do include a chapter on the de facto interaction of the executive with the legislature, chiefly in terms of legislative oversight or control of administrative agencies. Still, the perspective is always that of the executive and how it operates within the relationship, rather than vice versa.

Thus John M. Pfiffner has a chapter on "External Controls" in which he speaks of legislative controls and investigations.[13] Dimock and Dimock include a section on "Legislative Relationships." [14] And Golembiewski indexes his three selections on legislatures under the heading, "legislative-administrative relations." [15]

The perspective on this relationship that the authors reflect frequently betrays an unabashed executive bias. Millett places his discussion of legislative relations in a chapter on "Public Relations." [16] Herbert A. Simon, D. W. Smithburg, and V. A. Thompson include an extended section on "Techniques for Securing Legislative Support" in their chapter entitled "The Struggle for Existence." [17]

The Morstein-Marx book precisely states the treatment given legislatures in the texts: "With proposals for the purely internal reorganization of the legislative process, we have no concern. However, the various suggestions for alteration of the relationships between the legislative and executive branches are of interest." [18]

Legislative Compliancy

Several textbooks that do mention legislatures manifest a disposition to treat the legislature not in terms of effectiveness or improvement but in terms of making it more responsive to executive operations. Graves speaks of legislative "interference" with and "obstacles" in the way of executive agencies. He suggests that if only the legislature would follow the advice of the executive, government would be better.[19] And in the Morstein-Marx volume it is suggested that the legislature can best carry out its functions by heeding executive leadership: "The great advances in attaining administrative responsibility to the legislative branch have been made possible by strengthening the chief executive. . . . The chief executive is most effective in contributing to the democratic workings of administration if he combines with his machinery of coordination a policy or a philosophy that will inspire the support of . . . the legislative body." [20]

LEGISLATIVE EXCLUSION

Most texts treat legislatures as a subject external to public administration. Some specifically exclude legislatures from the purview of the field. Most address legislatures merely in terms of an environmental factor with which the executive must deal.

Simon, Smithburg, and Thompson were very clear: "By public administration is meant, in common usage, the activities of the executive branches. . . . Specifically excluded are judicial and legislative agencies." [21] Even Dimock and Dimock, who in their editions were more attentive to legislatures than most writers, listed the components of the field and placed legislatures in the category of "External Controls." [22]

The Morstein-Marx book, which consists of articles by fourteen of the then leading scholars in the field, contains many references to the legislature but consistently as part of the environment that affects "day-by-day administration" through its power of the purse, through statutes, and through appointment confirmations.[23] Again, it is Simon et al. who, in self-consciously clarifying their approach, characterize the assumption that is unstated in other texts: "Legislatures and courts are, however, a part of the environment within which public administration must be carried on. The activities, attitudes, and methods of these agencies will often powerfully influence the process of administration. . . . And so, while the operations of legislatures and courts will not be examined here directly or systematically, their effect upon public administration will have to be considered as the discussion progresses."[24]

ANTILEGISLATURE TONE

An antilegislature tone is evident. Frequently, legislatures are referred to as obstructionistic, and texts manifest a perspective of competition between the legislature and the executive—a rivalry syndrome. These books reflect a nonsymbiotic, nonsystemic vision of government and administration.

White's pathfinding text incorporated a grain of antipathy toward legislatures. Undoubtedly and understandably bothered by the complicating effects of legislative expressions of power over administration, White echoed a refrain that "legislatures have done far more harm than good by too detailed control of the organization of the administration."[25] He criticized Willoughby for exaggerating the role of the legislature.[26] And in his fourth edition he wrote: "The influence of Congress is thrown both for unity and for dispersion—the former sporadically, the latter more or less continuously. John Adams declared that the legislative branch was inevitably the enemy and rival of the executive."[27] Morstein-Marx's text concurs: "Congress, in its relations with the executive branch, tends to atomize rather than integrate the administrative structure and public policy."[28]

More recently, Golembiewski's volume presents, without rejoinder, the following statement of James Burnham: "In their endogamous conversations, at their parties, the upper strata of the bureaucracy do not hide their feeling that Congress is a roadblock that they must somehow bypass if the country is to progress, a kind of idiot boy who must be pushed, teased, and cozened." [29] Perhaps it is noteworthy that many of the authors of public administration textbooks were at various times "upper strata" bureaucrats.

Closely connected with the antilegislature tone, but worthy of separate observation, is the competitive rather than complementary perspective evinced in many texts. In addition to White's tacit endorsement of John Adams's opinion, numerous other indications appear in the texts. Morstein-Marx went as far as asserting that "our constitutional system assumes the desirability of ... rivalry between chief executive and legislature." [30] Pfiffner and Robert Presthus take the legislature to task for what they call antipathy toward the executive branch: "Perhaps the most descriptive trait of the legislative mind is its intuitive mistrust of the bureaucrats and experts." [31] V. O. Key, in an article in the Morstein-Marx volume, stresses that "in essence," legislatures and the executive "tend to be rivals" for the control of administration.[32] And, still in his final edition, White saw a "never-ending competition for power between legislative and executive branches." [33] There is, in no text, any serious reflection or consideration of a symbiotic relationship between the legislature and the executive. The adversary image appears dominant.

LIP SERVICE TO LEGISLATIVE IMPORTANCE

Many texts give lip service to the importance and needs of legislatures. The significance of a functioning legislature is widely cited, and internal needs of legislatures are frequently recognized. But there is seldom any attention to the implications of the expressed desire for an effective legislature, seldom any analysis of internal legislative requirements, seldom any discussion of the application of public administration skills to assisting in ensuring a functioning legislature.

Graves characterizes this lip service phenomenon when he insightfully identifies basic administrative problems of legislatures as being information gathering, committee procedures, and budget review; and then gives only superficial discussion to solving these problems, even though public administration possesses considerable expertise in these areas.[34] Corson and Harris are even more abrupt: "It is high time Congress improved its budgetary review process."[35] This pronouncement is followed by neither specification of what is administratively wrong nor any analysis of how the situation might be improved. Ira Sharkansky's 1970 volume is a bit more specific: "The major problems that the legislature faces are the fragmentation of its energies and a lack of information about policy issues."[36] But then he, too, makes no suggestion that public administration could help in these areas.

Earlier, Harvey Walker had been rather more blase and considerably less perceptive of the level of administrative requirements of legislatures: "Of course they [legislatures] all have administrative problems of their own—appointing clerks and stenographers, buying, printing, etc."[37] At about the same time, Pfiffner recognized serious administrative needs of legislatures; he spoke of essential needs of legislative committees and opined that a legislature should have its own staff of administrative personnel.[38] But at no time does he suggest that the field

[17]

of public administration should service those needs. A little later, Don Price, writing in the Morstein-Marx text, was more specific in recognizing legislative needs but equally silent on whether or how public administration should act on those needs: "... the legislature needs staff assistance in the review and interpretation of facts, the appraising of programs, the drafting of bills, and other technical work. It must have committee secretariats, legislative reference aids, and parliamentary counsel to fit itself for its tasks of general surveillance, just as the chief executive needs the tools of management that are appropriate to executive control." [39] The lack of any analysis of these needs leaves the impression that they are to be attended to by some other, unnamed field.

The lip service characteristic of texts generally can be epitomized by reference to the same Morstein-Marx edition. Early in that tome it is said that "it is a matter of highest concern whether or not the legislative marching orders for administrative officials are framed effectively and in full recognition of the public interest." [40] Near the end of the work George Graham writes: "Many things can be done to improve and expedite the work of Congress and of state legislatures." [41] At the front of the book writers affirm the importance of legislatures. At the back they express the need for improvement. And in between they mention specific administrative needs. But nowhere are legislative needs analyzed. Nowhere is there testimony that the field of public administration, recognizing the importance of legislatures and the need for improvement, could or should assist, or has assisted.

INCONSISTENCY IN TREATMENT

The textbooks are frequently incongruous in their treatment of the subject of legislatures. Many texts state the importance of legislatures on one page, then deride or dismiss legislatures in a following section. A large number of texts make statements that logically include and necessitate discussion of legislatures, but then proceed to make no mention of legislatures at all or to exclude them specifically without explanation. Similarly, several textbook authors make apparently prolegislature statements, but then, by omission of serious discussion or by later disparaging remarks, present a book that is fundamentally unresponsive if not antipathetic to legislative administration.

The field's first text dismissed legislatures immediately after noting their constitutional importance: "While in the intent of the Constitution the legislative branch is primary, in the actual operation of our government institutions leadership has often been, and now is usually found in the chief executive and his official subordinates." [42] In making no further comment, White appears to place the Constitution itself in support of the importance of legislatures and then to dismiss this design as inoperable and insignificant.

Similarly, Simon et al. affirmed that "we can not talk of making administration more responsible without considering the organization of political interests, the mechanisms that define and record the public will, the procedures of legislative bodies...." [43] Yet they had previously excluded legislative administration from the text and immediately discussed "Strengthening the Chief Executive" instead.

Examples of incongruous omission of mention of legislatures are more numerous. Pfiffner and Presthus preface their volume with the observation that public administration, and their text, are focused on the shaping and carrying out of public policy.[44] Surely legislatures are involved in the *shaping* of public policy, yet the authors omit any serious concern with Congress or state legislatures. Golembiewski's stated guidelines in choosing selections for his volume were to "illuminate the most diverse possible classes of administrative phenomena" and to raise "the widest possible range of philosophical and empirical issues." [45] Yet, though he believes that all organizations can be viewed usefully in terms of general managerial process,[46] legislative administration is not treated.

Certainly legislative administration is a key ingredient of public control of government, but Alan A. Altshuler avoids discussing it despite his apparent intentions: "The plain fact is that only the crudest beginnings have yet been made toward building a democratic theory that grapples seriously with the realities of the bureaucratic state—one which explains how 'adequate' public control ought to be redefined in the light of modern conditions, and how the public can be rendered capable of exercising such control ... this reader rests ultimately on my concern with these cardinal issues." [47] Finally, Sharkansky's book asserts that its emphasis is on "the contribution of public administration to public policy making." [48] He leaves legislatures out of the discussion by a definitional exclusion. The logic of such an omission is not presented.

LACK OF REASONED ARGUMENT

Typically, legislatures are blithely excluded from the realm of discussion without reasoned argument. In the several texts that speak to the question of whether or not legislatures are a concern of the public administration field, legislatures are normally judged to be outside the field's purview for vague or admittedly unknown rea-

sons. The dismissal is characteristically casual and un-
defended, even in contexts where there is a strong logical
implication for discussion of legislatures.

The Morstein-Marx volume maintains that public
administration may "even" be taken to include the formal
processes and operations through which the legislature
functions, "for there is much adroit management in the
conduct of legislative business." But the book then excludes legislatures from the field simply for reason of
"established usage." [49] Simon et al., also citing "common usage," restrict public administration to the executive branch and concede that the restriction is "arbitrary." Moreover, they acknowledge that legislatures
have special administrative needs that do require extensive treatment.[50]

Stein limits his work to the executive branch for the
admitted reason of mere "convenience." [51] Sharkansky
gives no authority whatsoever for his exclusionary con-
ception of the field. And even Dimock and Dimock, who
in other editions of their text include legislatures, say
cryptically in the third edition that matters of legislative
improvement "go beyond the legitimate scope of public
administration." [52]

Even in contexts that appear logically to warrant attention to legislatures, unsupported exclusion is common.
White recognizes that "legislative bodies now are generally unable to initiate within themselves solutions for the
extraordinarily complex and often technical problems
with which they are faced." [53] Then he says not a word
about how they might remedy this. The Morstein-Marx
book argues that the principal error made by congressional reformers is that they isolate Congress instead of
including the entire government.[54] Was Morstein-Marx

[21]

oblivious that the same criticism can be leveled against his text for limiting administration to only the executive part of government?

Graves is directly incongruous in this regard. His preface stresses his "recognition of the basic concept of administration as concerned with the transaction of *all* of the public business, whether legislative, executive, or judicial," [55] but the chapters that follow have nary a word on legislative administration. Corson and Harris declare that "public administration relates to the activities carried on by government" [56] but omit legislative activities. Michael D. Reagan ambitiously sets out to discuss aspects of administration which have grown rapidly in the real world, "but which have not yet received proportionate space in textbooks." [57] Legislatures still have not. And Gerald Caiden observes that the field has neglected the search for alternatives to bureaucratization, but he does not suggest a look at the largely nonbureaucratized legislatures.[58]

SOME INCLUSION OF LEGISLATURES

A few textbooks do clearly include legislative administration within the field. These appear to take legislatures seriously and devote some pages to a discussion of the subject. But even these texts generally fail to incorporate legislatures into general administration discussions throughout the chapters.

Willoughby was the first to make the point: "[Public administration] denotes the work involved in the actual conduct of governmental affairs, regardless of the particular branch of government concerned. It is thus quite proper to speak of the administration of the legislative branch of government...." [59] He then wrote a complete textbook on legislative administration, the first and last of its kind.[60] The first "reader" in the field, written by Albert Lepawsky, included a selection on congressional organization, thus placing legislative administration in the field, though giving it only brief attention. Significantly, Lepawsky made an observation that public administration has yet to heed properly: "If one is willing to cross the rigid line which separates the legislative and executive branches of American government, one can observe significant lessons for the science of organization in the structure of the American legislative system." [61]

Marshall Dimock, a student of Willoughby at Johns Hopkins University and once a member of the Vermont legislature, has given strong support in his texts to the notion of including legislative administration in the field: "If the term 'administration' is understood to apply to all kinds of situations where a definite program is to be carried out, then it should be clear that public administration covers all three branches of government, not just the executive branch alone. Congress ... is a large institution that must be managed by its own system of internal administration, by public servants." [62] And later in the same edition he makes the timely assertion that: "What must be guarded against—if popular government is to endure—is the weakening of legislative assemblies ... to the point where they virtually abdicate in favor of an executive branch characterized by vitality and efficiency of administration. In a healthy government both branches are strong and both are equal." [63] In subsequent editions he continues to delineate administrative needs of legislatures.[64]

Just as strong a case for attention to legislative administration is found in Felix Nigro's text editions. He forthrightly contends that "in the American scheme of things, the legislature is supposed to have a vital role in public administration." Moreover, "if it is to do its job well, the legislature must be concerned with constantly improving its own internal organization and procedures." [65] In his second edition Nigro makes the not unimportant remark that a chief reason why public administration should not exclude legislatures from its concern is that legislatures view themselves as heavily involved in administrative matters.[66]

Nevertheless, with the exception of Willoughby, none of these authors really incorporates legislatures into the field. While recognizing one benefit public administration could gain from legislatures, Lepawsky makes no comment on what assistance the field could provide; and there is no reference to legislative application in the numerous other discussions throughout his lengthy volume.

Similarly, both the Dimocks and Nigro, in spite of their insistent words for including legislatures within the purview of public administration, make little reference to legislatures in their subsequent chapters on various managerial processes. Moreover, their books do not even footnote the Willoughby book on legislative administration. In brief, though they do give attention to the legislature, they give it more a "brush job" than a helpful study.

HISTORICAL TRENDS

A review of the textbooks from a historical perspective confirms the conclusion of consistency in the neglect of legislatures. Indeed the few inclusive efforts stand out as anomalies. The first two textbooks went in different directions. White's book (1926) set the tone. It excluded legislatures in its definition of the field, neglected them throughout, and gave brief lip service to legislatures in a closing section on control of administration. White clearly focused the field on the executive. Willoughby

(1927) just as clearly placed legislative administration within public administration. Faced with these alternatives, the field, for a number of reasons analyzed in Chapter 6, overwhelmingly accepted White: Willoughby's book sold a single printing; White's went through four editions and eight printings of the fourth edition and is still a widely used text. White's book is listed among the most frequently cited books in the field of public administration in a recent study by Howard E. McCurdy.[67] Willoughby's book is not included in the list.

Moreover, White's four editions are consistent in their neglect of legislatures, though statements on the importance of legislative bodies increase with each edition. The 1939 volume mentions the importance of legislative bill drafting, auditing, and committee work.[68] By 1955 he was asserting that legislative improvement was crucial to the field.[69] But White never suggested that public administration could assist legislatures.

Pfiffner (1935) has gone through five editions, each one as executive-focused as the last; and it, too, is listed by McCurdy among the most frequently cited books in the field. The first edition mentioned legislatures chiefly in terms of legislative control being "a by-product of the American distrust of executive power" [70] and spoke with a decidedly antilegislature tone. By the fifth edition (1967), coauthored with Presthus, Pfiffner does briefly discuss informational and managerial needs of the legislature,[71] but not in terms of assistance from public administration.

The fourth major text, Harvey Walker's (1937), broke ground in that it had a chapter on judicial administration, thus extending the purview of the field beyond just the executive.[72] The neglect of legislative administration in this volume is thus all the more striking.

[25]

The Morstein-Marx volume appeared just after World War II, during which most of the contributors to this text had worked in the executive bureaucracy. Predictably, the work is heavily devoted to the executive, and there is a noticeable theme of executive-legislative rivalry.[73]

By 1950 the entrenched pervasiveness of the executive focus was evident when an employee of the Library of Congress wrote a text excluding the legislature from public administration.[74] Even Graves's traditional section on control of the bureaucracy stressed "legislative interference with administration." [75]

Simon, Smithburg, and Thompson's effort, the next text to appear (1950), went through six printings and has been described as "one of the most ambitious and complete textbooks in public administration." [76] It makes the rare concession that legislatures do have administrative needs, but then, true to custom, excludes legislative administration from the study. Despite their recognition of the fact of legislative administration, and their compilation of an extensive bibliography, Simon et al. neither footnote nor in any way mention Willoughby's unique work on legislative administration.

Harold Stein (1952) followed suit, but by this time there appeared to be a desire to state that legislative administration is excluded without prejudice. Stein calls his exclusion of legislatures "arbitrary," "unimportant," "convenient," and "not intended to prove anything." [77]

Lepawsky's reader (1952) was the first real breakthrough since Willoughby. Though his treatment is extremely brief, he does include "Congressional Organization" as a *substantive* part of the volume. Of course, Lepawsky was careful to title his tome "Administration" and not *"Public* Administration." Marshall and Gladys Dimock (1953) opened the door that Lepawsky had left ajar, forcefully including legislative administration in the field, and generally treating legislatures favorably. Significantly, this text has gone through four editions and is also listed by McCurdy among the most widely cited books in the field. It remains the single most salient, though by no means adequate, demonstration (since 1927) of a perspective encompassing legislative administration. One irregularity in the work is that Dimock fails to footnote Willoughby's book on legislative administration while he does cite his mentor's *Judicial Administration.*

Millett corrected Dimock's diversion by producing a text the following year totally ignoring legislatures and even relegating legislative-executive relations to a section on "public relations." Waldo (1955) set out to provide an "introduction to the textbooks." [78] In omitting legislative administration from his discussion, he properly portrayed the content of the past texts. Corson and Harris's text (1963), in following tradition, is a bit surprising only in that the latter author had previously been, and later was, one of the more productive observers of Congress.[79]

The second, and thus far last, offshoot to legislative administration was Felix Nigro's *Modern Public Administration* (1965). His qualified title for the text (*"Modern"*) is perhaps particularly appropriate in indicating that his approach, at least concerning legislatures, differs from "traditional" public administration. Early in the narrative Nigro speaks of the internal administrative needs of legislatures; he does, however, end the discussion in short order and, like Dimock and Dimock, without citing Willoughby's book. His 1970 edition continues the strong, but brief, recognition of legislative administration.

All the remaining recent textbooks follow the traditional line. Golembiewski's second edition (1972) appears even more remotely concerned with legislatures than his first (1966). Altshuler (1968), Reagan (1969), Sharkansky (1970), and Caiden (1971) all reflect the executive focus. The distinguishing trait of these recent works is that in espousing a "public policy" perspective, their neglect of legislatures can be deemed more illogical than that of the previous studies.

Finally, the conclusion that legislative administration is ignored in the textbooks is sustained by John C. Buechner (1968) and Paul Bartholomew (1972). Both of these provide an overview of material treated in previous texts. Neither of them mentions the administration of legislatures.[80]

NOTES FOR CHAPTER 1

1. Bertram M. Gross, *The Managing of Organizations* (New York: Free Press, 1964), pp. 226–227.

2. Leonard D. White, *Introduction to the Study of Public Administration* (New York: Macmillan, 1926).

3. W. Brooke Graves, *Public Administration in a Democratic Society* (Boston: Heath, 1950), p. 3.

4. Marshall E. Dimock and Gladys O. Dimock, *Public Administration* (New York: Holt, Rinehart, and Winston, 1953), p. 2.

5. John D. Millett, *Management in the Public Service* (New York: McGraw-Hill, 1954), p. viii.

6. Fritz Morstein-Marx, ed., *The Elements of Public Administration* (Englewood Cliffs, N.J.: Prentice-Hall, 1946), p. 147 ff.

7. White, *Introduction to the Study of Public Administration*, 4th ed. (1955), p. 44 ff.

8. For example, see White, Chapter 12, and Gerald E. Caiden, *The Dynamics of Public Administration* (New York: Holt, Rinehart, and Winston, 1971), p. 118 ff.

9. Robert T. Golembiewski et al., *Public Administration* (Chicago: Rand McNally, 1966), p. xiii.

10. Ibid., p. 372. Italics added.

11. Harold Stein, *Public Administration and Policy Development* (New York: Harcourt, Brace, 1952), p. x. This book's focus is all the more striking because Stein's effort was

[29]

a hallmark of the case method approach in public administration—an approach, very influential in the 1950s and 1960s—that purported to "tell it like it is." It might be argued that in neglecting legislatures, the case method school failed to portray the reality of the administrative system. Furthermore, because it was so vogue for so long, its neglect of legislatures may have entrenched the habit of neglect in the field generally.

12. Ibid., p. xii.

13. John M. Pfiffner, *Public Administration* (New York: Ronald Press, 1935), chapter 7.

14. Dimock and Dimock, *Public Administration*, 4th ed., p. 76 ff.

15. Golembiewski, *Public Administration*, index.

16. Millett, *Management in the Public Service*, chapter 6.

17. Herbert A. Simon, D. W. Smithburg, and V. A. Thompson, *Public Administration* (New York: Knopf, 1950), chapter 18.

18. Morstein-Marx, *The Elements of Public Administration*, 2nd ed., p. 330.

19. Graves, *Public Administration in a Democratic Society*, chapter 28.

20. Morstein-Marx, *The Elements of Public Administration*, 2nd ed., pp. 71, 82, 83.

21. Simon et al., *Public Administration*, p. 7.

22. Dimock and Dimock, *Public Administration*, first ed., p. 6.

23. Morstein-Marx, *The Elements of Public Administration*, 2nd ed. See, for example, p. 157.

24. Simon et al., *Public Administration*, p. 8.

25. White, *Introduction to the Study of Public Administration*, 2nd ed., p. 577.

26. Ibid., p. 567, footnote 3.

27. Ibid., 4th ed., p. 45.

28 Morstein-Marx, *The Elements of Public Administration*, 2nd ed., p. 317.

29. James Burnham, "Some Administrators' Unkindly View of Congress," in Golembiewski et al., *Public Administration*, p. 76.

30. Morstein-Marx, *The Elements of Public Administration*, 2nd ed., p. 340.

31. John M. Pfiffner and Robert Presthus, *Public Admisistration* (New York: Ronald Press, 1967), 4th ed., p. 416.

32. Morstein-Marx, *The Elements of Public Administration*, 2nd ed., p. 312.

33. White, *Introduction to the Study of Public Administration*, 4th ed., p. 289.

34. Graves, *Public Administration in a Democratic Society*, pp. 316–317.

35. John J. Corson and Joseph D. Harris, *Public Administration in Modern Society* (New York: McGraw-Hill, 1963), p. 122.

36. Ira Sharkansky, *Public Administration* (Chicago: Markham, 1970), p. 201.

37. Harvey Walker, *Public Administration in the United States* (New York: Farrar and Rinehart, 1937), p. 93.

38. Pfiffner, *Public Administration*, first ed., pp. 122, 128.

39. Morstein-Marx, *The Elements of Public Administration*, 2nd ed., p. 71.

40. Ibid., p. 98.

41. Ibid., p. 467.

42. White, *Introduction to the Study of Public Administration*, 2nd ed., p. 568.

43. Simon et al., *Public Administration*, p. 555.

44. Pfiffner and Presthus, *Public Administration*, 5th ed., p. 5.

45. Golembiewski et al., *Public Administration*, p xiii.

46. Ibid., p. xv.

47. Alan A. Altshuler, *The Politics of the Federal Bureaucracy* (New York: Dodd, Mead, 1968), p. vi. He focuses on mediation of public interest directly in the bureaucracy as Herring did.

48. Sharkansky, *Public Administration*, p. x.

49. Morstein-Marx, *The Elements of Public Administration*, 2nd ed., p. 6.

50. Simon et al., *Public Administration*, pp. 5–6.

51. Stein, *Public Administration and Policy Development*, p. x.

52. Dimock and Dimock, *Public Administration*, 3rd ed., p. 111.

53. White, *Introduction to the Study of Public Administration*, 4th ed., p. 7.

54. Morstein-Marx, *The Elements of Public Administration*, p. 330.

55. Graves, *Public Administration in a Democratic Society*, p. vii.

56. Corson and Harris, *Public Administration in Modern Society,* p. 11.

57. Michael D. Reagan, *The Administration of Public Policy* (Glenview, Ill.: Scott, Foresman, 1969), p. iii.

58. Caiden, *The Dynamics of Public Administration,* p. 20.

59. William F. Willoughby, *Principles of Public Administration* (Washington, D.C.: Brookings Institution, 1927), p. 1.

60. William F. Willoughby, *Principles of Legislative Organization and Administration* (Washington, D.C.: Brookings Institution, 1934).

61. Albert Lepawsky, *Administration* (New York: Knopf, 1952), p. 268 ff.

62. Dimock and Dimock, *Public Administration,* first ed., p. 8.

63. Ibid., p. 64.

64. Ibid., 3rd ed., p. 110.

65. Felix A. Nigro, *Modern Public Administration* (New York: Harper and Row, 1965), pp. 5–7.

66. Ibid., 2nd ed., p. 6.

67. Howard E. McCurdy, *Public Administration: A Bibliography* (Washington, D.C.: American University Press, 1972).

68. White, *Introduction to the Study of Public Administration,* 2nd ed., pp. 576–577.

69. Ibid., 4th ed., p. 508.

70. Pfiffner and Presthus, *Public Administration,* first ed., p. 87.

71. Ibid., 5th ed., pp. 396–398.

72. Walker, *Public Administration in the United States,* p. 409 ff.

73. See, for example, Morstein-Marx, *The Elements of Public Administration,* first ed., pp. 7, 81, 321, 331, 340, 407, 465.

74. Graves, *Public Administration in a Democratic Society.*

75. Ibid., p. 711.

76. McCurdy, *Public Administration: A Bibliography,* p. 75.

77. Stein, *Public Administration and Policy Development,* p. x.

78. Dwight Waldo, *The Study of Public Administration* (Garden City, N.Y.: Doubleday, 1955).

79. See, for example, his *Congressional Control of Administration* (Washington, D.C.: Brookings Institution, 1964).

80. A review of textbooks published since this study was completed indicates little, if any, change from the observations of this chapter.

2

Literature: Periodicals

Periodicals in the field of public administration, again reflective of the eclectic nature of the field, are various and numerous. A comprehensive and acceptable identification is difficult. Many public administrationists would cite such journals as *Administrative Science Quarterly, Public Personnel Management,* and the *Bureaucrat.* Some would include *Human Relations, Modern Government, Public Managment,* and the *Journal of Comparative Administration.* But virtually all public administrationists would consider the *Public Administration Review* as *the* periodical of the field. It is the most all-encompassing and representative periodical for public administration.

For present purposes, only volumes that are clearly recognized as, and are "self-consciously," journals of the core of the public administration field are utilized for demonstrating the treatment that has been accorded by the field to legislatures and legislative administration. Certainly it could legitimately be argued that, for example, neglect of legislatures by *Administrative Science Quarterly* would not be evidence of neglect of legislatures by the public administration field. But, unquestionably, the record of the *Public Administration Review (PAR)* would be a valid indicator. Thus, a comprehensive study of the content of *PAR*, in terms of its treatment of legislatures, was undertaken.[1]

From its launching in 1940 the *Public Administration Review* had produced 146 issues containing approximately 1,454 selections, chiefly articles and book reviews, by 1973. Twelve different editors-in-chief have been at the helm. A review of these thirty-three years of volumes indicates that this, *the* journal for public administration, has largely ignored legislatures and legislative administration. The following sections outline the general findings of the study.

NEGLECT OF LEGISLATURES

Public administration periodicals manifest a consistent neglect of legislatures. Selections dealing with legislatures generally have been scant; pieces addressing legislative administration specifically have been exiguous.

In the first article directly addressing legislative administration in *PAR*, Gladys M. Kammerer testified that "little thought has been given ... by students of administration, or the general public to the development of efficiency or responsibility in the management of the daily routine business that makes our national legislative body function."[2] A 1953 analysis of the content of *PAR* confirmed Kammerer's observation: Ernest A. Engelbert found that of 234 general selections in *PAR* between 1940 and 1952, only four dealt with legislatures, and this was the least number for any subject area he listed.[3] Ten years later Edward V. Schten indicated that the trend had not changed: "Analysis of legislative service organizations generally has not dealt closely with the administrative process underlying the research programs."[4]

The current investigation further confirms and updates these conclusions. By 1973 *PAR* had published only twenty-five selections dealing directly with legislatures (see Table 2). This figure represents less than 2 percent of all selections. Of the twenty-five, seven were book reviews. And of the total, only sixteen actually concerned administrative aspects of legislatures. Clearly, the conclusion that *PAR* has given little attention to legislative administration is warranted.

TABLE 2
SELECTIONS ON LEGISLATURES
Public Administration Review
(1940–1973)

Year	Subject	Author(s)
1942	Administrative aspects of coordinating national legislation with state legislation	Engelbert and Wernimont
1944	The budget as an instrument of legislative control	Smith
1946	Assistance by the bureaucracy in the legislative process	Sapp
1946	Congressional reorganization (book review)	Harris
1948	Congressional reorganization (book review)	Young
1949	Administration of Congress	Kammerer
1950	State legislative oversight	Kammerer
1951	Executive-legislative relations (book review)	Fainsod
1952	Legislative budgetary process	Harris
1953	Executive-legislative relationship in budgetary matters	Lawton

TABLE 2 (Continued)

Year	Subject	Author(s)
1954	Reorganization of local legislatures in Great Britain (reprint)	*The Economist*
1955	Legislative processes (book review)	Bone
1958	Legislative-executive relationship	Kampelman
1963	Legislative research administration	Schten
1964	Legislative budgetary procedures	Patterson
1964	Legislative processes (book review)	Burdette
1965	Legislative oversight	Kerr
1966	Legislative staffing	Butler
1966	Executive liaison with the legislature	Pipe
1966	Change of terms of congressmen	Polsby
1967	Legislative reform (book review)	Gibert
1968	Legislative process (book review)	Olson
1969	Congress and PPBS	Wildavsky
1970	Congress and PPBS	Lyden
1973	Local legislatures' oversight	Koehler

The first article dealing directly with legislatures did not appear until the seventh issue of *PAR*.[5] It discussed legislative procedures in states as well as Congress and the need for coordinating legislation at the two levels of government. Though Engelbert and Kenneth Wernimont did not rigorously address internal legislative management, and though their chief concern involved the needs of administrative agencies, their article did recognize the importance of legislative administration. Yet it was not until seven years later that Kammerer's article appeared on the administration of Congress and not until another fourteen years had passed that Schten treated the administration of legislative research. Three years later a piece on legislative staffing appeared.[6] In 1954 a selection on the organization of local legislatures in Great Britain was printed, but this was merely a reprint of an article from the London *Economist*, and there was no comment on its application to local legislatures in the United States.[7]

[38]

Five articles on legislative budgetary procedures[8] and three on oversight[9] can be added to those mentioned above to produce a total of thirteen *articles* dealing with legislative administration in the history of *PAR*. The other articles listed in Table 2 are concerned with legislative-executive relationships.

It is striking that the subject of legislative reorganization was featured only in *book review* form.[10] Even during the period of the Legislative Reorganization Act of 1946, not a single *article* on the subject was printed by *PAR*. It is further noteworthy that one of the best articles, a piece that rigorously analyzed organizational aspects and that clearly spoke in terms of legislative improvement, was contributed by an avowed economist, not by a writer identified as a public administrationist.[11]

EXTERNAL TREATMENT

The journal has tended to treat legislatures as an area external to the field of public administration. Of the few *PAR* selections that have concerned legislatures, several treated them only in terms of their impact on the bureaucracy. As already noted, many of the selections appeared as book reviews rather than as articles.

An article by Harold D. Smith was more concerned with the budget as an executive tool and portrayed Congress as a peripheral actor.[12] Franklin Burdette's book review discussed congressional elections, apportionment, and power systems, but included not a word on administration.[13]

A perspective of legislatures in terms of impact on the bureaucracy is unconcealed: Frederick J. Lawton's title included the phrase "as Viewed by the Executive."[14] Hugh A. Bone's book review spoke of administrators' becoming aware of the legislative environment so that "they will be better able to estimate prospects and opportunities for achieving their goals in Congress." [15] G. Russell Pipe's article concerned procedures developed by the bureaucracy for dealing with Congress, but said nothing about how the Congress is organized to deal with the bureaucracy. [16] Nelson N. Polsby analyzed a proposal to change congressional elections largely in terms of its effect on the executive. [17] And the tone of the seven book reviews that have discussed legislatures creates the impression that legislatures are not really a basic concern of the field but should be understood because they can impede the work of executive agencies.

SUPERFICIAL TREATMENT

The few pieces that do treat the subject of legislative administration tend to do so in a rudimentary and superficial fashion. There is little evidence of in-depth analysis or exploration. Moreover, the treatment appears more doctrinaire than pragmatic and frequently focuses on political rather than administrative questions.

Kammerer's article is restricted to "housekeeping," the "management of the routine functions" of Congress. [18] There is no analysis of committee work or plenary procedures, and even the sections on personnel and fiscal controls are basic, descriptive discussions. Stephen P. Gibert's piece analyzes legislative power distribution, the representative character of Congress, legislative innovative capacity, and congressional efficiency. [19] The last item receives the briefest treatment, and accordingly is only superficially reviewed. A proposed reorganization of local legislatures receives a cursory three-page presentation. [20]

Joseph P. Harris's contributions exemplify the doctrinaire perspective. In the only selection printed by *PAR* on the Legislative Reorganization Act of 1946, Harris presented an "all or nothing," dubiously realistic criticism: "Citizens ... will regard the passage of the act in the closing days of Congress this year as hardly more than a beginning of the needed reform of Congress, and not a very good beginning at that." [21] Instead of approaching the subject positively, he registered a disillusionment. He described new reforms as "clumsy" and "ineffective" and filled his prose with *shoulds* and *will have tos*. Further, the greater part of his discussion concerned political rather than administrative matters. He spoke of the caliber of members of Congress, of the "pernicious" patronage, of the power structure—all of which are matters more germane to general political science than to public administration. The administration concerns that Harris did consider received fleeting paragraphs of analysis. Regarding committees, for example, he said, "Limitation of the number of committees will, no doubt, make for more efficient operation of the committee system." [22] Instead of elucidating the organizational possibilities, he offered the reader a mere "no doubt."

In another article, six years later, Harris reflected a similar perspective. Analysis of administrative matters was cursory: "Somehow Congress must bring together its consideration of the whole budget." The treatment tended to be doctrinaire: "Congress should raise its sights." The focus was political more than administrative: "Congress should reconsider what its real function is...." [23]

Indeed, the apparent infatuation of the journal with political processes of legislatures, and the reluctance to really get into administrative processes, is evidenced by

[41]

the content of the relevant book reviews. Of six reviews on congressional reorganization, three deal almost solely with political practices.[24]

LIP SERVICE TO LEGISLATIVE IMPORTANCE

The periodical literature pays lip service to the importance of legislatures. The lack of serious attention to legislatures stands in contrast to these fervent expressions of concern.

In one of the very first issues it was asserted: "Since both are inseparable parts of policy formation and the execution of programs ... it is not possible to make a clear-cut separation between the legislative and administrative process."[25] But in largely ignoring legislatures, *PAR* gives the appearance of attempting such a clear-cut separation.

Relatedly, a suggestion that "because of its administration experience and technical knowledge, the executive branch can provide real assistance to the legislative branch"[26] was seemingly not endorsed by *PAR*, for there is little evidence of effort to foster such assistance.

More strikingly, the neglect of legislatures by *PAR* occurs in the face of persistent statements about the needs of legislatures, of definitions clearly including legislatures within the field, and of assertions that well-managed legislatures are requisite for well-administered government programs.

Kammerer observed in 1944 that "present administration of Congress probably stands in need of drastic reorganization more seriously than does the executive branch."[27] And she was merely echoing an earlier statement that "the need for the reform of Congress internally ... must be apparent to all."[28] Yet *PAR* gave minimal attention to these perceived needs, despite George A.

Graham's insistence that "students of administration must turn their attention to . . . the legislative process." [29]

In one of the few definitions of the field of public administration to appear in *PAR*, John C. Honey said: "Public administration is nothing more nor less than the art of conducting the affairs of government. Broadly conceived in a tripartite system, it extends beyond the executive branch to include the legislative and judicial functions as well." [30] A decade later he reasserted that view: "The realities of governmental operations dictate the pursuit of a much broader outlook and indeed of equating public administration with the total governmental process (executive, legislative, and judicial), in both its career and political manifestations." [31] Yet *PAR* consistently has appeared, by omission at least, to equate the field with the executive alone.

Finally, in recently observing that the way programs are structured is a reflection of the structure of the legislature, and that therefore legislatures need to be analyzed and improved,[32] Harold Seidman was merely adding a refrain to a point made by John M. Gaus in 1950.[33] Yet during that interval and after, *PAR* failed to act on those words. Lip service prevailed; legislatures were phantomized.

ANTILEGISLATURE EXPRESSIONS

Numerous antilegislature expressions appear in the journal. Some articles are passively negative by omitting legislatures from the scope of the field or from a subject particularly pertinent. Some selections pointedly attack legislatures.

Helen C. Hilling opined in *PAR* that "public administration encompasses a body of knowledge pertaining to the operational processes of the executive functions of government." [34] While her exclusion of legislatures from the definition of the field may not be particularly salient, certainly Comstock Glaser's omission of legislatures from his discussion of committees is remarkable.[35] Though legislatures have had enormous experience in working by committees, Glaser claims that committee management is a new field, that procedures are untested, and he never once mentions legislatures in this, one of the first articles of *PAR*. A similar article by Robert L. Hubbell, six years later, makes the same omission, thought it at least mentions that Congress has used committees.[36]

Paul Appleby, in reflecting on a long and distinguished government career, made the following observation in the pages of *PAR*: "The more I see of things, the more crucial I see the more frankly political structures and functions.... Adequate political organization is a very difficult matter with numerous aspects.... we must remember that we are looking for ways to improve the performances of government institutions." [37] Appleby's omission of a word on legislatures in this context is perhaps not noteworthy but for the breadth and prestige of the man.

But equally famous figures in the field have been pointedly antipathetic toward legislatures. John D. Millett and Lindsay Rogers have spoken of "legislative bickering and indecision." [38] Harvey C. Mansfield derided legislative incapacity to act.[39] And Merle Fainsod criticized one author's support of legislatures for being a "swim against the tide." [40]

BROAD ATTENTION TO OTHER AREAS

The neglect of legislatures is conspicuous in contrast to the attention given other identifiable areas of the field. Articles and full symposia on other purlieus with

[44]

administrative needs are prevalent. There has never been a symposium on legislative administration in the *Public Administration Review.*

As Table 3 indicates, *PAR* since its inception has included thirty-seven symposia covering nearly every area of administrative interest except legislatures. The executive has been the subject of four symposia, including the journal's first symposium in 1941. Moreover, every level of the executive—the president, the governor, the city manager—has been treated. Even the judiciary, which has not received adequate attention generally, has been the subject of a symposium.

Perhaps more telling is the absence of any reference to legislatures in symposia that have dealt with subjects quite relevant to legislatures. An otherwise excellent symposium on computers never mentioned their utility to legislatures, although legislatures have increasingly attemp-

TABLE 3
SYMPOSIA
Public Administration Review
(1940–1973)

Year	Topic
1941	Executive Office of the President
1944	Army Service Forces Administration
1945	Naval Procurement and Logistics
1958	Defense Administration
1958	Educating Executives
1960	Education Administration
1964	Government Decision-Making
1966	PPBS
1967	Science and Public Policy
1967	Higher Education for the Public Service
1968	Intergovernmental Relations
1968	Police Administration
1968	Computers in Public Administration
1969	The Presidency
1969	Diplomatic Administration
1969	PPBS Reexamined
1969	Decentralization and Participation

TABLE 3 (Continued)

Year	Topic
1970	The Governor
1970	University Administration
1970	International Civil Service
1970	Intergovernmental Relations
1970	Education and Public Policy
1970	Government and the Arts
1970	Governing Cities
1971	The City Manager
1971	Judicial Administration
1971	Planning
1971	Health Care Administration
1971	Criminal Justice
1972	Collective Bargaining
1972	Citizen Participation
1972	Regulatory Administration
1972	Productivity
1973	Canadian Public Administration
1973	Transportation Policy
1973	Future Organizations
1973	Continuing Education

ted to benefit from computer technology. Similarly, a discussion on science and public policy gave little attention to legislatures, as did others on citizen participation and on productivity.[41]

One noted public administrationist, when asked about the neglect of legislative administration by public administration, replied that it is no worse than the field's neglect of education administration or of health administration, that the field has only had time for the more pressing concerns of the executive bureaucracy.[42] Yet *PAR* has had time and space for symposia on education administration and health administration. Even subjects such as the arts and the diplomatic corps have been given the attention of *PAR* symposia;[43] but legislatures have not.*

*Partially as a result of this study a symposium on legislatures is planned for late 1975.

HISTORICAL PERSPECTIVE

A historical view of the treatment given legislatures by *PAR* does not attenuate the record of neglect. During its thirty-three-year lifetime and its twelve editors-in-chief, the neglect has been consistent. During its first decade, seven selections dealt with legislatures. Seven more appeared during the fifties; ten were printed in the following decade; and only two have thus far emerged in the 1970s. Under all of the editors-in-chief the record is equally sparse. The one moderate exception is Vincent Ostrom's stewardship (1963–1966), during which six legislative selections appeared. Six selections have also appeared under Dwight Waldo, but his tenure has thus far been twice as long as that of any predecessor.

Historical events seem not to have inspired much diversion from the neglect trend. The activity surrounding the Legislative Reorganization Act of 1946 might have prompted some *PAR* analysis of congressional management; but only a single selection appeared in 1946, and that was a book review.[44] The Watergate affair, which may to some degree be a result of the type of executive mesmerization that *PAR* has manifested, has not yet inspired any new *PAR* treatment of legislatures. Nor has the recent movement toward state legislative improvement resulted in *PAR* selections. The one event that appears to have produced some attention from *PAR* was a television show. In 1965 NBC television produced a program on improving the management of Congress.[45] In 1966 *PAR* published the most legislative selections (three) in any one year of its history.

Warren H. Butler has observed: "After a prolonged fling at romancing the presidency, students of American national government have lately been rediscovering Congress. Articles, symposia, management studies, television programs, all have produced suggestions for reforms to improve the functioning of the Legislative Branch." [46] It is ironic that Butler should make this statement in the pages of *PAR*, for the public administration journal has yet to end that "prolonged fling" at attending the executive to the exclusion of the legislature.

NOTES FOR CHAPTER 2

1. In addition, a survey of the content of the other journals mentioned was conducted. It revealed a nearly total neglect of legislative administration by these "peripheral" periodicals. One major exception is Samuel C. Patterson, "The Professional Staffs of Congressional Committees," *Administrative Science Quarterly* 15, no. 1 (March 1970): 22–38.

2. Gladys M. Kammerer, "The Administration of Congress," *Public Administration Review* 9, no. 3 (summer 1949): 175.

3. Ernest A. Englebert, "The Content of PAR, 1940–1952," *Public Administration Review* 13, no. 4 (autumn 1953): 258.

4. Edward V. Schten, "Administration and Legislative Research," *Public Administration Review* 23, no. 2 (June 1963): 81.

5. Ernest Engelbert and Kenneth Wernimont, "Administrative Aspects of the Federal-State Legislative Relationship," *Public Administration Review* 2, no. 2 (spring 1942): 126–138.

6. Warren H. Butler, "Administering Congress: The Role of Staff," *Public Administration Review* 26, no. 1 (January 1966): 3–13.

7. "New Broom at the Town Hall?" *Public Administration Review* 14, no. 2 (spring 1954): 128–130.

8. Harold D. Smith, "The Budget as an Instrument of Legislative Control," *Public Administration Review* 4, no. 3 (summer 1944): 181–188; Joseph P. Harris, "Needed Reforms in the Federal Budget System," *Public Administration Review* 12, no. 4 (autumn 1952): 242–250; Kenneth D. Patterson,

"Legislative Budget Review: An Economist's Viewpoint," *Public Administration Review* 24, no. 1 (January 1964): 7–12; Aaron Wildavsky, "Rescuing Policy Analysis from PPBS," *Public Administration Review* 29, no. 2 (March–April 1969): 189–201; Fremont J. Lyden, "Congressional Decision Making and PPB," *Public Administration Review* 30, no. 2 (March–April 1970): 167–168.

9. Gladys M. Kammerer, "Legislative Oversight of Administration in Kentucky," *Public Administration Review* 10, no. 3 (summer 1950): 169–175; James R. Kerr, "Congress and Space: Overview or Oversight?" *Public Administration Review* 25, no. 3 (September 1965): 185–192; Curtis T. Koehler, "Policy Development and Legislative Oversight in Council Manager Cities," *Public Administration Review* 33, no. 5 (September–October): 433–442.

10. Joseph P. Harris, "The Reorganization of Congress," *Public Administration Review* 6, no. 3 (summer 1946): 267–282; Roland Young, "Legislative Reform," *Public Administration Review* 8, no. 2 (spring 1948): 141–146; Stephen P. Gibert, "Congress: The First Branch of Government," *Public Administration Review* 27, no. 2 (June 1967): 178–189.

11. Kenneth D. Patterson, "Legislative Budget Review: An Economist's Viewpoint."

12. Smith, "The Budget as an Instrument of Legislative Control."

13. Franklin L. Burdette, "Congress, the People, and Administration," *Public Administration Review* 24, no. 4 (fall 1964): 259–264.

14. Frederick J. Lawton, "Legislative-Executive Relationships in Budgeting as Viewed by the Executive," *Public Administration Review* 13, no. 3 (summer 1953): 169–176.

15. Hugh A. Bone, "On Understanding Legislatures," *Public Administration Review* 15, no. 2 (spring 1955): 121–126.

16. G. Russell Pipe, "Congressional Liaison: The Executive Branch Consolidates Its Relations with Congress," *Public Administration Review* 26, no. 1 (January 1966): 14–19.

17. Nelson N. Polsby, "A Note on the President's Modest Proposal," *Public Administration Review* 26, no. 3 (September 1966): 156–159.

18. Kammerer, "The Administration of Congress," p. 175.

19. Gibert, "Congress: The First Branch of Government," p. 178.

Literature: Periodicals

20. The London *Economist,* reprint, *Public Administration Review* 14, no. 2 (spring 1954): 93.

21. Harris, "The Reorganization of Congress," p. 268.

22. Ibid., p. 273.

23. Harris, "Needed Reforms in the Federal Budget System," p. 250.

24. Namely, Hugh A. Bone, "On Understanding Legislatures"; Franklin L. Burdette, "Congress, the People, and Administration"; and David M. Olson, "Studies in American Legislative Process," *Public Administration Review* 28, no. 3 (May–June): 280–286.

25. Engelbert and Wernimont, "Administrative Aspects of the Federal-State Legislative Relationship," p. 129.

26. Carl R. Sapp, "Executive Assistance in the Legislative Process," *Public Administration Review* 6, no. 1 (winter 1946): 19.

27. Kammerer, "The Administration of Congress," p. 180.

28. Harris, "The Reorganization of Congress," p. 268.

29. George A. Graham, "Trends in Teaching Public Administration," *Public Administration Review* 10, no. 2 (spring 1950): 74.

30. John C. Honey, "Research in Public Administration," *Public Administration Review* 17, no. 4 (autumn 1957): 239.

31. John C. Honey, "A Report: Higher Education in the Public Service," *Public Administration Review* 27, no. 4 (November 1967): 294.

32. Harold Seidman, "New Aspects for Attention," *Public Administration Review* 30, no. 3 (May–June 1970): 273.

33. John M. Gaus, "Trends in the Theory of Public Administration," *Public Administration Review* 10, no. 3 (summer 1950): 165.

34. Helen C. Hilling, "Public Administration: Study, Practice, Profession," *Public Administration Review* 26, no. 4 (December 1966): 320.

35. Comstock Glaser, "Managing Committee Work in a Large Organization," *Public Administration Review* 1, no. 3 (spring 1941): 249–256.

36. Robert L. Hubbell, "Techniques for Making Committees Effective," *Public Administration Review* 6, no. 4 (autumn 1946): 348–353. Admittedly, there are significant differences between legislative and executive committees as well as useful similarities.

37. Paul Appleby, "Making Sense out of Things in General," *Public Administration Review* 22, no. 4 (December 1962) : 178–179.

38. John D. Millett and Lindsay Rogers, "The Legislative Veto," *Public Administration Review* 1, no. 2 (winter 1941) : 189.

39. Harvey C. Mansfield, "The Legislative Veto," *Public Administration Review* 1, no. 3 (spring 1941) : 281.

40. Merle Fainsod, "The Presidency and Congress," *Public Administration Review* 11, no. 2 (spring 1951) : 123.

41. References in *Public Administration Review* to the symposia cited are as follows: the president, *PAR* 1, no. 2 (winter 1941) and *PAR* 29, no. 5 (September–October 1969); the governor, *PAR* 30, no. 1 (January–February 1970); the city manager, *PAR,* 31, no. 1 (January–February 1971); the judiciary, *PAR* 31, no. 2 (March–April 1971); computers, *PAR* 28, no. 6 (November–December 1968); science and public policy, *PAR* 27, no. 2 (June 1967); citizen participation, *PAR* 32, no. 3 May–June 1972); and productivity, *PAR* 32, no. 6 (November–December 1972).

42. Personal letter to the author in response to the inquiry reprinted as Appendix B.

43. References in *Public Administration Review* to the symposia cited are as follows: education administration, *PAR* 20, no. 1 (January 1960) and *PAR* 30, no. 2 (March–April 1970); health administration, *PAR* 31, no. 5 (September–October 1971); the arts, *PAR* 30, no. 4 (July–August 1970); the diplomatic corps, *PAR* 29, no. 6 (November–December 1969).

44. Harris, "The Reorganization of Congress," p. 268.

45. The results of the program are published in Philip Dunham and Robert J. Fahey, *Congress Needs Help* (New York: Random House, 1966).

46. Butler, "Administering Congress: The Role of Staff," p. 3.

3

General Literature

Identifying, surveying, and characterizing the literature of any large discipline or field of study is a difficult undertaking. It is all the more formidable in a field as interdisciplinary and diffuse as public administration. This field draws from and attempts to knead the literature of so many other fields that it is no simple task to clarify just what constitutes the general literature of public administration.

Fortunately, for present purposes, an effort at clarifying and listing the relevant literature has recently been completed—namely, Howard E. McCurdy's study.[1] McCurdy studied numerous bibliographies and reading lists and sought the counsel of fifty public administration scholars in putting together a list of one thousand books that he asserts are "recognized as important in the discipline of public administration." [2] Of that total, he identifies the 187 books that were most often cited in the course of his research. This latter group was primarily utilized in the present study for purposes of unfolding what attention general public administration literature has given legislatures.

Admittedly, this procedure may not be totally valid and the conclusions that result may thus be incomplete and somewhat slanted, for McCurdy's methodology is not without shortcomings. Nevertheless, the McCurdy bibliography is broad, current, and the only timely effort available. While his inventory of the relevant literature may not be altogether comprehensive, and although his measures of importance may not be universally representative, his study can be deemed sufficiently broad to present an acceptable version of what constitutes public administration literature. Moreover, the objective of this chapter is to discover general characteristics of the public administration literature as a whole with regard to attention to legislatures, not to specify categorically the treatment given by every relevant work.[3] For this limited objective, use of McCurdy is considered sufficiently valid. Following are the general findings.

NEGLECT OF LEGISLATURES

The fundamental finding that again emerges is that public administration literature has neglected legislatures. Of the 187 books identified by McCurdy as those most frequently cited in public administration, none concerns legislative administration or management, and only five deal directly with legislatures in any thorough manner.[4] In fact, in the entire list of one thousand books, not a single work is cited on legislative reform, improvement, management, or even overall legislative process, although many books on these subjects are in print.[5] The few books listed that do deal with legislatures are focused on Congress; state legislatures are entirely neglected.

The five works mentioned tend to discuss Congress

primarily in terms of process rather than organization and as a factor external to administration. The book by Stephen Bailey is largely a description of the process of passing a bill and an analysis of the power influences involved. Freeman analyzes the relationship between congressional committees and executive agencies in terms of policy-making roles. Aaron Wildavsky describes and analyzes the role Congress plays in the national budget. Hyneman and Harris deal with the Congress as the external control of administration. The former presents and defends the theoretical basis for legislative supremacy; the latter (who was a vice-president of the American Society for Public Administration) describes and critiques the mechanisms used by Congress for control.[6]

The Harris book, both because of the background of the author and because of the subject addressed, might be expected to treat the internal management of Congress. Early in his discussion, Harris notes: "A reason for the increase in Congressional influence on administration is that Congress is becoming far better equipped to exercise control."[7] He seems to recognize that legislative control is largely a function of internal legislative management. Yet throughout the book he tends to identify broad problem areas of congressional control and to ignore analysis of managerial approaches to those problems. He observes that the budget control process is too dispersed, yet he does not comment on organizational possibilities for producing better focus.[8] He criticizes the congressional auditing system yet fails to suggest concrete administrative improvements in this area.[9] He maintains that "a basic defect in the organization and procedures of Congress . . . is that responsibility is hopelessly divided";[10] yet he does not suggest administrative approaches to this situation and does not even evaluate, in terms of their administrative merits, reforms proposed by others.

Thus, a review of the McCurdy list reveals a distinct lack of attention to legislative administration by the literature as a whole, and an examination of Harris's work and others indicates similar neglect by the few books that do concern legislatures generally.

This neglect contrasts with the marked attention given to executive administration. Included in the McCurdy list of most cited books are works by Gawthrop, Miller and Starr, Neustadt, Warner, Bernstein, Barnard, and Selznick, all of which concern the executive specifically.[11] Nearly exclusive identification with the executive appears dominant. Paul Appleby, in *Big Democracy*, seems to reflect the consistent perspective of the literature: "It is the whole contribution of the executive branch I have in mind when I think of 'public administration.' "[12] A survey of works published since McCurdy's study indicates no change in approach. Uveges's best-selling volume contains thirty-seven selections, only one of which concerns legislatures.[13] Frederick C. Thayer's recent book is an example of the literature neglecting legislatures even in a most eminently relevant context: It is a "search for . . . a formal theory of structured nonhierarchy,"[14] yet legislatures are not mentioned, even though many of them are operating examples of "structured non-hierarchy." And John Rehfuss's recent book similarly fails to alter the course.[15]

FAILURE TO USE AVAILABLE SOURCES

The public administration field appears not only to be failing to produce literature on legislative administration, but also to be little utilizing such literature available from other sources.

In addition to study of the McCurdy bibliography, a search was conducted for books dealing with legislatures and authored by recognized public administrationists. Three other works were discovered, none of which focuses on administration. Marshall Dimock's first book, written as a doctoral dissertation under William Willoughby, analyzes the causes and effects of congressional investigations but says little pertaining to the organization and procedures of the committees involved.[16] Bertram M. Gross wrote a book designed as a guide for administrators and others faced with the handling of legislative problems. He analyzes the power system of the Congress and discusses the legislature in terms of clarifying the process. He devotes no attention to administrative improvement.[17] Finally, in the only work found emanating from the public administration field that deals with state legislatures, William J. Siffin discusses the need to be aware of political realities in legislative research; he gives administrative aspects of the research only cursory treatment.[18]

Thus, the only work discovered in public administration literature that deals directly with legislative administration is Willoughby's 1934 classic,[19] and, according to McCurdy, it is not utilized.

It is also noteworthy that many other legislative works, produced by authors not normally recognized as public administrationists, also fail to appear in McCurdy's study. Given the stress on legislative process rather than administration in the titles that do appear in McCurdy, the absence of Jewell and Patterson's standard, of John S. Saloma's volume, and of Huitt and Peabody's collection,[20] is perhaps unexpected. Less salient, considering the particular neglect of state legislatures revealed by McCurdy's list, is the disregard of the edition by Herzberg and Rosenthal, the Jewell work, and the best seller by William J. Keefe and Morris S. Ogul.[21]

But perhaps most telling in the present context is the apparent nonutilization of works directly addressing legislative management. Neither the book by Alfred de Grazia, nor that by Donham and Fahey, nor the widely used work by the Citizens Conference on State Legislatures[22] appear in McCurdy.

ANTILEGISLATURE TONE

There is some evidence in the literature of an antilegislative bent. No attempt was made to document this observation extensively, but in the course of the survey some statements stood out.

Ordway Tead, in his influential *The Art of Administration*, asserted: "Our method of political government ... leaves to legislative bodies powers of determination over matters which might better be dealt with by ... administrative agencies."[23] John M. Gaus, one of the guiding lights in the field of public administration, apparently believed he was reflecting the consensus of the literature when he maintained that "there is general agreement among students of administration that generally legislatures have done far more harm than good by too detailed control of the organization of administration."[24]

And O. Glenn Stahl, in his very widely used *Public Personnel Administration*, portrays legislatures as obstructionary to a good civil service: "The transfer of control to the legislative body brought with it abuses which are still notable in various countries, including to some extent our own. Members of parliaments tended to look with apprehension upon the kind of efficient administration fostered by their royal forebears.... Thus, the first effect of the new dominance of elected legislative bodies was demoralization of the civil service."[25] This untoward treatment of legislatures merely echoed the sentiments of William E. Mosher and J. Donald Kingsley in the first edition of the same volume: "The problems of modern government are too complex to be coped with successfully by untrained legislators, 'fresh from the people.' " [26] Later in the book the authors spend several pages discussing "legislative interference." [27]

SUBFIELD RECORD

An initial review of various subfields of public administration indicates that, relatively speaking, the literature of comparative and development administration has given the most attention to legislatures. The budgeting literature has recognized and analyzed the role of legislatures in the budgetary process (for example, see Wildavsky's *The Politics of the Budgetary Process*), but more from a political than a managerial perspective.[28] The "new public administration" evinces no interest in legislatures despite its avowed concern with "participation" and "representation." [29]

Organization theory gives legislatures some attention: Though Luther Gulick and L. Urwick's famous collection of *Papers* holds that "public administration... concerns itself primarily with the executive branch," it also recognizes that "there are obviously administration problems in connection with the legislative and the judicial branches." [30] Though March's *Handbook* speaks of legislatures only in terms of relationship to the bureaucracy,[31] his coeffort with Simon appears to encompass open, environmentally complex organizations such as legislatures.[32] And though Gross's monumental study does not specifically treat legislatures, he clearly includes legislatures in his quest for "common elements in the administration of different types of organizations" and does refer to legislative bodies throughout the volumes.[33] Gross was once staff director of a U.S. Senate subcommittee, and he acknowledges the organizational aspect of that experience: "It [organizational concerns] entered into my daily efforts to get things done in Congress— from the conduct of a hearing to the drafting of a bill and the enactment of a law." [34]

But comparative and development administration literature, relative to the other subfields, has manifested the greatest interest in legislatures. Although the writers do generally tend to focus on the bureaucracy and neglect legislatures,[35] and even to deride legislatures[36] (perhaps largely because they were conditioned to this perspective by American public administration), experiences seem to have led some of them to a concern for legislatures.

As far back as 1954 David E. Apter spoke of developing a parliament simultaneously with economic development.[37] He suggested an unfolding conviction, based on actual efforts to improve bureaucratic organization in developing countries, that *effective administration* requires a functioning political institution. By 1963, Pye contended that "most transitional societies will realize more effective administration only if they broaden and more explicitly organize the non-bureaucratic components of the political process." [38] Indeed, he bluntly asserted that "administration cannot be greatly improved without a parallel strengthening of the representative political processes." [39] Fred Riggs echoed a similar refrain.[40] And Warren Illchman's review of the literature on development in 1965 revealed the same interest in political institutions as requisite for effective administration.[41]

A related, but distinguishable, reason for the concern of some comparative and development literature for legislatures may have been the view, again based on actual experience, that *national development* was dependent on effective political institutions in addition to a strong bureaucracy: "It can be argued that at present in most situations rapid economic growth is more likely to be stimulated by ... an increase in popular participation in the nation-building process." [42] Samuel Huntington, though referring to political parties more than to legislatures, said that modernization creates an "overriding need for political institutions." [43] Edward Weidner was more specific: "The role of the legislature is of fundamental importance.... The strengthening of the administrative side of government should be accompanied by a strengthening of the policy role of the legislative body." [44]

But, unlike public administration literature generally, some literature in comparative and development administration did not stop at merely recognizing the importance of legislatures; it went beyond "lip service," attempted to apply public administration expertise to legislatures, and analyzed how to improve them.

Immediately after his observation of the importance of legislatures, Weidner made a concrete proposal: "Establishment of a special legislative committee, commission, or council, supported by staff, to oversee planning matters might partially fill the need." [45] He urged that technical assistance be provided to legislatures. La Palombara discussed development in terms of both bureaucratic and political development, urged that public administration assistance be provided for the latter, and included a section, written by Riggs, specifically analyzing the administrative needs of legislatures.[46] Riggs identified budgetary, bill drafting, and information

[61]

needs[47] and discussed them in terms of legislative improvement, not of executive desires.

In 1969 Ralph Braibanti's volume stated the problem: "The role of American foreign aid in improving legislature capability has . . . been virtually nil." [48] He specifically identified areas for assistance: "The infrastructure of most parliamentary bodies in developing states can be vastly improved. Adequate office staff, committee staff, and a research service . . . are needed." [49] Finally, Kornberg and Musolf compiled an entire volume on *Legislatures in Developmental Perspective*,[50] a work completed in cooperation with the American Society for Public Administration, and most of which speaks affirmatively of legislatures.

In brief, the literature in the subfield of comparative and development administration, when compared with the writing of other subfields of public administration, appears to have given some significant attention to legislative administration. Some observations regarding this phenomenon are noteworthy. First, the literature of this subfield reflects its origin in general public administration in that most of it does neglect or deride legislatures; but it was forced by experience to give at least some attention to legislative administration. As will be shown in Chapter 7, the direct result of this turn is that American public administration, prompted partially by that overseas experience, is now showing signs of concern for legislative administration in the United States. In other words, the process of transferring American public administration knowledge abroad may be resulting in a development of American public administration at home.[51]

Second, public administration literature views administrative matters in the United States almost exclusively in terms of the bureaucracy, while in young countries problems of development appear to have necessitated a more systemic perspective of government and prompted the insight that functioning legislatures can be an important element for effective government. Within the United States, because legislatures have existed and have had some effect, the result of a lack of systemic perspective has perhaps not been so clear and rapid. Watergate, fiscal crises, and program failures are conceivably, to some degree, the slower and less explicit results of neglect by public administration of legislatures in the United States.

In sum, general public administration literature, like the textbooks and journals, has neglected legislatures. With the partial exception of comparative and development administration, the field has neither produced nor utilized literature dealing with legislative administration.

CONCLUSION

The evidence is impressive. Public administration literature is heavily focused on the executive to the exclusion of the legislature. The little interest in legislative activities has stemmed largely from concern over the manner in which legislatures relate to and impinge on management practices in the executive. Attention to legislative administration in particular has been extremely shallow. Neither the textbooks, nor the periodicals, nor the general literature seems to veer from this track.

NOTES FOR CHAPTER 3

1. Howard E. McCurdy, *Public Administration: A Bibliography* (Washington, D.C.: American University Press, 1972).

2. Ibid., p. 3.

3. Further research would be useful in clarifying the attention given legislatures by the several subfields of public administration—e.g., budgeting, organization theory, management science, etc.

4. Stephen Bailey, *Congress Makes a Law* (New York: Columbia University Press, 1950); J. Leiper Freeman, *The Political Process: Executive Bureau Legislative Committee Relations* (New York: Random House, 1965); Joseph P. Harris, *Congressional Control of Administration* (Washington, D.C.: Brookings Institution, 1964); Charles Hyneman, *Bureaucracy in a Democracy* (New York: Harper, 1950); Aaron Wildavsky, *The Politics of the Budgetary Process* (Boston: Little, Brown, 1964).

5. See Chapter 7.

6. Harris, *Congressional Control of Administration*, p. 3.

7. Ibid., p. 10.

8. Ibid., p. 103.

9. Ibid., p. 162.

10. Ibid., p. 287.

11. Louis C. Gawthrop, *Bureaucratic Behavior in the Executive Branch* (New York: Free Press, 1969); David W. Miller and Martin Starr, *Executive Decisions and Operations Research* (Englewood Cliffs, N.J.; Prentice-Hall, 1960); Richard Neustadt, *Presidential Power* (New York: Wiley, 1960); W. Lloyd Warner, *The American Federal Executive*

(New Haven: Yale University Press, 1963); Marver H. Bernstein, *The Job of the Federal Executive* (Washington, D.C.: Brookings Institution, 1958); Chester I. Barnard, *The Functions of the Executive* (Boston: Harvard University Press, 1938); Philip Selznick, *Leadership in Administration* (New York: Row, Peterson, 1957).

12. Paul H. Appleby, *Big Democracy* (New York: Russell and Russell, 1970), p. viii.

13. Joseph A. Uveges, *Dimensions of Public Administration* (Boston: Holbrook, 1971). The book discusses congressional oversight of NASA on pp. 521–535.

14. Frederick C. Thayer, *An End to Hierarchy* (New York: Franklin Watts, 1973).

15. John Rehfuss, *Public Administration as Political Process* (New York: Scribner, 1973). This book does contain a discussion on "legislative-bureaucratic relations," but nothing on internal legislative management.

16. Marshall E. Dimock, *Congressional Investigating Committees* (Baltimore: Johns Hopkins University Press, 1929).

17. Bertram M. Gross, *The Legislative Struggle* (New York: McGraw-Hill, 1953).

18. William J. Siffin, *The Legislative Council in the American States* (Bloomington: Indiana University Press, 1959).

19. William F. Willoughby, *Principles of Legislative Organization and Administration* (Washington, D.C.: Brookings Institution, 1934).

20. Malcolm E. Jewell and Samuel C. Patterson, *The Legislative Process in the United States* (New York: Random House, 1966); John S. Saloma, *Congress and the New Politics* (Boston: Little, Brown, 1969); Ralph K. Huitt and Robert L. Peabody, eds., *Congress: Two Decades of Analysis* (New York: Harper and Row, 1969).

21. Donald G. Herzberg and Alan Rosenthal, eds., *Strengthening the States* (New York: Doubleday, 1971); Malcolm E. Jewell, *The State Legislature* (New York: Random House, 1969); William J. Keefe and Morris S. Ogul, *The American Legislative Process* (Englewood Cliffs, N.J.: Prentice-Hall, 1964, 1972).

22. Alfred de Grazia, ed., *Congress: The First Branch of Government* (Washington, D.C.: American Enterprise Institute, 1966); Philip Donham and Robert J. Fahey, *Congress Needs Help* (New York: Random House, 1966); Citizens Con-

ference on State Legislatures, *The Sometime Governments* (New York: Bantam, 1971).

23. Ordway Tead, *The Art of Administration* (New York: McGraw-Hill, 1951), p. 86.

24. John M. Gaus, et al., *The Frontiers of Public Administration* (New York: Russell, 1936), p. 33. His observation was undoubtedly justified to some degree, but led to a warped perspective of the legislature.

25. O. Glenn Stahl, *Public Personnel Administration*, 5th ed. (New York: Harper and Row, 1962), pp. 5–6.

26. William E. Mosher and J. Donald Kingsley, *Public Personnel Administration* (New York: Harper, 1936), pp. 11–12.

27. Ibid., p. 66 ff.

28. A notable exception is Jesse Burkhead, *Government Budgeting* (New York: Wiley, 1956). Although his discussion of legislatures is brief, Burkhead manifests both a systemic perspective and an appreciation of the organizational dimension of legislative action. He speaks of a "working partnership" between the executive and the legislature and the need to approach improved budgetary processes through existing committee structures and operations in the legislature. See pp. 321–339.

29. Frank Marini, ed., *Toward a New Public Administration* (Scranton, Pa.: Chandler, 1971).

30. Luther Gulick and L. Urwick, eds., *Papers on the Science of Administration* (New York: Institute of Public Administration, 1937), p. 191.

31. James G. March, *Handbook of Organizations* (Chicago: Rand McNally, 1965), p. 820 ff.

32. James G. March and Herbert A. Simon, *Organizations* (New York: Wiley, 1958).

33. Bertram M. Gross, *The Managing of Organizations* (New York: Macmillan, 1964), p. vii.

34. Ibid., p. v.

35. Ferrel Heady's *Public Administration: A Comparative Perspective* (Englewood Cliffs, N.J.: Prentice-Hall, 1966) is representative.

36. See, for example, Robert Packenham, "Legislatures and Political Development" in Allan Kornberg and Lloyd D. Musolf, eds., *Legislatures in Developmental Perspective* (Durham, N.C.: Duke University Press, 1970). For a comprehensive analysis of this bent, see Abdo I. Baaklini, *Legislatures and Political Development* (Durham, N.C.: Duke University Press, 1975).

General Literature

37. David E. Apter, "Some Economic Factors in the Political Development of the Gold Coast," *Journal of Economic History* 14, no. 4 (fall 1954): 409–427. Though Apter is generally not viewed as a "public administrationist," his writings have been widely used in the development administration subfield.

38. Lucian W. Pye, "The Political Context of National Development" in Irving Swerdlow, *Development Administration* (Syracuse: Syracuse University Press, 1963), p. 41.

39. Ibid., p. 33.

40. Fred W. Riggs, "Relearning an Old Lesson," *Public Administration Review* 25, no. 1 (March 1965): 70–79.

41. Warren F. Illchman, "Rising Expectations and the Revolution in Development Administration," *Public Administration Review* 25, no. 4 (December 1965): 314–328.

42. Pye, "The Political Context of National Development." p. 41.

43. Samuel P. Huntington, *Political Order in Changing Societies* (New Haven: Yale University Press, 1968), pp. 460–461.

44. Edward W. Weidner, *Technical Assistance in Public Administration Overseas* (Chicago: Public Administration Service, 1964), pp. 210–211.

45. Ibid., p. 211.

46. Joseph La Palombara, ed., *Bureaucracy and Political Development* (Princeton: Princeton University Press, 1963).

47. Fred W. Riggs, "Bureaucrats and Political Development" in La Palombara, *Bureaucracy and Political Development*, p. 151.

48. Ralph Braibanti, ed., *Political and Administrative Development* (Durham, N.C.: Duke University Press, 1969), p. 94.

49. Ibid., p. 91.

50. Allan Kornberg and Lloyd D. Musolf, eds., *Legislatures in Developmental Perspective*.

51. For a discussion of general transfer processes and the benefits derived by the United States, see Brack Brown, "Lessons from Foreign Administrative Experience," paper presented at the annual meeting of the American Society for Public Administration, Syracuse, N.Y., 1974.

4

Institutions: Schools and Organizations

Key institutional manifestations of a professional field are its schools and organizations. Schools provide education and research; professional organizations afford continuous interchange through conferences, special studies, and regular meetings. This chapter reviews the attention given to legislatures by academic programs and research centers of public administration schools and by the American Society for Public Administration.

Academic programs in public administration are relatively easy to identify because of the existence of the National Association of Schools of Public Affairs and Administration (NASPAA), which is a close affiliate of the American Society for Public Administration. NASPAA periodically publishes a membership directory (reprinted as Appendix C) and maintains a library of catalogues of member institutions.

In order to ascertain the present attention given legislatures by schools with public administration programs, three avenues were pursued: first, a questionnaire, reprinted in Appendix B, was sent to all programs listed in the NASPAA directory; second, the NASPAA library of catalogues was canvassed; third, the director of NASPAA was consulted. These vehicles provided information on the recent place of legislatures in public administration programs; evidence of the historical attention given to legislatures was derived from various available documents and literature and from NASPAA records. The study sought evidence of attention to legislatures generally and to legislative administration specifically. Findings reveal some interest in legislatures as a factor in the public administration environment but neglect of the administration of legislatures.

Curriculum

The NASPAA directory lists over eighty programs of public administration across the country. Some programs are not listed by NASPAA, but the directory includes most schools and is certainly representative. The conclusion that legislatures are neglected is warranted on the basis of (1) a review of the catalogues of all the listed programs, (2) twenty-six questionnaire responses received from the schools listed in Table 4, and (3) consultations with various public administrationists and NASPAA officials (see Appendix A).

General Findings

No school has had a program or even a single course dealing with legislative administration until just recently.[1] Several schools that totally neglect legislatures do have programs in judicial administration. State University of New York (SUNY) at Albany has begun a legislative administration concentration within a master of public administration (MPA) degree program. (See Chapter 7 for a discussion of this development.) This is the only program of its kind in the United States.

TABLE 4
SCHOOLS RESPONDING TO QUESTIONNAIRE*

California State University, Chico
California State University, San Diego
Fairleigh Dickinson University
George Washington University
Harvard University
Indiana University
Northern Illinois University
Northwestern University
Nova University
Pennsylvania State University
Princeton University
State University of New York at Albany
Syracuse University
University of California, Riverside
University of Dayton
University of Illinois
University of Massachusetts
University of Michigan
University of Nebraska at Omaha
University of North Carolina
University of Pennsylvania
University of Pittsburgh
University of Southern California
University of Texas at Austin
University of Washington
West Virginia University

*These schools include most of the largest public administration programs in the country.

The absence of curricular attention to legislatures is most conspicuous at Roosevelt University, Texas Christian University, University of Southern California, San Diego State University, Chico State University, and

Golden State University because they do have programs in judicial administration.

Some schools manifest interest in legislative organization by offering legislative internships and legislative courses, which partially treat administrative questions, to public administration students. Indiana, Sangamon State, Memphis State, Buffalo State College, and the University of Texas at Austin indicate that they offer legislative internships. The best course discovered in the study—that is, the one most apparently geared to administrative aspects of legislatures—is offered by Howard University. This course, "Legislatures and Legislative Behavior," is part of Howard's MPA program and deals with committee systems, legislative reorganization schemes, and state and local legislatures.

New York University offers a course on "Legislative Review of Administration," which treats legislative control mechanisms. Northeastern lists a course on "Legislative Process" as an elective in the MPA curriculum, as does Southern Methodist. And Princeton has a seminar on "Legislation and Legislative Action," which focuses on bill drafting procedures.

Several schools report that their public administration students are able to take a course on "legislative process" as offered in the university's political science department. While several of these courses appear to give some attention to organizational aspects of legislatures (notably those at Colorado, Hawaii, Drake, Illinois, and South Dakota), most of them are concerned with the behavior or role of legislatures rather than with their administrative or managerial improvement.[2] The salient point is that they are listed as political science rather than public administration courses, implying that legislatures are external to the field of public administration.

In sum, most public administration curricula indicate no attention to legislatures; several programs provide a nonadministrative legislative process course; some permit a legislative process course that includes administrative concerns; a few curricula offer legislative courses as part of an MPA program; and only one public administration program offers a concentration in legislative administration.

Historical Perspective

Back catalogues of public administration schools were not available; thus, historical neglect of legislatures in curricula cannot be rigorously documented. What was available consisted of NASPAA records, reports from elder statesmen and scholars of the field, and George A. Graham's book on public administration education.[3]

NASPAA records indicate no past curricular attention to legislative administration and only infrequent inclusion of "legislative process" courses. None of the public administrationists consulted indicated that there were any past academic programs on the subject.[4] And Graham's review of the curricula of public administration programs at Michigan, Syracuse, Cincinnati, California, Minnesota, Harvard, and Pennsylvania revealed no departure from the record of neglect.[5]

RESEARCH

In addition to the questionnaire sent to research arms of public administration schools and a search through the literature for written products of research, legislators and legislative staff were asked if public administration schools have provided any assistance to legislatures (Appendix B). The following record emerged.

NASPAA lists indicate that formal research bureaus or institutes, linked with public administration programs, exist at Alabama, Arizona, Long Beach State, Berkeley, Georgia, Indiana, Michigan, Mississippi, Fairleigh Dickinson, SUNY Albany, Penn State, Memphis State, Tennessee, and Texas. While several, or all, of these centers may in the past have conducted legislature-related research, only the examples noted below were found cited in literature or by legislators and staff.

The Bureau of Public Administration of the University of California, forerunner of the present research centers at Berkeley and Long Beach, is the earliest example discovered of a public administration research arm, connected with a university, assisting a legislature. As early as 1935, the Bureau operated a legislative information service to prepare reports on current legislative problems for members of the California legislature.[6] However, the Bureau apparently limited its assistance chiefly to information on subject areas of proposed legislation; there is little evidence that it concerned itself with other internal administrative needs of the legislature.[7]

The only other early example of attention to legislatures is that of the Institute of Local and State Government of the University of Pennsylvania. Graham reported in his survey of public administration programs that this institute provided research assistance to a Pennsylvania legislative commission.[8]

Finally, in 1956, the Bureau of Government Research of the University of Maryland, in conjunction with the College of Business and Public Administration, sponsored and published a series of lectures on legislative reform by George B. Galloway. The resulting volume analyzes the results of the Congressional Reorganization Act of 1946, directly addressing questions of committee structure, workload, staffing, and fiscal controls.[9]

These are the only historical examples discovered of public administration schools conducting research related to legislatures. Recent examples are similarly sparse. Of the fifteen research institutes listed by NASPAA, only three report that they devote a significant part of their efforts to legislative improvement. The University of Georgia's Institute of Government undertakes considerable work for the Georgia state legislature,[10] and the Bureau of Public Administration at the University of Alabama expends nearly half its resources on assistance to the Alabama legislature. [11] The most extensive research assistance to legislatures appears to be provided by the Comparative Development Studies Center of State University of New York at Albany. It devotes the major part of its efforts to legislative administration research (see Chapter 7). The Institute of Public Administration at Arizona State, the Bureau of Public Administration of the University of Tennessee, the Institute of Governmental Studies at Memphis State, and the Bureau of Governmental Research at Mississippi do direct some of their attention to legislatures, but the efforts appear to be a relatively minor part of their programs.

In sum, the research arms of public administration schools appear to have widely ignored legislatures. Only a few research centers of those schools conduct much significant legislative research, though several more do show some interest. Historically, the record is even leaner.

Thus, schools of public administration, in both curriculum and research, evidence inattention to legislatures generally and neglect of legislative administration specifically. This record is in spite of exhortations from the field on the importance and feasibility of education. Fritz Morstein-Marx wrote that "however diverse the forms of government action may be, the management of public business is recognized as a field of career activity for which it is possible to provide training." [12] Leonard White maintained: "In the race with events, institutions of higher learning have their special responsibilities. They ought to produce a considerable share of the leadership of the oncoming generation. They will produce a due portion of the administrative talent upon which political leadership must depend." [13] And Edward Schten specifically noted in *Public Administration Review* that public administration schooling is important for legislative staff researchers.[14] Yet schools of public administration have paid little attention to legislatures.

ORGANIZATIONS

Various organizations could be considered as public administration bodies. Numerous management groups, political science fraternities, and government-related organizations are concerned with public administration. But in judging the attention of the organized field of public administration to legislatures, the record of the recognized organizational representation of the field is considered the most significant, and perhaps the only clearly admissible, evidence. Clearly, the American Society for Public Administration (ASPA) is the prime organizational representation of the field; thus the record of that organization was examined in terms of attention to legislatures.[15] The examination reveals a rarefied record.

The society was founded in 1939 and by 1975 had a membership of nearly 15,000 in eighty-four chapters across the country. It holds an annual national conference at which panels convene to discuss a wide range of topics considered pertinent to the field. The expressed purpose of the society is "to improve the administration of the public service at all levels of government and in all functional and program fields."

For evidence of attention to legislatures, records of the society were examined and officials were consulted. Membership of the society's national council, topical content of the national conferences, and areas of committee work were particularly studied. Evidence of interest in legislatures by local chapters of the society was also sought. In general, the society has demonstrated little attention to legislatures, although there is evidence that its local chapters have devoted somewhat more.

In an article noting administrative needs of legislatures, G. Russell Pipe listed organizations that had shown interest in improving legislative institutions.[16] He mentioned the American Political Science Association, the American Enterprise Institute, the American Assembly, and various foundations. Excluded from his inventory was the American Society for Public Administration.

Perhaps the most compelling justification for that exclusion is the record of the content of the annual national conferences of the society. There is no record of a conference panel on legislatures until 1972, when one session urged that the society give more attention to legislatures.[17] Indeed, at the 1946 national conference, during a time when congressional reorganization was receiving wide attention elsewhere, ASPA not only ignored legislatures but had a panel on *executive* reorganization instead.[18] This neglect at the conference was consistent with neglect by committees of ASPA. The Morstein-Marx volume notes that the American Political Science Association had a Committee on Congress, which contributed to and analyzed the Legislative Reorganization Act of 1946.[19] The American Society for Public Administration had none. In fact, the society has never had a committee on legislatures, nor has it conducted any studies on legislative administration.[20] In fact, when the society co-sponsored, with the American Academy of Political and Social Science, a special conference in 1967 on "Theory and Practice of Public Administration," no mention was made of legislatures. A major part of the conference, however, focused on "The American Public Executive." [21]

Undoubtedly the personal interests of the membership spurred the neglect of legislatures. A membership survey conducted in 1955 asked ASPA members to indicate areas of interest. Executive development was widely listed, as were municipal management, police, and public relations. Legislatures were mentioned by fewer than 1.5 percent of the members, though legislative-executive relations were frequently cited.[22] There has never been a president of ASPA who has had any significant experience with legislatures, nor have there been many executive council members with links to the legislative branch.[23]

Just as the only notable attention to legislatures in public administration literature came from the subfield of comparative and development administration, so too the only significant ASPA interest in legislatures was manifested by its Comparative Administration Group (CAG). And, as in the case of development literature, attention by CAG was relatively late and sparse. Nevertheless, in 1966 the CAG of ASPA, prompted largely by requirements of the U.S. Foreign Assistance Act, Title IX, did become concerned with legislatures and cause ASPA to contract with the Agency for International Development (AID) for a CAG study of legislatures.[24] Not coincidentally, a member of the CAG, James J. Heaphey, convened the first ASPA national conference panel on legislatures in 1972.

The overall ASPA record of inattention to legislatures is not mitigated by reference to its prehistory. The Committee on Public Administration of the Social Science Research Council, which began in 1928 and in many ways can be regarded as the predecessor of ASPA, similarly gave legislatures little attention. Between 1938 and 1944 the committee sponsored thirty-eight conferences, none of which dealt with legislatures.[25] It published twenty-four books and monographs, including one on judicial administration,[26] but none on legislatures.[27] And although it did form a subcommittee on Research in the Legislative Process,[28] no activity of that committee is evident.

There is evidence that local chapters of ASPA have been more interested in legislatures than the national organization. One monthly meeting in 1947 of the Albany, New York, chapter featured a panel on "Legislative Review of Administration" chaired by Donald Axelrod,[29] who later became the chairman of an academic program for public administration. The Washington, D.C., chapter in 1948 held a meeting on "Reappraisal of the Congressional Reorganization Act." [30] The same chapter elected an officer of the Library of Congress, George Galloway, as its vice-president in 1949, and in 1965 featured an address by a former congressman on congressional processes.[31] The secretary of the New York state senate, Albert J. Abrams, was elected president of the Albany, New York, chapter during the late 1960s. That chapter has periodically held panels dealing with legislatures. Similarly, in 1974, the Kentucky chapter held a meeting on "Self-Analysis of the Kentucky General Assembly."

In summary, the American Society for Public Administration has demonstrated little concern for legislatures, as did its forerunner, the Committee on Public Administration of the Social Science Research Council. Neither its national conferences, nor its committees, nor its special studies have evinced much attention to legislative bodies. Local chapters have been somewhat more attentive.

NOTES FOR CHAPTER 4

1. It should be noted that these findings are based largely on 1972–73 catalogues. Programs may have changed since that time.

2. The following schools offer courses that appear to fit this description: Arizona State, American University, Chico State, Harvard, Western Kentucky, Northern Illinois, Golden Gate, Virginia, West Virginia, Michigan, Nova, Sangamon State, Dayton, Massachusetts, Nebraska, and Washington.

3. George A. Graham, *Education for Public Administration* (Chicago: Public Administration Service, 1941).

4. Donald C. Stone reports that a study he recently conducted indicates that early education in public administration did emphasize legislative processes more than it does today. (Personal letter to the author dated February 20, 1974.)

5. Graham, *Education for Public Administration*, pp. 147–256.

6. The activity of the bureau is reported and described in the *Final Report* of the New York State Joint Legislative Committee on Legislative Methods, Practices, Procedures, and Expenditures, Legislative Document No. 31 (Albany: Williams Press, 1946), p. 148 ff.

7. The only evidence discovered is Dorothy C. Culver, *Legislative Reorganization*, 1941, and Eugene C. Lee, *The Presiding Officer and Rules Committee in Legislatures of the United States*, 1952, both published by the California Bureau. See also Victor Jones, *The Legislature and the Budget*, 1941.

8. Graham, *Education for Public Administration*, p. 252.

9. George B. Galloway, *Congressional Reform Revisited*

(College Park: University of Maryland Press, 1956).

10. For example, the institute has published *Handbook for Georgia Legislators* (1973) and *Strengthening the Georgia General Assembly* (1970).

11. For example, see James D. Thomas, *The Alabama Legislature* (University of Alabama: Bureau of Public Administration, 1974).

12. Fritz Morstein-Marx, ed., *The Elements of Public Administration*, 2nd ed. (Englewood Cliffs, N.J.: Prentice-Hall, 1959), p. 34.

13. Leonard D. White, *Introduction to the Study of Public Administration*, 4th ed. (New York: Macmillan, 1955), p. xii.

14. Edward V. Schten, "Administration and Legislative Research," *Public Administration Review* 23, no. 2 (June 1963): 84.

15. Evidence was also sought of attention to legislatures by other public administration-related organizations, such as the Institute of Public Administration. No significant activity was discovered.

16. G. Russell Pipe, "Congressional Liaison," *Public Administration Review* 26, no. 1 (March 1966): 22.

17. See James J. Heaphey, "Technical Assistance in the Administration of Legislatures," paper delivered at the annual meeting of ASPA, New York, March 1972.

18. Reported in *Public Administration Review* 6, no. 1 (winter 1946): 93.

19. Morstein-Marx, *The Elements of Public Administration*, 2nd ed., p. 536, note 6.

20. This fact was verified by the executive director of ASPA in personal communication with the author.

21. See James C. Charlesworth, ed., *Theory and Practice of Public Administration* (Philadelphia: American Academy, 1968).

22. "Membership Survey, ASPA," *Public Administration Review* 15, no. 1 (winter 1955): 46–47.

23. The only examples discovered are Barbara Matula and June Martin of central staff of the New York state assembly, who joined the ASPA executive council in 1970 and 1973, respectively; and Norman Beckman of the Library of Congress, who chaired a major ASPA committee in 1973.

24. This history is reported by Allan Kornberg and Lloyd D. Musolf, eds., *Legislatures in Developmental Perspective* (Durham, N.C.: Duke University Press, 1970), pp. 3–5.

25. William Anderson and John M. Gaus, *Research in*

Public Administration (Chicago: Public Administration Service, 1945), appendix 4.

26. Charles U. Samenou et al., *Research in Judicial Administration* (Washington, D.C.: Committee on Public Administration, 1942).

27. Anderson and Gaus, *Research in Public Administration,* appendix 5.

28. Ibid., appendix 3.

29. Reported in *Public Administration Review* 8, no. 1 (winter 1948): 78.

30. Ibid., p. 76.

31. Roger H. Davidson et al., *Congress in Crisis* (Belmont, Calif.: Wadsworth, 1966), p. 118, note 42.

5

Commentary: Summary and Perceptions

Examination of the record of the institutionalized field of public administration has revealed a considerable neglect of legislatures generally and of legislative administration specifically. The literature of the field has been largely empty or negative on the subject. Schools of public administration have offered few courses and little research concerned with the administration of legislatures. The national organization for the field has avoided activity concerned with legislatures. On the whole, every institutional manifestation of the field of public administration appears to have developed a virtually exclusive identification with the executive bureaucracy and a consequent inattention to the legislature. As Emmette S. Redford has noted: "The methods of Congress...have not had adequate consideration." [1] More basically, to borrow the incisive words of Herbert Emmerich: "While we have been repenting that it took us so long to perceive the political aspects of administration, we still have to explore the high administrative content of politics." [2]

One palliative: As noted at the beginning, this examination of the record of public administration has encompassed only the chief institutional manifestations of the field; thus the judgment of neglect of legislatures is here laid specifically against schools, ASPA, and basic literature, not necessarily, for example, against all individual public administrationists. For, as Luther Gulick has reminded us, several noted members of the field have demonstrated serious interest in legislatures.[3] Gulick himself served on the staff of the New York state legislature during the 1920s; Marshall Dimock was a member of the legislature of Vermont; and Bertram Gross was director of a congressional committee staff in the 1940s. Nevertheless, the absence of any significant institutional attention by public administration to legislatures, in contrast to the plethora of assistance it has rendered the executive, supports a considerable indictment.

Thus far the judgment of neglect is based solely on an examination of the record of identifiable representations of the field. Considering the difficulty, previously noted, in defining the field for examination, and the caveat that frequently apparent facts do not tell the whole story, it was deemed important to measure the perceptions of participants concerning the past relationship of public administration to legislatures. Do public administration scholars perceive the field as having neglected legislatures? Do legislators themselves consider that public administration has been inattentive to legislative bodies? Do legislative administrators and staff believe the field of public administration has excluded them? A negative reading would conflict with the evidence gleaned from the record and would compel serious re-examination of the indictment. On the other hand, an affirmative response could confirm and broaden the charge of neglect, for it might suggest that the record of neglect is more extensive than portrayed above.

Thus, a questionnaire was prepared to query noted scholars in the field on the matter of the attention of public administration to legislatures. Separate questionnaires were designed for legislators and legislative staff (see Appendix B). Appendix A identifies the respondents.

PERCEPTIONS OF SCHOLARS

The academicians, all of whom are recognized leaders of the public administration field, were asked generally for their thoughts on the subject of public administration and legislatures; they were not given a strictly designed series of questions. Though this methodology is surely not rigorous, the responses are nonetheless interesting and suggestive as well as corroborative of the recorded evidence. The perceptual evidence presented in this section is merely a check, or secondary reading, on the primary evidence already presented. Hence, any shortcomings in the questionnaires utilized are not considered critical.

As Table 5 indicates, the comments of the scholars

TABLE 5
PERCEPTIONS OF SCHOLARS
(Total Number of Respondents = 18)

	Number	Percentage
Perceive Neglect	18	100
Concerned about Neglect	15	82
Unconcerned about Neglect	2	12
Ambivalent about Neglect	1	6

reflect a perception that public administration has neglected legislatures. Two respondents, while conceding inattention, suggested that it has not been total. Said one, "My point is that the approach [including legislatures within the field] has not been neglected; instead, it has not been supported as much as in my opinion it needs to be." But most of the comments dwell on explanation: "I am not certain why these fields [legislatures and the judiciary] have been neglected by students of administration. There may be many reasons for the neglect. Since I am among the neglectful, I can only give you my own view."

Some were defensive: "Legislative administration ... is only one of a score of a hundred specialties under the general rubric of administration and ... the neglect of legislatures is no greater than the neglect of public school administration. ... The executive branch is large enough, complicated enough, to absorb the energy and attention of students." "There are so many other fields of neglect by our apparently limited number of public administration scholars that I cannot enthusiastically endorse a plea for attracting such scarce resources to the study of legislative administration."

One respondent begged the question: "I have considerable doubt about the feasibility of studying legislatures as an integral part of Public Administration study."

But most of the scholars expressed concern: "I think public administration should show as much interest in improving the organization and functioning of the legislature as in the departments and agencies." "The functioning of legislatures and their role in the political/administrative process needs much more attention."

[88]

Thus, public administration scholars do acknowledge the record of the field's overlooking legislatures.

PERCEPTIONS OF LEGISLATORS

Elected members of legislatures were specifically asked this question: "In your view has the field of public administration in the past abandoned or neglected legislatures?" As Table 6 indicates, three out of four legisla-

TABLE 6
RESPONSES OF LEGISLATORS
Question: "In your view has the field of public administration in the past abandoned or neglected legislatures?"

	Number	Percentage
Yes	34	72
No	13	28
Total	47	100

tors answered affirmatively. Moreover, the respondents hail from Congress and thirty states representing every region of the country. Several legislators supplied amplifying comments: "Let me say that it seems to me in general that public administration has neglected legislatures without a doubt." A few noted the field's emphasis: "Public administration has overlooked legislatures in favor of the executive branch." And several remarked that legislatures have neglected public administration as much as vice versa: "Public administration has not had a receptive audience." "Legislatures have frequently neglected the expertise and knowledge of competent public administrators."

In sum, legislators themselves seem to perceive that public administration has not been of assistance to their needs. It is noteworthy that the legislators' responses were based on a question that did not define or restrict the field of public administration. It might thus be inferred that the perception of neglect applies not only to institutional public administration but to individual and peripheral activity as well.

PERCEPTIONS OF LEGISLATIVE STAFF

Professional legislative staff members, representing various functions and legislatures (see Appendix A), were asked: "How do you see the past role of the public administration field (schools, organizations, and scholars and practitioners who identify with public administration) in legislative processes? Did the field abandon legislatures? Has it made any significant efforts or contributions that you know of?"

Table 7 depicts the response: over 90 percent of the

TABLE 7
PERCEPTIONS OF LEGISLATIVE STAFF
(Total Number of Respondents = 23)

	Number	Percentage
Perceive Near Total Neglect	15	65
Perceive Much Neglect	6	26
Perceive Some Attention	2	9
Perceive Much Attention	0	0
Total Perceiving Neglect	21	91
Total Perceiving Attention	2	9

respondents perceive public administration as having neglected legislatures. Descriptions of the attention of public administration to legislatures included the following: "near nonexistent," "passive," "minimal," and "not significant." One high-ranking staff official said: "I get the impression that schools of public administration are not particularly interested in state legislatures and have therefore contributed very little." A key legislative aide remarked: "Most of the literature has tended to emphasize the executive side of governmental activities and to have ignored the potential for public administration participation in the professional/technical sense with legislatures." A staff director commented: "The past role of public administration has greatly overlooked the need for administrative study and development of management expertise within the legislative branches of government." And a staffer of a committee on legislative improvement reflected: "I think we can all agree that this [public administration and legislatures] is a neglected linkage."

Several respondents emphasized false impressions of legislatures: "Public administration has misrepresented legislative processes." "Scholars of P.A. are not familiar with legislative process." "As a legislative staff person, I see a lack of understanding on the part of administrators of the legislative process."

One committee director was specific: "Some otherwise excellent products of public budgeting writers have treated the role of legislatures only in passing in their call for budget reform." And a veteran in legislatures made a significant distinction: "The field of political science itself has shown interest in state legislatures, but not the field of public administration."

In short, legislative staff seem to perceive public administration neglect of legislatures in clear and specific terms; and they express this perception more consistently than either legislators or scholars.

To summarize, perceptions of those involved in the field of public administration and in legislatures support the conclusion derived from the record examination: public administration has neglected legislatures.

Notes for Chapter 5

1. Emmette S. Redford, *Democracy in the Administrative State* (New York: Oxford, 1969), p. 131.

2. Herbert Emmerich, "The Scope of the Practice of Public Administration" in James C. Charlesworth, ed., *Theory and Practice of Public Administration* (Philadelphia: American Academy of Political and Social Science, 1968), p. 96. While it is doubtful whether Emmerich had legislatures in mind, his point is nonetheless an appropriate recognition that political institutions, such as legislatures, do have administrative needs.

3. Personal letter to the author dated April 4, 1974.

6

Analysis:
Why the Neglect?

Considering the importance of legislatures to governmental systems and, more particularly, the presence of W. F. Willoughby's perspective during the formative period of the public administration field, the record of neglect, documented in the previous chapters, may at first be somewhat surprising, if not quite astounding. A number of factors, however, help explain the record. Although analysis of these explanatory causes is largely a historical undertaking, it is pertinent to the present study because it can provide additional perspective for judging the propriety of any future involvement of public administration with legislatures.

The following depiction of past influences does not presume to be definitive but rather is illustrative and suggestive of external and internal factors that may have affected the direction the field took relative to legislatures. Seven explanatory classifications are utilized as a convenience, not as a rigorous categorization; for many of the phenomena identified or suggested overlap and interact and could validly be discussed under more than one of the general groupings.

Although Woodrow Wilson's 1887 article is usually cited today as the beginning of the public administration field in the United States,[1] Frank Goodnow's *Politics and Administration*,[2] published in 1900, has been recognized as the *principia* for public administration writings.[3] Leonard White's *Introduction to the Study of Public Administration* (1926), the first textbook in the field, crystallized the executive bent that has characterized public administration. What factors between 1900 and 1926 can account for White's perspective and for his book's being so successful? And what influences after 1926 contributed to the prevalence of the executive oriented tone set by White?

HISTORICAL FACTORS

Significant events and pervasive attitudes can be determinants of the course of individual lives and careers as well as of institutional, disciplinary, or professional development. Certainly the direction of the public administration field was influenced by the character of the period of its emergence and maturation. Specific events, sources of origin, popular perceptions, and manifest needs and opportunities peculiar to the time may provide some insight into the field's relative disregard of legislatures.

Events

Two pre-1926 events are noteworthy: World War I and the League of Nations experience. The war, in its enormity and challenge, undoubtedly had a telling impact

[94]

on attitudes. As Dwight Waldo has written: "The un-
questioned faith in democracy as a superior way of life
and the boundless confidence in its ultimate triumph
were shaken by the smooth precision and smashing
power of Germany at war." [4] Doubts and self-examination resulted in an emphasis on efficiency, which the Ger-
mans had demonstrated: "If democracy were to survive
it had somehow to add efficiency to its ideals of liberty
and equality." [5] Legislatures were not a likely source of
increased efficiency, but new administrative organs and
devices in the executive were.

At the same time a world legislature, the League of
Nations, was instituted. It faltered and eventually failed,
providing more possible cause for disillusionment and
cynicism about legislatures.

Shortly after White's textbook appeared, the de-
pression and Franklin Roosevelt's administration resulted in a tremendous expansion of the executive branch
and in the creation of numerous and varied administrative
agencies. Given these opportunities and needs, public administrationists focused on the executive bureaucracy,
and White's book stressing executive management was
one of the few written sources available that specifically
addressed the needs of the new public managers.

Willoughby's perspective, with its broader scope and
inclusion of legislative and judicial administrative needs,
was not so pertinent to the exigencies and realities of the
times. Legislatures were not doing nearly as much as the
executive and thus may have appeared to have little need
of administrative attention. Furthermore, the FDR era
witnessed a focus on the federal government in Washington, with only one legislative institution, and a relative
decline in state and local government. Public administration turned its attention to where the big action was.

White's book, again, was more attuned to this focus, while Willoughby gave states equal time in his writings.[6]

World War II added to the momentum by further increasing both the size of and focus on the executive bureaucracy. Thousands of public administrators, academic as well as professionals, gained experience in and commitment to the executive branch. More and more, the public administration field identified with the executive.

Origins

The historical origins of the field may also have influenced the trend toward the executive and away from legislatures. Public administration can trace its strongest roots to political science and business, both of which, during the period of the emergence of public administration, tended to emphasize a strong executive. As Waldo has noted, political science after the Civil War became increasingly sympathetic to the notion of a strong executive: "It [that view] found its justification in the unhealthy condition of our government and politics. It was nourished by admiration for... American business organization."[7] Political scientist Gamaliel Bradford articulated the sentiment of the time when public administration was beginning to emerge:

> No government has ever been permanently able to maintain itself where a numerous legislature has taken upon itself directly the work of administration.... At present the question is by what method can public opinion be most effectively brought to bear upon the powers of government, and we have reached the conclusion that to this end public opinion is to be concentrated on individuals. It is evident that this can only be effectively done in the executive branch.[8]

A judgment of this extent by a leading political science reformer, at a time when public administration was developing from the political science discipline, can shed considerable light on the record.

During the first decade of this century, business organizations were recognizing and espousing the principles they practiced, and this development constituted the first rigorous theories of administration. Frederick Taylor's *Principles of Scientific Management* is the chief espousal.[9] These theories stressed division of labor, efficiency, and executive control, and had considerable influence on the emerging field of public administration. Needless to say, their application to collegial, "inefficient" legislative organizations might not have been altogether convenient. On the other hand, they undoubtedly abetted the emphasis of public administrationists on the executive.

Finally, the public administration field was emerging during an age when the popular image of and attitude toward state and local legislatures in particular (and occasionally even toward the national Congress) were not inducive of administrative concern. Legislatures seldom appeared to affect people's lives, and the notion of the "citizen legislature" was strong. The legislature was widely viewed as "a sometime thing, made up of friends and neighbors who, out of a sense of patriotic duty, sacrifice some time every two years to consider questions of general concern." [10] With serious government business at hand in the executive branch, disregard of these legislatures by the public administration field is not wholly surprising.

SOCIOLOGICAL ELEMENTS

The social backgrounds of public administrationists, both civil servants and academics, may have contributed to the tendencies of the field. Three observations are suggestive in this regard. First, several influential writers and practitioners in the field were raised and educated in countries with a tradition of executive dominance. Carl Friedrich and Fritz Morstein-Marx, for example, were both educated in Germany, as were Frank Goodnow and William E. Mosher. Morstein-Marx became editor of the *Public Administration Review*. Mosher was the premier dean of the first school for public administration in the United States. Their backgrounds, and those of others, may have predisposed them to identify administration with the executive and to disregard legislatures.

Second, a strong moralistic grain, which can tend to produce a "right-wrong" perspective and a distaste for compromise, has frequently appeared in the field. Indeed, the Pendleton Act, which established the civil service on a "merit system," was largely based on an evangelical outrage at previous abuses by public administrators and on a commitment to place the civil service on a high moral plane. As Frederick Mosher remarks of the Pendleton Act: ". . . its essence was moral at a time when American thinking was heavily moralistic. Few reform movements in American history could draw so clear a distinction between right and wrong, between the 'good guys' and the 'bad guys' " [11] It is noteworthy that this act, which created a formal institution for public administrators to identify with, applied only to the executive bureaucracy, not to staff of the legislature, and that Leonard White later served as commissioner of the civil service.

Frederick Taylor viewed scientific management nearly as a moral crusade. William Mosher and Donald Stone, both former deans of graduate schools of public administration, are rightly recognized as men of exceptionally strong moral convictions.

Legislatures are *sui generis* compromise institutions in which political considerations can occasionally blur moral principles, and which in the past have frequently been prime targets for charges of corruption. People of strong moral belief might tend to avoid such institutions and concentrate their energies instead on more "principled," less "political" institutions such as executive-administrative agencies.

Third, and perhaps most saliently, there has been a strong association of lawyers with legislatures and a sometimes intense aversion to legalists by public administrationists. Norton Long expressed a popular view in the public administration field when he observed that legislatures have long been the domain of the "upper class," of professional lawyers, while the bureaucracy has been the natural home of the common man.[12] This perception of distinct social groupings for particular branches of government has been accompanied by a not always suppressed antipathy, as Waldo noted: "The anti-legal temper of public administration is obvious and its import clear. In fact, one does not need to go far in the literature of public administration to find that if any person is to count for less than one in the New Order it is the lawyer! The lawyer suffers from a meager social outlook; the spirit of the New Management does not abide with him...." [13] White's textbook expressed a distinctly antilegal bias,[14] and John Pfiffner's 1935 textbook labors under little inhibition: "The twentieth century social scientist feels that the lawyer should not have the predominant part in molding political and social thought... the eighteenth century legalistic approach to government must give way to the realistic scientific method." [15] In view of such expressed disdain for the professional class that dominated legislatures, it is little wonder that the public administration field did not rush to serve with them.

In sum, the educational background, moral bent, and

social identification of some leading public administrationists may help explain why the field has neglected legislatures.

IDEOLOGICAL CURRENTS

Perhaps the most effective influences on the field relative to involvement with legislatures were the ideological perspectives and guides that dominated. Several strong currents can be identified that plausibly prevailed against the possibility of attention to legislatures.

Politics-Administration Dichotomy

The most evident of these influences is the theory of the politics-administration dichotomy, which crystallized during the very early years of the field and largely held sway until after World War II. The first substantial book of the field, Goodnow's *Politics and Administration*, drew the distinction clearly. There were two basic functions of government—decision and execution. The legislative body was to carry out the political aspect; the executive was to implement the policy decisions. Politics was the realm of the party and the legislature; administration that of the executive.[16] Woodrow Wilson's original essay made a similar distinction,[17] and the dichotomy was further developed and fortified as the field of public administration grew. Pfiffner clearly stated the sentiment in 1935: "It [politics] must be controlled and confined to its proper sphere which is the determination, crystallization, and declaration of the will of the community. Administration, on the other hand, is the carrying into effect of this will once it has been made clear by political processes." [18]

This ideological principle had a strong hold into the 1940s, and in its explicit as well as implicit characterization of the legislature and the government system, provided a significant raison d'etre for neglect of legislatures. It made administrative students, as one critic noted, disposed to deal with questions of administration as if they were separate from the general political system.[19]

It is further remarkable that even when systemic questions were considered, the legislature was frequently shunned. For example, Goodnow did speak to questions of administrative accountability but turned to the political party, not the legislature directly, as the instrument of control. The party, he argued, is the necessary device both for expressing and executing policy.[20]

In brief, an ideological dichotomy between politics and administration may have conditioned the perspective of public administrationists in such a way that legislative involvement would be either not considered or quickly rejected as inappropriate.

Gospel of Efficiency

Most periods in history can be epitomized by a few key words, and, as Dwight Waldo has observed, *efficiency* was the national catchword during the period of the development of public administration: "It is amazing what a position of dominance 'efficiency' assumed, how it waxed until it had assimilated or overshadowed other values, how men and events came to be degraded or exalted according to what was assumed to be its dictate. It became a movement...a 'Gospel.'" [21] Public administrationists embraced the doctrine without restraint. As Frederick C. Mosher notes: "The field proclaimed a new gospel to a new deity: efficiency.... Efficient administration was 'good'; inefficient administration was 'bad.'" [22] Indeed, it was in the name of the canons of efficiency that both the Brownlow and Hoover Commissions urged that the executive be fortified as "the center of energy." [23]

Legislatures would be among the most likely institutions to be "degraded" by apostles of such a gospel. They were not only notoriously "inefficient" but by their nature could easily be viewed as having little hope of salvation. Under the efficiency gospel legislatures were the temples of the pagans. Combined with the politics-administration dichotomy, the gospel of efficiency can be seen as a strong ideological obstruction to any relationship between the field of public administration and legislatures.

Scientism Syndrome

Closely related to the gospel of efficiency is the commitment to science that took hold during the formative period of public administration. Inspired by the achievements of the physical sciences and discouraged by the problems of human affairs, many came to believe that science could solve all difficulties, that the scientific method, when applied to social affairs, would produce the golden age.[24] This faith in science and in the efficacy of the scientific method is manifest in the literature of public administration. Waldo has portrayed the tenets of the writers: "Science relies upon exact measurement: so let the data of administration be measured. Science is concerned only with facts: so let the 'facts' be sovereign. Science makes use of experiment: so let the mode of administrative advance be experimental." [25]

Legislatures frequently require avoidance of clearcut determinations for the sake of political realities. And their data frequently include intangibles. They routinely must go beyond, behind, and underneath facts and

[102]

concern themselves with immeasurables. And they regularly must rely on precedent, because the risks of experiment are often politically intolerable. The field of public administration, enamored of science, was thus not a natural ally of legislatures. Alfred de Grazia puts it bluntly: "In all of the scientific thought about administration, much of which was of a high order, there was little place for the concept of government by legislature. How could one organize a legislature to 'get things done' according to the principles of hierarchy, subordination, efficiency, integration, delegation with strict accountability, and so on, with the jargon of the new science? And how could one do so without taking the heart and soul out of the legislature? It could not be." [26]

After World War II, what Sayre calls "prophets of a new science of administration" emerged.[27] Herbert Simon was the chief representative.[28] He advocated a scientism based on the argument of logical positivism that facts must be separated from values. Legislatures, being arenas for fact-value synthesis, were not likely clients of Simon's scientists.

Focus on Rationality

Waldo has identified rationalism as one of the most outstanding characteristics of American administrative study.[29] While this is closely related to the ideologies of efficiency and scientism discussed above, it merits separate notation not only because of its explanatory utility but also because it will be an important guide when exploring the future relationship between the public administration field and legislatures (see Chapter 9).

During its development, Waldo suggests, the field was largely undisturbed by discoveries from psychology concerning the irrational forces influencing human be-

[103]

havior.[30] That is, in spite of new insights[31] and disillusionment about the rationality of men, the field tended to assume rationality when it faced administrative questions: "One gets the impression from some of the literature that organizations can be designed according to blueprints, fabricated of standardized parts, crated, shipped, and assembled on order at any time or place." [32]

An example of this perspective was the apparent surprise of public administrators at the opposition to the 1937 Brownlow federal reorganization proposal. The focus on rationalism had seemingly created a righteousness mentality within the public administration field, an aloofness from nonrational factors, and an expectation that its superior arrangements would, of course, be desired and adopted.

The volume of the imponderables that operate in legislatures—the political realities, the emotional elements, and the unmistakably "irrational" influences—probably were evident even to the astigmatic rationalists and thus further diminished any inclination to get involved with legislatures. Furthermore, given the rigid perspective, any attempted relationship might have been doomed.

The rationalism focus began to attenuate after World War II with the efforts of Alexander Leighton, Philip Selznick, and others,[33] but its latent influence in the field will have to be recognized and understood in any future efforts to relate the field to legislatures.

Expertise Complex

Conviction of the necessity for "experts" in government was widespread during the development of the public administration field. The tenet generally entailed notions of permanency, training, and specialization and was based on the vision that experts were needed in govern-

ment in order to preserve modern bureaucracy.[34] Waldo
felt as late as 1948 that this ideology still prevailed.[35]

Connected with the expertise complex, there appears
to have been a commandment against experts serving political purposes. Legislatures were examples par excellence of nonexpertise. They convened infrequently; their
members were quite impermanent; and political considerations prevailed in their deliberations. The "expertise"
complex could conceivably have caused legislatures to appear to be inappropriate territory for "expert," "nonpolitical" public administrators. Or, if not that, then the
complex perhaps fostered a view of legislatures as hopelessly immune to the benefits of expertise.

Professional Identification

The expertise complex helped produce a professional
self-awareness among public administrationists. The
character of that "class consciousness" was shaped by
many factors and resulted in an ideological professional
identity that may have inhibited a relationship with legislatures; for that identity was largely with the executive
branch. As Willoughby wrote: "In the threefold classifi-
cation of government powers this [administration]is
confused with, or treated as part of, the executive. To so
great an extent is this true that the two terms, executive
and administration, are used almost interchangeably."[36]

This ideological identification had its source in early
administrative writings and was fortified by experience.
During the period of the emergence of the field, writers
such as Woodrow Wilson were proclaiming a need for
stronger executive leadership and urging an increase in
the power and responsibilities of the president. In
Waldo's characterization of the period: "Students home
from the Continent were anxious to find a formula that

would enable democracy to secure the manifest advantages of autocracy." [37] Exaltation of the executive became the Holy Grail.

Historical experience solidified the perspective. The civil service, of course, was already associated primarily with the executive. But then the New Deal of FDR brought an increase in involvement of public administrationists with the executive and a change in the type of involvement. Public administration academics and writers in the field took full-time administrative positions in government for significant periods of time, then returned to academia. World War II blended into and increased this development. Waldo, who was among those who went to Washington and then returned to the university, feels that this experience caused public administrationists like himself to identify as "The President's Men" and to view the legislature as "the enemy." [38]

Thus, the social group comprising the field of public administration gained experiences that tended to crystallize identification with the executive and to cause not only a neglect of legislatures but a "rival" perception of them.

Antilegislature Ambience

Throughout the development of public administration there have been pervasive expressions of pessimism and distaste concerning legislatures that may have abetted the "enemy" view mentioned above.

At the very beginning of the development of the field, Goodnow referred to legislatures in cynical terms: "The form of a legislature survives, but the substance and spirit have vanished. The legislative power is exercised by one man or a small self-constituted group through dummies who are still in name representatives of the people." [39]

[106]

Fifty years later the view was a bit altered, but the cynicism undiminished: "...conditions are too anarchical in our Congress to permit that body to try to organize its experience for the production of knowledge." [40] Norton Long proclaimed that legislators instinctively disassociate themselves from administrative concepts,[41] implying that public administration should have no interest in Congress. Indeed, when a prolegislature book appeared in 1950,[42] *Public Administration Review* commented on it with rather unctuous but unmistakable obloquy: "Hyneman's book is a sharp challenge to the doctrinal orthodoxies which have dominated public administration circles over the last years. His iconoclastic thesis is developed with a rigorous logic and courageous consistency which compels admiration even when it does not induce assent." [43] And consistently during the past two decades there have been declarations from political scientists that legislatures are in decline, that they are archaic and relatively powerless.[44] The dissemination of views such as these conceivably further inclined the public administration field away from involvement with legislative institutions.

Furthermore, antilegislature inclinations of public administrationists may have been nourished by an "antipublic administration" bent within legislatures. Several legislators consulted during the present study expressed the view that a past lack of receptivity by legislatures inhibited interest by public administration.

In brief, ideologies concerning politics and administration, efficiency, science, rationality, expertise, professional identity, and the status of legislatures are distinguishable and of explanatory utility. The ideologies do overlap, and their categorization may be somewhat contrived. But the perspectives they suggest were present in the field to a significant degree, and they do provide considerable insight for explaining the neglect of legislatures.

ECONOMIC INFLUENCES

While financial factors may not be as compelling as economic determinists would have us believe, people do tend to go where the jobs are. For the public administration field, the jobs have been in the executive branch. In particular, positions for practitioners have generally been coordinated through the civil service, which, as has already been noted, did not apply to the legislature. Even had the civil service included positions with the legislature, the overwhelming number of jobs would still have been with executive agencies; professional legislative staffs have, until recently, been very small.[45] Further, the civil service provided economic security, which legislative work did not.

Several scholars consulted during this study cited the job situation as the key cause of public administration's neglect. One remarked: "The executive branch has 100 career jobs to offer for every one that legislatures can offer. Legislative staff jobs are notoriously insecure—or are so regarded." Another commented: "The general practice of legislatures to use a patronage system has caused those concerned with professional administration to not pay heed to the legislative needs in the administration area."

Second, research money—dollars for scholars—was frequently available for studies of executive-oriented matters, but seldom for legislative studies. The beginning of public administration research was the establishment in 1906 of the New York Bureau of Municipal Research, the spirit of which has deeply affected the field.[46] It, and other research organs that followed the bureau, were very close to the business community and committed to the idea of "efficiency." Its leaders reportedly "detested politicians" [47] and were thus not inclined to spend research money on legislatures. Considering the influence of the bureau movement on the field, as well as the need of researchers for financial support, the propensity of the bureau and its offshoots may be a substantial reason why the public administration field disregarded legislatures.

POLITICAL TEMPERAMENT

Association of legislatures with the political aspect of government, and the general disposition of the public administration field against politics per se, may have influenced the direction of the field. Generally, politics and politicians per se appear to have been anathema to public administrationists. (Of course, as discussed earlier, public administrationists have in fact often been involved in reconciliation functions through the bureaucracy, but it is doubtful that this was recognized as politics. Similarly, devotion to the president was to the office more than to the political man.)

On an intellectual level, the politics-administration dichotomy for some time freed public administrators from political "bacteria." But when that illusion disintegrated, the field still hesitated to approach political questions and institutions.[48] There appears to have been a reluctance to consider administration in terms of the political system or to recognize administration as systemic at all. Hence, the field showed little positive concern about legislatures.

On an emotional level also, politics has appeared to be distasteful to students of administration. Waldo de-

scribes a "strong feeling of revulsion toward 'politics'"
as a characteristic of the field during its development,
and he found that in 1948 the prevailing attitude was still
that "politics is a low form of activity." [49] Indeed, when
the first school of public administration was founded in
the United States, in 1924, the mere suggestion of the
word "politics" caused a stern reprimand: The founder
and endower wrote officials at Syracuse University that
the new school must not be named the "Maxwell School
of Politics" but rather the "Maxwell School of Citizenship." He fully chronicled the evils of politics and expressed his hope that students of the school would avoid
it.[50] This disdain of political matters conceivably contributed in some measure to the trend of ignoring legislative
bodies.

Psychological Proclivities

It might reasonably be argued that psychological
factors, such as illusions of power and insecurity, affected the course taken by the field. On one hand administrative writings tended to portray the public administration field as a "governing class," a power unto itself,
an independent and essential part of government, a
prime force, "not a mere tool of the legislature." [51]
There appears to be a power complex that may have
tended to drive the field away from the legislature, which
might subjugate it.

On the other hand, given the relative newness of the
field, fears of weakness and apprehensions caused by insecurity may have led to a desire for isolation from the
political "germs" of legislatures. The strength of the new
field was largely in its claim of being a science, an asset
that might prevail in executive administration but not
immediately in the legislature.

[110]

Relatedly, a territoriality factor may have been influential. Altshuler has noted: "At the birth of public administration as an academic discipline, quite naturally a need was felt to explain with the greatest possible clarity what distinguished it from other subjects within the broad field of government. The constitutional distinction between legislative and executive institutions provided an obvious foundation on which to build." [52] In this perspective the field of political science can be seen as having co-opted the area of legislatures, and the new public administrationists were not about to invade. This can be seen in Simon's explanation for limiting public administration to the executive: "The selection of the problem area is an arbitrary one, made partly because of a traditional academic breakdown of specialties." [53] In any case, these and other psychological influences may further explain the record of avoidance of legislatures.

FORTUITOUS PHENOMENA AND EXPEDIENCY

Finally, having developed a rather lengthy scheme of causation, the analysis should recognize and consider the element of chance. Surely to some degree it may have been just "in the stars" that public administration would neglect legislatures.

Specifically, if we consider the success of White's 1926 book, relative to Willoughby's effort, as a key turning point in the development of the field, the function of chance cannot be ignored. As fate had it, White was considerably younger than Willoughby (thirty-five, whereas Willoughby wrote *Principles of Public Administration* at sixty). White therefore was perhaps more aggressive and intent on furthering his fame and influence. As fate had it, White's book was published by a commercial, profit-oriented New York house that conducted a sales campaign in behalf of the book. Willoughby's work came out of the Brookings Institution, where publishing and salesmanship were secondary to research and intellectual reward. In effect, it can be argued that White's perspective was propagandized by an ideologically disinterested but profit-intent vehicle. Had Willoughby been published by a commercial firm, things might have been different.

Numerous other occurrences can be analyzed in terms of fortuity, such as the coincidence of FDR's election and the outbreak of war at a critical period in the development of the field. The point is that though there are many logical explanations for the neglect of legislatures, some or all of them might have become inoperative were it not for some factors of chance and timing.

Elements of expediency also may have entered the picture. It could have appeared easier to highly motivated public administrationists to effect change and good government through the executive than through the legislature. One enlightened administrator with sufficient power would be easier to secure than hundreds of enlightened legislators. And there seems to have been a sense of urgency. As the Brownlow Committee prefaced its 1937 report: "Without results we know that democracy means nothing and ceases to be alive in the minds and hearts of men." [54]

Finally, the effect of momentum should not be overlooked. Once a trend begins, it is difficult to change let alone stop it. While several of the influences identified above may have been substantial, even compelling, at the time, many of them later lost strength; yet legislatures continued to be neglected. The politics-administration dichotomy was challenged. The zeal for efficiency was tempered. Noted figures in the field, including Leonard White, even urged that attention be given to legislatures.

Yet the neglect phenomenon prevailed. Certainly momentum, and perhaps a feeling that the field was already committed to the huge executive and did not have time for legislatures, contributed to the continuance. (The fact that the field is committed to the executive is still cited by some scholars as a reason for not assisting legislatures today.)

Whereas at the beginning the presence of "good" reasons may have influenced the direction of the field, later the mere absence of compelling cause may have inhibited a change or branch-off of direction. Indeed, legislatures may not have been interested in any relationship with public administration due to a distrust of public administrationists because of past criticisms.[55] As the following chapter will show, some provocative reasons have finally appeared, and a new direction in the field may be taking shape.

SUMMARY

In brief, the record of the neglect of legislatures by public administration is not altogether unfathomable. To wit, there are historical, sociological, ideological, economic, political, psychological, and fortuitous circumstances that shed light on the development. The presence of White's perspective in 1926 is scrutable and the prevalence of his vision is understandable. But adherence to that direction is neither inevitable nor necessarily desirable, nor, as the next chapter discloses, is it unmitigated.

Notes for Chapter 6

1. Woodrow Wilson, "The Study of Administration," *Political Science Quarterly* 2, no. 2 (June 1887): 197–222.

2. Frank Goodnow, *Politics and Administration* (New York: Macmillan, 1900).

3. Dwight Waldo, *The Administrative State* (New York: Ronald Press, 1948), p. 106.

4. Ibid., p. 10.

5. Ibid., p. 11.

6. Indeed, his *Principles of Public Administration* (Washington, D.C.: Brookings Institution, 1927) was subtitled "With Special Reference to the National and State Governments" and included extensive discussion of state organization.

7. Waldo, *The Administrative State*, p. 105.

8. Gamaliel Bradford, *The Lesson of Popular Government* (New York: Macmillan, 1899), pp. 43–46.

9. Frederick Taylor, *Principles of Scientific Management* (New York: Harper, 1911).

10. Citizens Conference on State Legislatures, *The Sometime Governments* (New York: Bantam, 1971), p. 32.

11. Frederick C. Mosher, *Democracy and the Public Service* (New York: Oxford University Press, 1968), p. 76.

12. Norton E. Long, "Bureaucracy and Constitutionalism," *American Political Science Review* 46, no. 3 (September 1952): 813–814.

13. Waldo, *The Administrative State*, p. 79.

14. Leonard D. White, *Introduction to the Study of Public Administration* (New York: Harper and Brothers, 1926), p. ix.

Analysis

15. John M. Pfiffner, *Public Administration* (New York: Ronald Press, 1935), p. 18.

16. Goodnow, *Politics and Administration*, p. 22.

17. Wilson, "The Study of Administration," p. 210 ff.

18. Pfiffner, *Public Administration*, p. 9.

19. A. C. Millspaugh, "Democracy and Administrative Organization" in C. G. Haines and M. E. Dimock, eds., *Essays on the Law and Practice of Governmental Administration* (Baltimore: Johns Hopkins University Press, 1935), pp. 47–93.

20. Goodnow, *Politics and Administration*, pp. 199–202.

21. Waldo, *The Administrative State*, p. 19.

22. Mosher, *Democracy and the Public Service*, p. 71.

23. See Wallace S. Sayre, "Trends of a Decade in Administrative Values," *Public Administration Review* 11, no. 1 (winter 1951): 13.

24. See Bernard Crick, *The American Science of Politics* (Berkeley: University of California Press, 1964). Although he does not address public administration writings specifically, Crick traces the development of scientism in political science generally.

25. Waldo, *The Administrative State*, p. 21.

26. Alfred de Grazia, *Congress: The First Branch of Government* (Washington, D.C.: American Enterprise Institute, 1966), p. 4.

27. Wallace S. Sayre, "Premises of Public Administration: Past and Emerging," *Public Administration Review* 18, no. 2 (spring 1958): 104.

28. Herbert Simon, *Administrative Behavior* (New York: Macmillan, 1945).

29. Waldo, *The Administrative State*, p. 25.

30. Ibid.

31. Notably Elton Mayo, *Human Problems of an Industrial Civilization* (New York: Viking, 1933).

32. Waldo, *The Administrative State*, p. 26.

33. Alexander Leighton, *The Governing of Men* (Princeton: Princeton University Press, 1945); Philip Selznick, *TVA and the Grass Roots* (Berkeley: University of California Press, 1949).

34. For example, see A. L. Lowell, "Expert Administrators in Popular Government," *American Political Science Review* 8, no. 1 (February 1913): 45–62.

35. Waldo, *The Administrative State*, pp. 91–92.

36. Willoughby, *Principles of Legislative Organization and Administration*, p. 8. Wilson, "The Study of Administra-

tion," p. 198, had explicitly identified administration with the executive.

37. Waldo, *The Administrative State,* p. 36.

38. Dwight Waldo in personal interview with the author, December 3, 1973, at Syracuse, New York. See also Roger H. Davidson et al., *Congress in Crisis* (Belmont, Calif.: Wadsworth, 1969), p. 39, for a discussion of causes of identity with the executive.

39. Goodnow, *Politics and Administration,* p. 170.

40. Long, "Bureaucracy and Constitutionalism," pp. 815–816. See also Pendleton Herring, *Presidential Leadership* (New York: McGraw-Hill, 1940), chapters 1–4. Herring argues that legislative interference is the greatest obstacle to improving efficiency in government.

41. Roland A. Young had previously suggested this in *This Is Congress* (New York: McGraw-Hill, 1943), chapter 1.

42. Charles Hyneman, *Bureaucracy in a Democracy* (New York: Harper, 1950).

43. Merle Fainsod, "The Presidency and Congress," *Public Administration Review* 11, no. 2 (spring 1951): 122.

44. For example, see Samuel Huntington, "Congressional Responses to the Twentieth Century" in D. B. Truman, ed., *Congress and America's Future* (Englewood Cliffs, N.J.: Prentice-Hall, 1965); C. Hollis, *Can Parliament Survive?* (London: Hollis and Carter, 1949); and G. Lowenberg, ed., *Modern Parliaments: Change or Decline* (Chicago: Aldine Atherton, 1971).

45. For the example of the staff size of the New York state legislature, see Alan P. Balutis, "Professional Staffing of the New York State Legislature" (Ph.D. diss., State University of New York at Albany, 1973), pp. 55–56.

46. According to Waldo, *The Administrative State,* pp. 31–32.

47. Ibid., p. 32.

48. See Dwight Waldo, "The Administrative State Revisited," *Public Administration Review* 25, no. 1 (March 1965): 21.

49. Waldo, *The Administrative State,* p. 25.

50. Letter of George Maxwell to Vice Chancellor W. P. Graham of Syracuse University, dated August 18, 1924.

51. Waldo discusses this in *The Administrative State,* pp. 92–93. See also W. E. Mosher, "The Making of a Public Servant," *National Municipal Review* 28, no. 2 (June 1939): 416–419; and Pendleton Herring, *Public Administration and*

the Public Interest (New York: McGraw-Hill, 1936) as examples of Waldo's point.

52. Alan A. Altshuler, *The Politics of the Federal Bureaucracy* (New York: Dodd, Mead, 1968), p. 56.

53. Herbert A. Simon et al., *Public Administration* (New York: Knopf, 1950), p. 7.

54. President's Committee on Administrative Management, *Report* (Washington, 1937), p. 1.

55. See Davidson et al., *Congress in Crisis,* p. 41.

7

Augurs of Change: Efforts at Legislative Improvement

The lack of attention to legislatures by public administration, while extensive, is not inveterate. Moreover, indications are that a new trend is developing, that the field may indeed be turning some attention to legislatures. An examination of the record would be incomplete without mention of these new developments. Additionally, the study would be lacking without reference to efforts at legislative improvement that have originated outside the field of public administration. These "external" activities have entered the void partially created by the inattention of public administration and may have prompted new awareness on the part of people in the field. Furthermore, such activities have helped clarify the need for public administration skills within legislatures and conceivably could be significant vehicles for channeling future public administration assistance.

[119]

Examination of the Record

This chapter, then, describes recent and developing indicators of public administration interest in legislatures, suggests some factors facilitating these developments and pointing to a new trend, and examines major efforts at legislative improvement from outside the field of public administration.

RECENT DEVELOPMENTS WITHIN THE FIELD

The first major break in the record of neglect can be traced to the Comparative Administration Group and to the action of a legislature itself—namely, the U.S. Congress. In 1967 Congress adopted an amendment to the Foreign Assistance Act of 1961. The new directive, designated Title IX, required that "emphasis shall be placed on assuring maximum participation in the task of economic development on the part of the people of the developing countries, through the encouragement of democratic private and local governmental institutions." The Agency for International Development (AID), the federal bureau charged with administering U.S. foreign assistance, was little prepared for this new mandate for "political" development and sought ideas. Within AID Raymond Randall was directed to find ways of implementing Title IX. By chance, Randall had previously been on the faculty of Indiana University, where he was a colleague of Professor Fred Riggs, a recognized scholar in development processes.[1] Randall quite naturally turned for assistance to Riggs, who at the time happened to be chairman of the Comparative Administration Group (CAG) of the American Society for Public Administration (ASPA).

Riggs informally proposed some ideas for improvement of legislatures as a way of implementing the congressional directive. As a result of these contacts, AID formally contracted with ASPA for the CAG to conduct an extensive study of the feasibility of assisting legislatures in the context of political development.

As part of the grant contract, CAG convened a conference of scholars and legislative practitioners at "Planting Fields" near Oyster Bay, Long Island, in December of 1967.[2] The conference facilities were provided by the State University of New York (SUNY), whose chancellor, Samuel Gould, had a special interest in international programs. The New York state senate, through its secretary, Albert J. Abrams, cooperated with the conference, and among the convenors were James J. Heaphey, a professor of public administration from the State University of New York at Albany who had acquired practical legislative experience as an intern with the California assembly; and Larry Margolis, now the executive director of the Citizens Conference on State Legislatures.

This conference crystallized ideas from previous meetings and resulted in a recommendation to AID that a few Comparative Legislative Studies Centers be established at appropriate universities as resources for legislative improvement in developing countries. Because a viable research center was already established at SUNY Albany (Heaphey had organized the Comparative Development Studies Center with state funding), and due to the support of the New York legislature, the Albany campus was one of the recommended locations for such a center.

The CAG report was acted on in 1969 by Princeton Lyman at AID, who contracted with the Comparative Development Studies Center (CDSC) of SUNY Albany to conduct a pilot study of assistance to legislatures in developing countries. As a result of all these efforts, it was proposed that legislative improvement become a major focus of CDSC. AID accepted the proposal and contracted to support what was to become the chief institutional vehicle for linking the public administration field with legislatures.[3]

The Comparative Development Studies Center

The Albany Center was associated with the Graduate School of Public Affairs, and the work with legislatures increasingly led to a direct relationship with the Department of Public Administration; for as projects developed it became clear that the resources in the public administration field were most pertinent to the needs of legislative development. This evolution continued, and in 1972 Donald Axelrod, who had authored a pioneering study of legislative administration in New York,[4] became chairman of the Department of Public Administration, further melding the legislative work with public administration resources.

CDSC's legislative program began with pilot projects for legislative improvement in Brazil, Costa Rica, Ghana, and Ethiopia. Its efforts, based primarily on public administration resources, have developed to the extent that the center now is involved in legislative improvement work on five continents, in several U.S. states, and with a growing number of local jurisdictions. It has, for example, assisted the New York senate in strengthening its committee system, the Brazilian Congress with information technology, and the Costa Rican Legislature with bill indexing. The salient point in the present context is that increasingly and consistently the center's work has led to public administration resources. The following institutionalized expressions of that development have resulted.

Literature. The center has moved to have legislative administration included in public administration text-

books, periodicals, and general literature. Specifically
it has urged that textbook writers add a chapter on the
management of legislatures; it has begun a new publication directly concerned with the subject; it has explored the matter with editors of the *Public Administration Review*; further, it has been responsible for publication of various relevant works.[5] Indeed, this volume
is due to CDSC inspiration and support.

Schools. CDSC activity has been a key factor in legislative curriculum and research development within
as coordinator of the New York State Legislative Internship Program, which provides graduate credit from New
York universities for interns, most of whom are studying public administration. More significantly, and directly resulting from CDSC efforts, a master of public
administration (MPA) degree with a major in legislative administration has been developed at SUNY Albany.
Legislative officials help teach in the program as visiting
professors of public administration.

Finally, as previously noted, as a research arm of the
Albany Public Administration Program, CDSC concen-
trates its work on legislatures. In addition to providing
research assistance to numerous foreign legislatures, to
state legislative bodies, and to local legislatures, the center undertakes projects for the National Legislative Conference and for the American Society of Legislative
Clerks and Secretaries.

Organizations. The American Society for Public Administration, due largely to CDSC efforts, has indicated
an interest in these new developments. At its 1972 national conference, the society sanctioned a panel that discussed the inclusion of legislatures in public administration concerns. This was the first panel focused on
legislatures ever to be a part of an ASPA national con-

ference. The following year, in Los Angeles, a panel on legislative staffing was held at the national conference under the chairmanship of Milton Esman.[7] And in 1974 a panel was convened on legislative oversight.[8] Further, interest in embracing legislatures in ASPA activity has been expressed by officers of the society (see Chapter 10). This new ASPA recognition of legislatures was demonstrated in writing in the February 1974 issue of the society newsletter, *News and Views*. The issue included an article treating legislative administration. The author, Herbert Roback, suggested one current factor that may be prompting development of attention to legislatures: "The Watergate disclosures have strongly reinforced a belief in Congress that constitutional balance between the Executive and Legislative Branches is lacking and must be restored."[9]

INDUCEMENTS TO DEVELOPING ATTENTION TO LEGISLATURES

Roback's comments indicate one prod in the direction of increased attention to legislatures. Additional spurs can be suggested. In general, there are historical, ideological, economic, political, and fortuitous factors that help explain current developments.

Historical Factors

Watergate can be viewed either as a chief cause or as merely one of a sequence of factors ending the "era of the executive," which more or less began with Franklin D. Roosevelt. In either case, there is a discernible historical development in the United States today indicating a lessening of enchantment with executive power. Instead of efforts at elevating the executive, such as those of Neustadt and Burns,[10] books that deflate the executive are appearing.[11] Newspaper and magazine editorials are bemoaning executive excesses and urging more assertive legislatures.[12] Television's Capitol Hill correspondents are gaining some of the renown and special status previously reserved for White House reporters. Further, television itself has presented a study on the management of legislatures.[13] Surely the public administration field is not immune to these societal trends.

In particular, because of Watergate, there may be developing within the field of public administration an awareness of an observation made by Dwight Waldo nearly thirty years ago: "Gradually, in the public administration movement as a whole, research and facts have come to be regarded less and less as devices of citizen co-operation and control and more and more as instruments of executive management." [14] This, combined with a perception induced by Watergate of W. H. Allen's early caveat that "without intelligent control by the public, no efficient, progressive, triumphant democracy is possible," [15] may be of considerable motivating influence toward increased attention to legislatures. Indeed, the alumni publication of a major public administration school recently declared: "How to maintain the strength and direction provided by the President while guarding against the excesses which led to the great political crisis of the age is a major challenge confronting professional public administrators and every citizen of the United States." [16] Perhaps legislative improvement may be seen as one answer to that challenge.

A second historical factor may be the rise of the "new federalism" and the consequent turn of attention to states and localities. Whereas for the federal government there is only one legislature, which may not appear sufficiently expansive to justify special attention, states and localities have numerous legislative institutions that can absorb consequential attention.

A third suggested inducement is the post–World War II emphasis on overseas activity followed by the recently developing turn homeward. During the Marshall Plan, "communist containment," and "Point Four," hundreds of public administrationists gained experience in technical assistance projects in developing countries. This, in turn, produced an attempted broadening of public administration to enable the field to cope with "development." As previously discussed, this included an unaccustomed flirtation with legislatures. Neoisolationism is now returning those foreign-oriented perspectives to the domestic scene, and perhaps that broadened public administration field is now more apt to include legislatures in its homefront horizon as well.

Finally, the signing of the Congressional Budget Act of 1974 was a momentous assertion of the importance of the legislature. Congress's strengthened role in the budget process undoubtedly will tend to elicit interest from public administrationists.

Ideological Currents

There have been some recent ideological developments within both the field of public administration and the circle of legislative participants. On one hand, the "new public administration" ideology [17] and the acknowledged turbulence within the field [18] have mellowed previous dogmatic and structured inclinations and opened the field to a tolerance for ambiguity as frequently found in legislative processes. A subsequent easing of antilegislative biases may be in progress. Relatedly, the concept of the politics-administration relationship, first modified in the late 1940s in such a way as to reject any dichotomous description, may be undergoing a second adjustment. Whereas the first change resulted in a self-conscious affirmation of the political content of administration, a new twist may be recognizing the administrative content of politics,[19] which would encompass, for example, the managerial aspect of legislatures. In short, the politics-administration dichotomy may finally be developing into an androgyny.

Similarly, legislative participants are perhaps more receptive to assistance from public administration because of an ideological development on their part. Some time ago it was noted that democratic ideology and institutions matured in association with a belief in harmony, a conviction that things need not be managed but will run themselves: "The democratic philosophy at present is in the travail of being 're-thought' to accommodate the concept of management and democratic institutions in the throes of change to accommodate the fact of management." [20] In recent years that "re-thinking" has been institutionally manifested in legislatures.

Finally, there may be an increasing optimism and positiveness about legislatures. The old conventional wisdom about the "decline of legislatures" is being debunked by public administrationists,[21] and strains of negativism over the manageability of legislatures are apparently quieting in legislative arenas. All these ideological adjustments conceivably are facilitating public administration involvement with legislatures.

Economic Influences

Clearly, one of the most effective inducements to the recent attention described above has been the conditions attached to AID funds. After Congress passed Title IX, public administration had to look at legislatures if it wanted to further its role in foreign technical assistance. AID grants have continued in this vein and work of CDSC is in large measure due to AID financial support.

Two similar phenomena are noteworthy. One is the increasing availability of foundation funds for legislative management-related efforts; the other is the substantial proliferation of legislative staff jobs in recent years. The Ford Foundation, the Johnson Foundation, and the Carnegie Fund have given support to legislative internship programs, legislative evaluation projects, legislative committee studies, and the like. The Ford Foundation is even showing interest in legislative improvement abroad, an area it had previously avoided.

Moreover, government and business funds are increasingly available for legislative improvement work. The Law Enforcement Assistance Administration of the Department of Justice has financed a broad study of security administration for legislatures.[22] Large computer companies are supporting studies of the informational needs of legislatures. And legislatures themselves are allocating growing amounts of money to internal managerial improvement.

Job opportunities with legislatures are expanding. Not only are state legislatures requiring more manpower, but local legislatures are hiring administrators.[23] In 1974 the Graduate School of Public Affairs of SUNY Albany, one of the largest public administration programs in the country, experienced more job recruitment from legislatures than from executive agencies. Legislative agencies in Wisconsin, Texas, Illinois, Virginia, and New York all sought MPA graduates at the Albany school. At the local level there are nearly three thousand legislatures which are just beginning to create staff positions.

[128]

Political Temperament

Political factors could plausibly be inducements to a new relationship, for both the field of public administration and legislatures have "political" gains to make through association. Legislatures have been sensitive to their frequent domination by the executive; among other consequences, political pride has often been awakened, and there now appears to be a determination among legislators to harness their constitutional power. Public administration expertise may be regarded as a useful tool for producing political parity.

Public administrationists, on their part, appear increasingly aware of the need for political understanding and support for innovative action, and there seems to be a consequent interest in legislatures for development of these political requisites. As noted earlier, apostles of PPBS have identified lack of political requisites as a major cause of the failure of the budgetary advance.[24] Productivity analysts are stressing the need for political support,[25] as are program evaluation experts.[26] And the interest is not just in shrewdly gaining political favor but in helping develop in legislatures the political capacity for competently coping with and utilizing broad administrative advances.

In brief, the "political" climate appears ripe for a relationship between public administration and legislatures. Both can derive benefits.

Fortuitous Phenomena

Finally, the element of chance seems to have played a leading role in recent developments. As chance had it, the official at AID charged with implementing Title IX had been a colleague of the chairman of the Comparative Administration Group. By circumstance, a respected member of that CAG had been a legislative intern and had developed a special interest in and knowledge of legislatures. And fortuitously that member had institutional resources available for pursuing the ideas originated in CAG deliberations. It is further remarkable that those resources were centered in the capital of a large state where legislative contacts could easily be established.

In sum, not only are there some solid indications that the public administration field may be turning attention to legislatures, but there is a series of factors inducing and facilitating that embryonic trend.

DEVELOPMENTS OUTSIDE THE FIELD

A further inducement is the presence of several developments external to the public administration field. Both private and public efforts at improving legislative administration have blossomed. These efforts demonstrate the need and desire for public administration-type resources, and many of them could provide established channels for linking the field with legislative institutions. Legislatures themselves, the Citizens Conference on State Legislatures, the Eagleton Institute of Politics, the American Enterprise Institute, the Committee for Economic Development, the National Planning Association, the National Broadcasting Company, and the American Political Science Association have all undertaken significant efforts.

Legislatures

Legislatures have undertaken both individual and collective programs for administrative improvement. Collectively, they have organized into the National Conference of State Legislatures (NCSL). Individual efforts are exemplified by the Congressional Select Committee on Committees and the New York State Assembly reform movement.

National Conference of State Legislatures. The NCSL and its predecessors (the National Legislature Conference and the National Conference of State Legislative Leaders) have been serving state legislatures since 1948. Among its objectives is provision of information, analysis, and advice leading to the improvement of legislative organization and procedures. For this purpose it has organized a number of committees dealing with modernization, security, and evaluation and consisting of legislators and legislative staff from the states. Numerous publications have resulted from these efforts, including *Mr. President . . . Mr. Speaker . . .* (1963), which reports on legislative services organization; *American State Legislatures: Their Structures and Procedures* (1971), which outlines organizational and procedural aspects of the state legislatures; *Key Points in Legislative Procedure: Twenty Ways to Expedite the Legislative Process* (1970); *Handbook for Legislative Committees* (1969); and *Legislative Modernization* (1968). All of these are indicative of the administrative concerns of legislatures.

Congressional Select Committee on Committees. The U.S. Congress has made several efforts at administrative self-improvement, chiefly the Joint Committee on the Organization of Congress in 1946, which resulted in a Legislative Reorganization Act; the Joint Committee on the Organization of Congress in 1965, whose proposals failed enactment but led to a major bill in 1970; and the recent Select Committee on Committees, which was directed to conduct "a thorough and complete study with respect to . . . committee structure of the House, the number and optimum size of committees, their jurisdictions, the number of subcommittees, committee rules and procedures,

[131]

media coverage of meetings, staffing, space, equipment, and other committee facilities."[27]

The latter effort included extended hearings during the summer of 1973 and a series of invited working papers. Though many of the matters of concern to the committee were clearly within the competence of the public administration field, very few public administrationists appear to have assisted the committee; and though the Citizens Conference and the Eagleton Institute contributed to the hearings, no public administration institutional aid was evident. Indeed, though numerous political scientists participated in the hearings,[28] only four individuals generally identified as public administrationists appeared: Bertram M. Gross, Allen Schick, Elmer Staats, and Aaron Wildavsky.

Individual States. Several states have undertaken their own efforts at administrative improvement. Representative of these is the New York assembly's *Majority Report on Legislative Reforms, 1969–1973,* which utilizes standards formulated by the Citizens Conference. It is in many respects an effort at developing administratively effective yet politically feasible procedures.

A striking aspect of all the foregoing manifestations of legislative effort is that they deal largely with administrative questions yet receive no evident assistance from public administration.

Citizens Conference on State Legislatures

Formed in 1965 "in response to the legislatures' need for revitalization," the Citizens Conference on State Legislatures (CCSL) is a private, nonprofit organization that operates a program designed to strengthen legislatures at the state level. The work is supported by foundation grants, contract work, and contributions from private businesses. The conference conducts research into prevailing conditions and needs of legislatures, publishes related works, and designs and implements improvement programs. Among the major efforts of CCSL are an evaluation of the effectiveness of the state legislatures, published under the title *The Sometime Governments;* publication of numerous bibliographies on various topics of interest to legislatures; an extensive program for legislative improvement in seven states;[29] and a model committee staff program. The executive director of CCSL reports that the public administration field has not been helpful to the conference's efforts.[30]

Eagleton Institute of Politics

In 1966 the Eagleton Institute of Politics at Rutgers University established a Center for State Legislative Research and Service. It received financial support from the Ford Foundation and the Carnegie Corporation, and has completed organizational studies for a number of state legislatures.[31] The institute's studies have been designed to examine "organization, operations, and procedures, and to make recommendations for improvement."[32] As Eagleton's director rightly says: "Eagleton has played a significant role in the contemporary movement for legislative reform. It has exerted—and continues to exert—continuing energy on behalf of American state legislatures."[33]

American Enterprise Institute

The American Enterprise Institute (AEI) is a private research and educational organization that conducts studies of national policy problems. Its purpose is to assist policy makers, legislators, and educational leaders by providing them with factual analyses and studies of important current issues of national significance. In 1965 the institute sponsored a study of the functions of

Congress "with an eye to the needs of the currently operative Joint Committee on the Organization of the Congress."[34] Eleven political and behavioral scientists participated in the study and produced a volume, *Congress: The First Branch of Government*, directly addressing institutional needs of Congress. There was little input from the field of public administration. (Aaron Wildavsky was the only "public administrationist" participating.)

Committee for Economic Development

The Committee for Economic Development (CED) is a private group of businessmen and educators that seeks to improve the operations of the American economy through research and public policy studies. In 1963 it formed a Committee for Improvement of Management in Government, which published *Improving Executive Management in the Federal Government* the following year. The committee manifested a systemic perspective on government when it published *Making Congress More Effective* in 1970. The study analyzes structural and procedural problems that limit congressional effectiveness, and it proposes specific solutions. Although public administration did not cooperate in this latter effort institutionally, several noted public administrationists did assist as individuals.[35]

National Planning Association

One of the few groups to attempt to further the Legislative Reorganization Act of 1946 was the National Planning Association (NPA), a group of businessmen that conducted a study that same year. The resulting volume, authored by industrial engineer Robert Heller, deals with organizational and procedural questions within an "engineering approach and analysis."[36]

National Broadcasting Company

Television, too, undertook an effort to improve Congress. Prompted by correspondent David Brinkley, NBC employed the Arthur D. Little Company, a management consultant firm, to analyze the management of Congress in 1965. The stated purposes of the study were: (1) to define congressional methods, resources, and practices, (2) to identify operating problems, and (3) to suggest ways of applying management techniques to congressional operations. The resulting program was so well received, and the report so well balanced, that a book based on the show was published.[37]

American Political Science Association

Unlike the American Society for Public Administration, the American Political Science Association (APSA) has several times formed a committee on legislatures. In 1941 the organization established a Committee on Congress, which produced a volume detailing many of the reforms later to appear in the Legislative Reorganization Act of 1946.[38] George B. Galloway described the committee as "the chief catalytic agent of congressional reform."[39]

In 1950 the association formed a Committee on American Legislatures which four years later released a study dealing in part with legislative organization and procedure.[40] Public administrationist Donald Axelrod served on the committee along with W. Brooke Graves and Joseph P. Harris, both of whom authored public administration texts.

Then again, in the late 1960s, APSA inaugurated a State Legislative Service Project whose main function was the preparation of manuals for legislators concerned with immediate and practical problems of institutional life. Due to this project a series of books describing various state legislatures has appeared.[41]

Several observations regarding all of the above mentioned efforts are noteworthy:

1. Organizations of legislators, of businessmen, of journalists, and of political scientists—academic, private, and professional groups—have all attempted to provide for managerial needs of legislatures; but one source of both managerial and political knowledge, the American Society for Public Administration, has remained uninvolved.

2. Several of the involved groups have focused on state legislatures, several on Congress. But only one group, the Comparative Development Studies Center, a public administration group, studies and assists legislatures generically—that is, at all levels of government, whether local, state, or national, foreign or domestic.

3. The efforts of the several groups suggest the pertinence of public administration skills for legislative needs. Most of the efforts involved organizational and procedural problems of a government institution, subjects that are central to the field of public administration. It could be suggested that some of these efforts failed because public administration did not help. It might even be suggested that some of the efforts may have been initiated partly because neglect by the public administration field left a void that had to be filled by some effort. One legislator's comment that "we need more help but already have too many offers from the unqualified" may be related to this suggestion.

4. In any case, several of the groups described are excellent potential vehicles for assistance from public administration. In particular, the programs of legislators themselves, through the NCSL and unilateral projects of the CDSC, the Citizens Conference, and the Eagleton Institute, offer established channels for harnessing the re-

sources of the public administration field toward legislative improvement.

The following section, Part 2 of the book, explores the relevance of those public administration resources, offers a framework for involvement, and discusses specific means for bringing the institutional assets of public administration to bear on the expressed needs of legislatures.

NOTES FOR CHAPTER 7

1. For example, his *Administration in Developing Countries: The Theory of Prismatic Society* (Boston: Houghton Millfin, 1964) was a widely known work.

2. Papers presented at the conference are printed in Allen Kornberg and Lloyd Musolf, eds., *Legislatures in Developmental Perspective* (Durham, N.C.: Duke University Press, 1970).

3. Simultaneously, also as a result of these efforts, AID funded a Consortium of Legislative Study Centers, headed by Allen Kornberg. The consortium consisted of Duke University, University of Hawaii, University of Iowa, and later, State University of New York at Albany.

4. *Final Report* of New York State Joint Legislative Committee on Legislative Methods, Practices, Procedures, and Expenditures (Albany, 1946).

5. Notably Abdo I. Baaklini, *Legislatures and Political Development* (Durham, N.C.: Duke University Press, forthcoming); Abdo I. Baaklini and James J. Heaphey, *Legislative Institution Building* (Sage, forthcoming); Alan P. Balutis, "Legislative Staffing in New York" (Ph.D., diss. SUNY, Albany, 1973). Additionally, numerous articles and monographs have resulted.

6. James J. Heaphey and Abdo I. Baaklini of the CDSC convened this panel and presented papers: Heaphey, "Technical Assistance in the Administration of Legislatures," and Baaklini, "Comparative Legislative Process."

7. Papers were presented by Abdo I. Baaklini, "Legislative Staffing Patterns in Developing Countries," and Alan P. Balutis, "Legislative Staffing: Some Preliminary Findings."

8. Richard E. Brown of the New York State Legislative Commission on Expenditure Review presented a talk on "Legislative Auditing." James J. Heaphey and Ray D. Pethtel of the Virginia Legislative Review Commission participated.

9. Herbert Roback, "Congress in Transition," ASPA *News and Views* 24, no. 2 (February 1974): 3–5.

10. Richard E. Neustadt, *Presidential Power* (New York: Wiley, 1960); James M. Burns, *Presidential Government* (Boston: Houghton Mifflin, 1965).

11. For example, Arthur M. Schlesinger, *The Imperial Presidency* (Boston: Houghton Mifflin, 1973), and Rexford Tugwell and Thomas Cronin, *The Presidency Reappraised* (New York: Praeger, 1974).

12. See, for example, *New York Times* (February 13, 1973), and *New York Post* (June 11, 1972).

13. "Congress Needs Help," National Broadcasting Company television program, November 1965.

14. Dwight Waldo, *The Administrative State* (New York: Ronald Press, 1948), p. 33, note 28.

15. W. H. Allen, *Efficient Democracy* (New York: Dodd, Mead, 1907), pp. ix–x.

16. David Bennett, "From Teapot Dome to Watergate," *Syracuse Alumni Review* (spring 1974): 4.

17. See Frank Marini, ed., *Toward a New Public Administration* (Scranton, Pa: Chandler, 1971).

18. See Dwight Waldo, ed., *Public Administration in a Time of Turbulence* (Scranton, Pa.: Chandler, 1971).

19. This was suggested by Herbert Emmerich in James C. Charlesworth, ed., *Theory and Practice of Public Administration* (Philadelphia: American Academy, 1968), p. 96.

20. Waldo, *The Administrative State*, p. 101.

21. See Heaphey, "Technical Assistance in the Administration of Legislatures," pp. 7–9, and Abdo I. Baaklini "Legislatures in Developing Countries: Myths and Realities," paper presented at the annual convention of the Society for International Development, San Jose, Costa Rica, 1973.

22. See James J. Heaphey, ed., *Legislative Security* (Albany, N.Y.: Graduate School of Public Affairs, 1972).

23. For example, the Clinton County, New York, legislature in 1973 hired a full-time administrator and created part-time internships specifically earmarked for MPA students.

24. Allen Schick, "A Death in the Bureaucracy," *Public Administration Review* 33, no. 2 (April 1973): 145–156.

25. Walter Balk, "Decision Constructs and the Politics

of Productivity," paper presented at the annual convention of the New York Political Science Association, Albany, 1973.

26. Joseph S. Wholey et al., *Federal Evaluation Policy* (Washington, D.C.: Urban Institute, 1970).

27. House Resolution 132, 93rd Congress, first session.

28. For a listing see *Panel Discussions before the Select Committee*, vol. 2 (Washington, D.C.: U.S. Government Printing Office, 1973), pp. 865–869.

29. Massachusetts, New Hampshire, Ohio, Louisiana, Colorado, Arizona, and Minnesota.

30. Larry Margolis in personal interview with the author, January 1974.

31. Namely, Arkansas, Connecticut, Florida, Maryland, Mississippi, Rhode Island, and Wisconsin.

32. Alan Rosenthal, "Contemporary Research on State Legislatures" in *Political Science and State and Local Government* (Washington, D.C.: American Political Science Association, 1973), pp. 55–86.

33. Alan Rosenthal, *The Improvement of State Legislatures* (New Brunswick, N.J.: Eagleton Institute, 1971), p. 13. The institute has published many important works, including Alan S. Chartock and Max Berking, *Strengthening the Wisconsin Legislature* (New Brunswick, N.J.: Rutgers University Press, 1970); Donald G. Herzberg and Jess Unruh, *Essays on the State Legislative Process* (New York: Holt, Rinehart, and Winston, 1970); Donald G. Herzberg and Alan Rosenthal, eds., *Strengthening the States: Essays on Legislative Reform* (New York: Doubleday, 1971); David B. Ogle, *Strengthening the Connecticut Legislature* (New Brunswick, N.J.: Rutgers University Press, 1970); David B. Ogle, *Strengthening the Mississippi Legislature* (New Brunswick, N.J.: Rutgers University Press, 1971); Alan Rosenthal, *Strengthening the Maryland Legislature* (New Brunswick, N.J.: Rutgers University Press, 1968); Alan Rosenthal, "An Analysis of Institutional Effects: Staffing Legislative Parties in Wisconsin," *The Journal of Politics* 32, no. 3 (August 1970): 531–562; Alan Rosenthal, "Between Sessions: The Effectiveness of Legislative Study and Interim Work," *State Government* 44, no. 2 (spring 1971): 93–101; Alan Rosenthal, *The Interim Work of the Texas Senate* (New Brunswick, N.J.: Eagleton Institute, 1971); C. Lynwood Smith, *Strengthening the Florida Legislature* (New Brunswick, N.J.: Rutgers University Press, 1970); Charles Tantillo, *Strengthening the Rhode Island Legislature* (New Brunswick, N.J.: Rutgers University Press, 1968).

34. American Enterprise Institute, *Congress: The First*

Branch of Government (Washington, D.C.: AEI, 1966), p. v.

35. Namely, Luther Gulick, John J. Corson, and John W. Macy. Additionally, Frederick C. Mosher, James W. Fesler, Lyle C. Fitch, and Don Price serve on CED Advisory Boards.

36. Robert Heller, *Strengthening the Congress* (Washington, D.C.: National Planning Association, 1946). (Noted public administrationist Luther Gulick served on the board of trustees of the NPA.)

37. Philip Donham and Robert J. Fahey, *Congress Needs Help* (New York: Random House, 1966).

38. Committee on Congress, American Political Science Association, *The Reorganization of Congress* (Washington, D.C.: APSA, 1945).

39. George B. Galloway, *Congress at the Crossroads* (New York: Crowell, 1946).

40. Belle Zeller, ed., *American State Legislatures* (New York: Crowell, 1954).

41. James L. Best, *The Washington State Legislative Handbook*, 1971; William C. Chance, *A Guidebook for Ohio Legislators* (Columbus: Ohio Legislative Service Commission, 1970); Elmer E. Cornwell et al., *The Rhode Island General Assembly* (Washington, D.C.: American Political Science Association. 1970); Joel M. Fisher et al., *The Legislative Process in California* (Washington, D.C.: American Political Science Association, 1973); Edwin A. Gere, ed., *The Massachusetts General Court* (Washington, D.C.: American Political Science Association, 1972); Samuel K. Gove and Richard J. Carlson, *An Introduction to the Illinois General Assembly* (Urbana: University of Illinois Press, 1968); Ronald D. Hedlund and Wilder Crane, *The Job of the Legislator: Wisconsin* (Washington, D.C.: American Political Science Association, 1971); Daniel V. McGraw, *The Role of the Lawmaker in West Virginia*, (Washington, D.C.: American Political Science Association, 1970); Lawrence C. Pierce et al., *The Freshman Legislator* (Washington, D.C.: American Political Science Association, 1972); Arthur Ristau, *A Handbook for the New Hampshire General Court* (Hanover, N.H.: Dartmouth University Press, 1971); Wayne R. Swanson, *Lawmaking in Connecticut* (Washington, D.C.: American Political Science Association, 1972); and Sidney Wise, *The Legislative Process in Pennsylvania* (Washington, D.C.: American Political Science Association, 1971).

PART 2

Exploration
of
Potential

Introduction

The previous chapters examined the record of public administration in terms of its attention to legislatures and found a chronicle of neglect. The examination also, however, disclosed strong and widespread expressions from the field on the importance of legislatures, the existence of legitimate organizational aspects within legislatures, and the logical relevance of the public administration field to legislative operations. Moreover, this study has found a firm consensus among both public administrationists and legislators that the field should assist legislative bodies: Forty-six of forty-seven legislators indicated that attention by public administration would be welcome and/or useful; sixteen of eighteen noted scholars believed that the field should turn toward legislatures; every university research arm contacted concurred; 93 percent of public administration schools responding said legislative administration should be part of academic programs; and legislative staffers overwhelmingly expressed interest in assistance from public administration (see Chapters 8 and 10). Finally, Chapter 7 revealed some indication that public administration may now be on a threshold.

Prompted by all these expressions, this second part explores possibilities. What is the basis of these expressions? Do legislatures have organizational needs and what are those needs? Is public administration equipped to assist? Is the organizational dimension of legislatures different and, if so, how might a public administrationist proceed? How could the public administration field bring its resources to bear on legislative needs?

Foundations for involvement by public administration with legislatures are explored in the following chapter. Firm bases, both theoretical and pragmatic, are suggested. Chapter 9 searches for guidelines, grounded on the nature of legislatures, for approaching the administrative problem and proposes a framework for involvement. The final chapter recommends specific institutional means of allying the public administration field with legislative bodies.

8

Foundations for Involvement: The Organizational Dimension

The extent of public administration's neglect of legislatures has been indicated. This chapter explores foundations for charting a new course in the field. It discusses some theoretical issues; it investigates the organizational needs of legislatures and analyzes the suitability of public administration for addressing those needs; it considers some needs of the public administration field and asks whether legislatures can be useful for solutions; it examines mutual needs and interests and probes the benefits of alliance. Do legislatures really have institutional needs requiring organizational craft? Does the public administration field stand to advance its goals by turning attention to legislatures? Does it have pertinent resources to contribute?

THEORETICAL BASES

The very notion of treating a legislature as an organization is intellectually abhorrent to some reputable

[145]

scholars. They see an unfortunate dominance of organizational thought in a world that longs for "community." Wolin epitomizes the concern of Jacques Ellul[1] and others when he laments: "Today the individual moves in a world dominated by large and complex organizations. The citizen faces 'big government'; the laborer a large trade union; the white-collar worker, a giant corporation; the student, an impersonal university. Everywhere there is organization, everywhere bureaucratization; like the world of feudalism, the modern world is broken up into areas dominated by castles, but not the castles of *les chansons de geste*, but the castles of Kafka."[2] These thinkers decry an overemphasis on technique and power to the detriment of political fraternity.

Gene S. Poschman specifically applies this concern to the legislature. Cherishing the legislature as a representative institution embodying the unorganized characteristics of the masses, he reproves writers and observers who regard the organizational design of institutions as the decisive factor in determining the correct outcome of policy decisions.[3]

The argument of these thinkers should be well taken. There is an undeniable need for community, and the legislature is fundamentally a political body with a largely communal, consensual function (see Chapter 9). This purport is deemphasized, and often overlooked or denied, by those who regard the subject of legislative administration strictly in terms of management. Indeed, one public administrationist consulted during the present study declared: "If public administration gives more attention to legislatures, it should be from the point of view of 'management' and not 'politics.'"

A danger in both of these perspectives is that the nature of the legislature is dichotomized, with each notion isolated and regarded as the whole. On one hand, it is affirmed that the legislature is a community; on the other it is asserted that the legislature is an organization. The danger is in the tendency to assume that the two notions can only be disparate. It can be suggested that such dichotomizing produces an unrealistic view of the nature of the body, unrealistic at one extreme in denying an organizational dimension, unrealistic at the other extreme in obfuscating the political dimension.

One need only look at the New Hampshire state legislature, for example, to see a legislature as a community. In that body, over four hundred people, from every small area of the state, function with the "unorganized characteristics of the masses," and vigorously assert their desire and ability to so function. But at the same time, paradoxically perhaps, they express perceived organizational dimensions of their community. Indeed, some of the strongest expressions of desire for assistance by public administration came from legislators and staff of the New Hampshire legislature in response to the questionnaires appearing in Appendix B. This phenomenon supports the generalization Polsby has proffered: "For a political system to be viable, for it to succeed in performing tasks ... in behalf of a population of any substantial size, it must be institutionalized. That is to say, organizations must be created and sustained that are specialized to political activity. Otherwise, the political system is likely to be unstable, weak, and incapable of servicing the demands or protecting the interests of its constituent groups." [4]

This concept of viability, it is suggested, is a central theoretical basis for public administration involvement with legislatures. For a political community to be viable it must incorporate an organizational dimension. And

[147]

the organizational dimension can and must provide that viability without wilting the political dimension. The concept of mingling these dimensions can perhaps be clarified by reference to Philip Selznick's notion of institution.

In his *Leadership in Administration*, Selznick distinguishes between organization and institution: "The term 'organization' suggests a certain bareness, a lean, no-nonsense system of consciously co-ordinated activities. It refers to an expendable tool, a rational instrument engineered to do a job. An 'institution,' on the other hand, is more nearly a natural product of social needs and pressures—a responsive, adaptive organism." [5] Selznick portrays an institution as an engaged reconciliation of idealism with expediency, of freedom with organization, as a complex mixture of both designed and responsive behavior. It has a managerial dimension but also a community dimension of interaction and adaptation. Moreover, he cautions that institutional health requires delicate adjustment of the design aspect to the values engendered in the community aspect, and not vice versa. [6] Wolin describes a similar concept in terms of values of social stability, cohesion, and integration being more fundamental in these institutions than efficiency and rationality. [7]

Polsby's study of the House of Representatives found that this concept of mingling the organizational with the political is realizable. He suggests that the community of the House of Representatives has gradually and necessarily become more institutionalized and developed a greater managerial dimension, without impairing its communal dimension: "[The] findings suggest that increasing hierarchical structure is not a necessary feature of the institutionalization process. Organizations, other than bureaucracies, it seems clear, also are capable of having natural histories which increase their viability in the modern world without forcing them into uniformly centralized patterns of authority." [8]

These considerations lead to two pertinent contentions: First, those theorists who recoil from the suggestion that an organizational dimension is essential to a legislature may be unrealistically deemphasizing the modern environment. Whereas perhaps originally, or ideally, legislatures could be built on a solely "community" concept, modern complexities and demands necessitate, for the very viability of the "community," a broader concept that mingles an organizational dimension with the community notion. In the words of a state legislator: "If it is true that the citizen nature of a legislator must be preserved in order to best serve the goals of democratic self government and to protect the liberties of the people, then it is unquestionably true that in an age of increasing complexity, certain things must be done within the structure of the legislature in order to have it function well. . . ." [9]

Second, those theorists who suggest that the managerial or organizational dimension of legislatures can be approached in isolation from the political or communal may be in danger of injuring the nature of the institution they intend to assist. Accordingly, it is suggested that the concept of "legislative improvement," rather than of "legislative management," is more useful to the matter of public administration involvement with legislatures. Whereas "management" may imply a one-dimensional perspective, "improvement" suggests the political-organizational mixture described above. For example, legislative improvement might entail a certain amount of "mismanagement," "inefficiency," and so on for the sake of the political dimension (see Chapter 9). The immediate question, then, is whether the public administration field is attuned to such a multidimensional approach.

Admittedly, the field has frequently been characterized by notions of order and control. Hierarchical organization and unflinching efficiency have been passwords of the field from Gulick and Urwick's PODSCORB to Herbert Simon's fact-value dichotomy. As Wolin observed: "The writers who ranked organization foremost among social phenomena inevitably emphasized considerations far different from those preoccupying the theorists of community. The organizationists looked upon society as an order of functions, a utilitarian construct of integrated activity, a means for focusing human energies in a combined effort. Where the symbol of community was fraternity, the symbol of organization was power."[10]

However, again as Wolin recognizes, administrative theory has broadened to incorporate communal values in organization.[11] Elton Mayo and Selznick are examples of this growth, even if we accept Wolin's critique of their perspective as being basically manipulative. But more recent and less vulnerable examples exist. Warren Bennis speaks of the death of bureaucracy,[12] while Frederick C. Thayer calls for the end of hierarchy.[13] And Lewis A. Froman has specifically applied administrative theory to legislative organization and found them mutually insightful.[14] There are, in brief, firm indications that public administration has developed a flexibility enabling a multidimensional perspective. Involvement with legislatures might enrich that development.

Finally, the fundamental theoretical support for public administration involvement with legislatures is the concept of system. No matter how "ideal" it might be, a legislature exists within a system, within an environment that it must react to as well as shape. Those who would overstress the community dimension of the legislature appear to isolate it from the odious organizational world, to make it an island separate from the mainland, to see the legislature as a last bastion of a better society. They appear to disregard Waldo's observation that we do indeed live in an administrative culture and that survival in such an environment requires coming to terms with that reality.[15] More specifically, as Polsby suggests, legislatures are increasingly institutionalized and as such do have unavoidable organizational needs.[16] And, most trenchant, a legislature is a part of a system of government that has certain administrative needs that can be satisfied only in the legislature. Isolating the legislature as an ideal community and neglecting the organizational dimension thus endangers the viability not only of the community itself but of the system to which it belongs.

On the other hand, those who would overstress the managerial dimension of a legislature similarly appear to isolate it from the environment, to forget that we live in a community culture as well as an administrative one, and to overlook the political function of the legislature. In the governmental system the legislature is an essential political component in which representativeness, diversity, and elements of disorder are more important than strict efficiency and organizational control. Isolating the legislature from the political dimension and attempting to make it an "ideal" organization endangers the viability of the system. Samuel C. Patterson supports the point: "We will at our great peril persist ... in ignoring the purely political, symbolic, ameliorative function of collective institutions, of which the legislature is example

[151]

par excellence. We are too easily prepared to monkey with legislative organization and procedure in all innocence of the subtle institutionalized mechanisms of catharsis and symbolic satisfaction which, if grossly disturbed by reforms of efficiency and good management, may be eroded enough to let rancor, excessive conflict, raucous combativeness, and the evanescence of trust undermine the social fabric in unanticipated and unwanted ways." [17]

The systemic concept joins the political and organizational dimensions and can provide an appreciation enabling an enriching involvement of public administration with legislatures. The present chapter clarifies the organizational dimension; the following chapter attempts to join that with the political.

BACKDROP

Relatively recent developments support the argument of the institutionalization of legislatures and the growth of the flexibility of public administration. Further, these developments help explain why legislators and public administrationists might be interested in working together.

On one hand legislatures have undergone a major institutional evolution.[18] Legislators, who once were part-time amateurs, are now largely full-time professionals. Sessions that used to be brief and biennial are now continuous and annual. Staff that formerly was part-time and patronage-based is now full-time and professional. And public cynicism or apathy concerning legislatures is increasingly replaced by public expectations of service and solutions to problems. And legislators themselves are expressing a determination to realize legislative potential: "Congress has been content to be a passive audience when it could readily become a vast sounding board to arouse and educate the Nation." [19] All these developments are demanding improved organizational and managerial features within legislative bodies. As perceived capability is growing, perceived needs for improved organization are emerging.[20]

On the other hand the field of public administration has been experiencing times of turbulence, searching for a "new public administration," and generally mellowing its "president's men" stance. The subfield of comparative administration has tempered a focus on bureaucracy with a vanguard concern with legislatures.[21] Classical concepts of organization theory have been evolving with greater flexibility of norms and variety in description and analysis, tending toward a common ground of organization theory and legislative reality: The human relations element,[22] the "open systems" perspective,[23] and "end of hierarchy" broaches,[24] in finding strict bureaucratic structure lacking, have drawn organization theory closer to the organization phenomena existing in legislatures. And budgetary theory, which once largely ignored the legislative organization aspect, shows signs of concern for the implementive and evaluative roles of legislatures.[25] Each of these developments may tend to produce within the field of public administration more interest in legislatures.

Moreover, the field generally shows signs lately toward a more systemic, less exclusively executive-oriented, perspective. As noted earlier, judicial administration programs have begun at several public administration schools. And statements such as the following from the Bureau of Public Administration at Alabama are causing little objection: "If government is to be viewed as a system—and we think it must—it makes little sense for public administration to ignore legislatures or stay at arm's length from them." The Watergate developments have certainly not inhibited expression of this new outlook.

GENERAL INCENTIVES

Several broad incentives for legislative improvement support the case for collaboration between public administration and legislatures and could prompt mutual interest. These incentives include a concern for the American system of government, an awareness of and anxiety over possible domination by the executive branch, and recognition and distress over the new complexity of legislative operations. Additionally, the need for development of administrative theory, and the presence of favorable dispositions, are conducive to alliance.

Maintenance of the American System

Expressions of concern for legislative improvement frequently point to a regard for the American system as an underlying motive for assistance. Donald G. Herzberg and Alan Rosenthal said at the beginning of their book: "Checks and balances, we believe, is more than a notion willed to us by our Federalist forefathers. It is a necessary principle to follow if government is to be representative and effective. The executive branch, whatever its popularity, capability, or good faith, may commit errors. The legislature should be there to remedy them." [26] The Citizens Conference on State Legislatures was unhesitant in proclaiming one of its motives: "We are rediscovering the states and their legislatures ... for the most pragmatic of reasons: our federal system simply will not work well without them, and it is the only system we have." [27] And the Committee for Economic Development specifically linked organizational needs with maintenance of the system: "Continuing delay in modernization of Congressional structures and procedures will surely be injurious to the national interest...." [28] Justice Frankfurter's dictum is cited by many: "The history of American freedom is, in no small measure, the history of procedure." [29]

This recognition of the importance of legislative improvement to the American system may be filtering into public administration circles and shaping a foundation for involvement. Indeed, a recent effort at applying organization theory to legislative staff work manifested such a motive: "Legislatures must become viable institutions in order to maintain free and democratic societies." [30]

Executive Domination

Watergate dramatized the disproportionate power that had developed in the presidency. This awareness has crystallized similar concerns of imbalance in executive power over that of legislatures at state levels as well. Whereas frequently in the past hurt pride caused outcries from legislators against executive domination, increasingly the concern is based on cool assessment of an unhealthy situation. As one legislator reflected: "We have provided endless equipment for the executive and administrative agencies to take care of themselves; but we have not provided ourselves with the machinery to do those things that we ought to do." [31] A public administration proponent of improved legislative staffing recently pointed to escape from "complete dominance by the executive" as a widespread motive for interest in legislative improvement.[32] And Ralph Braibanti, in advocating legislative improvement in developing countries, expressed a similar concern as well as a belief that executive dominance fosters inferior bureaucratic administration: "The object is to accord the legislature all the facilities necessary to rectify the imbalance which now exists in expertise—an imbalance heavily weighted on the side of the executive. Ultimately the consequence of this [legislative] structural improvement will be more powerful and more rational control over bureaucracy and the gradual infusion into administrative decision-making of the basic polity reflected in the legislature." [33]

Clearly, recognition that executive dominance is an insalubrious condition of government appears to be an underlying inducement to efforts at legislative improvement.

Current Complexity of the Legislative Task

Donald R. Matthews has described modern legislation as complex and technical, and crushing in quantity.[34] A recent study of Congress sustained this limn in finding that four out of five congressmen consider "complexity of decision-making" and "lack of information" as the major problems preventing more effective performance.[35] These reactions are understandable considering the fact that annually thousands of bills pile up on the desks of legislators. For example, in New York in 1972 more than fifteen thousand bills were introduced at the legislative session. For each legislator to spend a mere ten minutes on each of these bills would have required a full year of ten-hour days. Moreover, the technical, as well as numerical, complexity of bills is increasing. Legislators are swamped by information that requires sophisticated processing in order to be usable.[36]

As a consequence, it is increasingly evident that, in the words of the former executive director of the National Legislative Conference, "the ability of the legislative branch to realize its full potential in the coming decade rests substantially on development of effective means of 'managing' itself." [37] Organizational development is more and more necessarily relevant to legislatures due to the sheer complexity of their tasks.

Development of Administrative Theory

Recently, inadequacies of traditional administrative theory have surfaced, and public administrationists have begun searching for remedies.[38] Thayer has described the task as a search for "a formal theory of non-hierarchy," [39] a search that Caiden says has too long been neglected.[40] Undeniably, legislative organization, with its long history and variety of structures, including considerable doses of non-hierarchy, is territory ripe for search. As Albert Lepawsky maintained some years ago: "... one can observe significant lessons for the science of organization in the structure of the American legislative system." [41] A personal comment by a legislative director of research clarifies the point: "I have potentially 236 bosses [the legislators] and this is a situation quite different from that of the bureau chief in an executive branch agency. I am also part of a very 'flat' organization which does much of its work through a system of 90 to 100 committees, joint committees, service agencies, etc., a situation that completely departs from the classical pyramid type of structure. At times, also, my bosses are 'warring' against each other and may come to me with competing demands that must be treated separately and confidentially. Moreover, outside forces in the executive branch, e.g., a budget bureau, a personnel agency, a general services administration, may try to control my operations in technical ways; how do I deal with them?"

It is eminently conceivable that application and adaptation of administrative theory to legislatures could prove to be enriching for administrative theory as well as beneficial to legislatures. Besides providing new dimensions for administrative concepts, such a course might provide public administration with a more integrated approach to all public organizations. Indeed Froman's study, as well as Polsby's suggests this.[42] As enthusiasm for improving administrative theory grows, the mere possibility of enlightenment from legislatures may prove an inducement to involvement.

Presence of Favorable Dispositions

One scholar interviewed was concerned about the receptivity of legislators to attention by public administration: "At least until relatively recently it was not entirely unreasonable to assume that few persons within the legislative branch would be responsive to efforts directed toward administrative improvements within that branch. In other words, the 'climate' for such efforts was not very encouraging." Thus, to test this concern, the perceptions of legislators were sought. Out of forty-seven legislators responding, forty-six indicated that attention by public administration to legislatures would be welcome and/or useful (see Table 8).[43] The legislators were asked whether they believed public administration could be useful to them in the areas specified in Table 9. As indicated, their responses reveal a rather favorable disposition toward public administration assistance. This apparent receptivity could be an additional inducement to public administration involvement. Further, it may be connected with a perception that legislative needs require external assistance.

ORGANIZATIONAL NEEDS OF LEGISLATURES

As Willoughby observed[44] and Marshall and Gladys Dimock echoed: "Like any organization, a legislature also must get the facts when there is a problem to be solved,

TABLE 8
INTEREST OF LEGISLATORS
(Total Number of Respondents = 47)

Question: In your view would increased attention and availability of the field of public administration to legislatures be (a) welcome, (b) useful, (c) dangerous, (d) extremely helpful, (e) undesirable?

	Yes	No
Welcome	40	1
Useful	39	1
Dangerous	2	27
Extremely Helpful	5	2
Undesirable	1	26

Note: Several respondents checked more than one description. A total of 46 checked *welcome* or *useful* or both.

TABLE 9
DISPOSITION OF LEGISLATORS TOWARD
PUBLIC ADMINISTRATION AREA ASSISTANCE
(Total Number of Respondents = 47)

Question: Do you believe the field of public administration could be useful to legislatures in (a) providing skilled staff, (b) assisting in managerial problems, (c) undertaking specific studies at your request, (d) exploring means of adapting administrative tools to political realities, (e) educating bureaucrats on legislative processes?

	Yes	No
Providing Skilled Staff	41	3
Assisting in Managerial Problems	35	7
Undertaking Specific Studies	44	2
Exploring Means of Adapting Administrative Tools to Political Realities	36	5
Educating Bureaucrats on Legislative Processes	32	11

analyze alternatives, organize so as to do its job effectively and responsibly, and concentrate on first things first. It must secure able personnel, arrange and oversee their responsibilities, and coordinate the whole effort to emphasize policy and accomplishment." [45] As an organization in its own right, a legislature needs good administration. As a part of the whole administrative system of government, a legislature requires sound organizational capacities in order, for example, to carry out its formulative and evaluative functions effectively.

In order to identify and clarify further the organizational needs of legislatures, legislative staff members (see Appendix A) were asked: "What role do you think the public administration field could usefully play in legislative improvement? What particular needs of legislatures might the field be helpful in?" Characteristic of the responses is the following from the clerk of a state assembly: "The prime objective of legislatures is to produce good legislation and how this is accomplished has many factors which public administration can help to evaluate and place in proper order. This implies management, staff and physical means to accomplish the purpose." And the director of a legislative service commission remarked: "If we zero in on 'improvement' the use of administration and managerial concepts in improving the legislature should be emphasized. Legislative administration suffers from a lack of savvy—of managerial technique, of planning and control approaches, and of use of modern techniques. Frequently where there is an awareness of the need for help or of modernization, the response is inefficient or 'gimmicky.' "

In general, the organizational needs expressed by the respondents defined three basic areas: housekeeping, operational requirements, and functional/systemic needs.

Housekeeping Needs

Routine management needs were frequently mentioned. Among these were those that Gladys M. Kammerer identified as "housekeeping" functions of legislatures: handling of payroll and accounts, recruitment and selection of administrative personnel, library and informational services, bill drafting, printing, handling mail, security, and building maintenance.[46] To this list we could add such tasks as preparation of the legislature's budget, procurement of supplies and equipment, allocation of office space, and coordination of routine operations. Personnel involved in these functions range from mail room attendants and Xerox machine operators to clerks and secretaries. Additionally, individual legislators need to organize and manage their own staffs and offices.

Not surprisingly, there is evidence that these needs are not being adequately met. One legislative staffer has remarked in *Public Administration Review* that "it is highly doubtful that Congress makes use of its present resources in the most effective manner." [47] It has also been reported that members of Congress, incumbents as well as freshmen, frequently seek advice on how to organize their offices more efficiently.[48] And the American Society of Legislative Clerks and Secretaries has contracted with a public administration research group for assistance in housekeeping tasks.[49] This latter development is not only reflective of housekeeping needs but also indicative that public administration resources are deemed pertinent.

Legislatures thus appear to have legitimate administrative needs, similar to those of executive agencies, merely for housekeeping purposes. Both the organization as a whole, and the office organizations of individual legislators, face administrative problems and demands. Moreover, as the volume, not to mention complexity, of legislative business increases, so do the administrative challenges of housekeeping.[50] And this holds true not only for the Congress in Washington and the legislatures at fifty state capitals, but for hundreds of local legislatures throughout the nation.

Operational Requirements

A broader level of identifiable legislative administration needs, beyond "mere" housekeeping, involves the
operational conduct of the legislature's specific function
of legislation and the myriad ramifications of that task.[51]
Among the elements referred to are staffing, committee
organization, procedures, external linkages, and organizational development.

Staffing. Many observers have complained of the
"inadequate staff support" available to legislatures.[52]
Under modern conditions of voluminous and technical
deluge, the administrative need entails both a quest for
managerially competent people and the efficient utilization of such staff.[53]

Some time ago Kammerer noted a difficulty in ob-
taining needed staff for legislatures. She specifically
traced one cause of the problem to the preference of people trained in public administration for the bureaucracy,
implying that such individuals are a key need of legislatures.[54] More recently the same need was affirmed in a
study of Congress that urged a strengthening of staff
resources by recruitment of highly qualified specialists,
specifically, "management experts." The study further
remarked that "serious attention should be given to professional training and development" of staffs.[55] Indeed,
the director of a state assembly agency commented: "The
growth of legislative staff offers the most fertile field in
which public administration can be of assistance. We es-
pecially need public administrators who will accept positions on these staffs."

The second aspect of staffing needs is effective utilization. As a noted author puts it: "Its [Congress's] further development, however, will require congressional
adaptation to a new era of governmental decision making. And not the least of these requirements for adapta-

tion will be the intelligent and effective use of congressional staff." [56] The need for knowledge of how best to use staff has often been noted, both in terms of efficiency of utilization[57] and from the viewpoint of effective control of staff: "Staffs may usurp congressional roles and become 'wheelers and dealers.' They may develop cozy relationships with congressmen, agency personnel, and interest group representatives and facilitate the growth of sub-governments that are difficult for both the President and Congress to control." [58] Legislatures clearly need organizational skill both within their staffs and over their staffs.

Committees. Committees are variously described by legislators themselves as "central to the operation of the House," [59] "essential," [60] and "the heart and soul of the legislative process." [61] Yet the same legislators decry the managerial condition of committees. As one senator expressed the situation: "The standing committees of the Senate are a hodge-podge of incongruous arrangements, more the result of precedent—or accident—than design." [62] Both legislators and outside reformists express a belief that committee structures need to be brought into harmony with changing needs of the country and that administrative skill is required toward that end. As Senator Bill Brock has said, "Committees are a management tool." [63]

Among the administrative needs frequently cited are jurisdictional definitions, intercommittee coordination, workload management, operating procedures, and information management. The extent of administrative needs of legislative committees is highlighted by the work of the Select Committee on Committees in the United States House of Representatives, the task force under the majority leader of the New York state senate, and numerous other reform efforts in state and local legislatures.

Procedures. Rules of procedure are fundamental in the management not only of legislative committees but also of the legislature as a whole. Procedures are required for an adequate flow of communication, for scheduling, for assigning priorities, for monitoring, for ensuring political access, and so forth. But there is frequent dissatisfaction expressed concerning the administrative quality of current legislative procedures. A congressman argues that no business corporation would permit the outmoded procedures that prevail in the House of Representatives.[64] A private study group sees a need to eliminate "anomalies and irrational procedures" in Congress.[65] A businessmen's group recommends "democratized procedures."[66] The point is that constant concern with administrative procedures faces legislatures just as it faces executive agencies.

External Linkages. Administrative mechanisms for links to clients are vital to government agencies. Representative legislatures have an obviously vital need for relationships with constituents, lobbyists, executive agencies, and local governments. And while political channels service many of these needs, there is a considerable administrative component as well. Information flow to the press and directly to constituents, contacts with lobbyists and public interest groups, public access to legislative sessions and the concomitant security needs, liaison with agencies, and so on, all require well-administered networks.

Organizational Development. Related to the needs already discussed, and to others not specifically mentioned, is a broad administrative need in legislatures for what can be called organizational development or continuing reorganization. Monitoring mechanisms for utilization, support, and preservation of legislative capabili-

[164]

ties are needed. Among other functions, these devices should be able to sense and analyze internal problems prior to crisis. And "feedback loops" among committees, leadership, legislative agencies, and external elements require continual maintenance.

The organizational needs mentioned are only illustrative of aspects of the legislative environment that require administrative skill. They are neither exhaustive nor necessarily separately distinguishable, nor do they require only administrative skill; as already suggested, and as the next chapter clarifies, the political context predominates. But there is a significant organizational component in legislative operations that benefits from administrative knowledge.

Systemic Needs

Perhaps the broadest level of administrative need stems from the place of legislatures in the overall, systemic government process. As Richard Neustadt and others indicate, American legislatures constitutionally hold four tangible administrative powers in the system of government administration: organization, authorization, appropriation, and oversight.[67] Joseph Harris calls it "congressional control of administration."[68] Allan Schick was referring to these powers when he lamented the past neglect of "the essential role of legislative bodies in the maintenance of responsive and effective government."[69] This level involves the public policy role of the legislature and includes managerial capacity in budgeting, program analysis, planning, and oversight. Fundamental to exercise of all these functions are information and evaluation capacities.

Information Systems. Information is crucial to all the systemic functions of legislatures, whether it be in budgetary deliberations, program planning, or evaluation. As Alexander Smith concluded, the whole legislative process is built around the acquisition of information and application of data to legislative tasks.[70] But more and more the need is not so much for access to information as it is for management of information.[71] Legislatures are increasingly overloaded with data, and their need is for input channels and tools and procedures enabling practical use of the data in decision-making. In a word, the need is for administration, for control over the facts, for the ability to research in depth and quickly. The director of a legislative staff was alluding to this when he responded: "Budget preparation and presentation is rudimentary and needs modernization. This could be the most useful contribution from public administration."

Standardization of format, mechanisms for definition, routinization of transmission, abstraction, and dissemination are some of the problems involved. Quite naturally, automated information processing systems are being employed for assistance.[72] The need for administrative skills in designing, implementing, and maintaining such systems was recently recognized when the National Legislative Conference turned to the Comparative Development Studies Center, a public administration group, for assistance in developing automated information systems for state legislatures.

Evaluation Technology. A few years ago Daniel P. Moynihan observed that "a new source of knowledge is coming into being." He referred to the product of evaluation research and cautioned that the executive was developing a monopoly over it and that this imbalance would be dangerous to the administrative system.[73] Etzioni issued a similar caveat.[74] Since that time legislatures have begun to improve their evaluation capacities. The General Accounting Office is serving a broader role for Congress; various "auditing" agencies have been created in state legislatures, and the Comparative Development Studies Center has received a grant to conduct a comprehensive study of legislative program evaluation.

Legislative program evaluation is a loosely used term that variously refers to auditing, expenditure review, program effectiveness, and so on. Broadly defined, it refers to legislative oversight and focuses on program performance in terms of both objectives and dollars. In any case, the point is that legislative evaluation or oversight is a key element in the system of government administration and that it requires administrative skill.

In sum, legislatures have a considerable organizational dimension. As organizations they need good management. As components in the government system they require administrative expertise. Clearly, housekeeping, operational areas, and systemic functions interrelate. And, in the words of a high-ranking legislative staffer who expressed many of the needs identified here: "[These needs] represent a series of very difficult problems, but they need to be solved, and the system will operate much better if public administration addresses itself to them."

RESOURCES OF PUBLIC ADMINISTRATION

Given the broad administrative needs of legislatures, what is the relevancy of the public administration field? What special contribution can it make to legislative improvement? How is it different from the general political science field? Much of the relevancy may be self-evident, since the field has been performing housekeeping, procedural, and substantive tasks such as budgeting and evaluation in the executive branch. Nevertheless, it is useful to clarify the resources of the field as they particularly relate to legislatures. Of chief pertinence in this regard are the operating perspective of the field and the expertise on which it can draw.

Operating Perspective

As Morstein-Marx long ago recognized, "political sense is generally more important than administrative experience"[75]; and clearly, pervading and transcending all the managerial needs of legislatures is the political function and dimension of the legislature. However, as suggested already, within the political dimension there is the unmistakable element of institutional action. In this sense the issue of legislative improvement can at least partially be defined in terms of managerial and organizational factors. A legislature is a political arena, but it is also an institutionalized structure, and it is for this latter reality in particular that the public administration field possesses a useful perspective.

Perhaps because the field is a thorough mix of practical experience and academic perception, it is institutionally geared and oriented toward action and problem-solving. Its work and its study are largely concerned with getting things done. It is an art-science "engage," and this perspective distinguishes it from political science. Heaphey has argued that political scientists tend to focus on sociopolitical factors of legislatures, not on organizational activities, that they are most interested in inputs, such as elections, parties, and social backgrounds, to the legislative process rather than on through-puts.[76] Rosenthal's survey of contemporary research on state legislatures confirms Heaphey's thesis.[77] He finds that most of the legislative research performed by political scientists has focused on the behavior of individual legislators and on external variables affecting collective legislative behavior. He points out that very little work has been done on institutional concerns such as committees, staffs, and performance. And an Urban Institute study of literature on local legislatures found what it calls a "political science viewpoint" and a lack of research directed toward helping local legislatures improve their work.[78]

While the perspective of political scientists is unquestionably useful and needed, it is not enough. Legislatures do need institutional attention as well. One scholar consulted put it thus: "Political scientists are intent on theory and make little contribution to institution. In the division of labor, public administrators should pick up the slack." And, as Heaphey advises: "Activities labeled legislative improvement by the persons pursuing them are not understandable solely in terms of political motivations. For example, you cannot understand the demand of a new Speaker of a lower house in the United States for new rules of procedure solely in terms of his personal political aspirations. His personal political aspirations will certainly affect his thinking, but his demands for new rules will be heavily influenced by what the organization structure with which he is dealing regards as reasonable."[79]

This typifies the public administration perspective and is a distinct resource of value to legislatures. A review of testimony before the Joint Congressional Committee on the Organization of Congress[80] confirms Stephen P. Gibert's contention: "Not all academic critics nor all Congressmen, of course, 'fit the pattern,' but a qualified generalization can be made that academic critics tend to concern themselves with more fundamental areas of concern such as party responsibility and Congress as a representative body. Congressmen themselves, in contrast, tend to be concerned with more limited, more mundane,' and pragmatic issues such as staffing, committee efficiency, and committee organization and procedures." [81] Moreover, though perhaps in the past many public administrationists' concepts of organizational action were too rigid to be of utility to "chaotic" legislatures, the field has developed an appreciation of loosely structured, complex conditions and has produced various concepts for operating within such environments. [82]

Expertise

This book previously alluded to the institutional, intellectual, and experiential content of the public administration field. The American Society for Public Administration lists over fourteen thousand members representing numerous administrative skills and eighty-four chapters across the country and in virtually every state capital. There are approximately one hundred schools for public administration and over fifteen research bureaus. These assets represent training and action resources in various specialized fields pertinent to legislatures, including organization theory, budgeting, program evaluation, and information systems. Moreover, the field is interdisciplinary—a mix of psychologists, sociologists, journalists, scientists, economists, and others. It thus might make significant contributions to public policy problems as well as to more narrow organizational questions. Additionally, the field has a comparative orientation linking jurisdictional and organizational divisions. Further, unlike business administration, the field has operated in a political environment and has a long tradition of public service. It could render considerable administrative assistance to legislatures.

MUTUAL INTERESTS

There is a general area of mutual interest that provides a basis for public administration—legislative alliance. It is a fundamental and mutual concern for the overall functioning of the government system. As Neustadt says: "Congress ... has at least as much to do with executive administration as does an incumbent of the White House." [83] Administration is a continuing function of both the legislative and executive branches, exercised through parallel organizations in the two branches interacting with each other. [84]

To begin with, public administrationists have correctly observed that the quality of administration depends in no small part upon the quality of legislation. [85] And the quality of legislation is in no small measure determined by the quality of legislative management: "The way programs are structured is a reflection of the structure of the legislature." [86]

Second, it may be of mutual interest to improve the oversight capability of legislatures. William M. Capron argues that better legislative evaluation and audit would be an incentive to better agency administration. [87] Implying the same thesis, V. O. Key judged that "legislative control is most effective when all administration is sufficiently integrated." [88] Their message is that good executive administration is a function of good legislative administration.

Third, it may be that legislatures and the public administration field need each other if good government is to prevail. The organizational expertise of public administration is essential to effective legislative functioning. But the political sense of the legislator is vital to effective administration: "The legislator's indispensable contribution to policy-making is his delicate feel for the political system.... His special expertise lies in his ability to inject the unique data of politics into this process, in order to render policy outcomes tolerable as well as rational." [89]

In sum, there is a solid basis for attention by public administration to legislatures. Legislative bodies, like every other organization, have administrative needs, and public administration, by its perspective and content, is particularly suited for helping fill those needs. And, most tellingly, the effectiveness of the government system as a whole argues for a joining of the legislative institution and the public administration field. The field's concern for administrative improvement should not be a locus, restricted to the executive, but rather an adaptable focus pertinent to all parts of the government system.

But recognizing the organizational dimension of legislatures and addressing the issue of legislative improvement are two different matters. The political dimension needs to be joined with the managerial effort. The following chapter suggests a framework for approaching that fusion.

Notes for Chapter 8

1. Jacques Ellul, *The Technological Society* (New York: Vintage, 1964).

2. Sheldon S. Wolin, *Politics and Vision* (Boston: Little, Brown, 1960), p. 354.

3. Gene S. Poschman, "The Images of Organization, Pluralism, and Community in American Social Science Literature on the Legislature" (Ph.D. diss., University of California, Berkeley, 1970).

4. Nelson W. Polsby, "The Institutionalization of the U.S. House of Representatives," *American Political Science Review* 62, no. 1 (March 1968): 144.

5. Philip Selznick, *Leadership in Administration* (New York: Harper and Row, 1957), p. 5; Chester I. Barnard develops the notion of rational organization in *The Functions of the Executive* (Cambridge: Harvard University Press, 1938), p. 73.

6. Selznick, *Leadership in Administration*, pp. 21, 141.

7. Wolin, *Politics and Vision*, p. 410.

8. Polsby, "The Institutionalization of the U.S. House of Representatives," p. 168.

9. Michael L. Strang, "The Case for the Citizen Legislator," *State Government* 47, no. 3 (summer 1974): 135.

10. Wolin, *Politics and Vision*, p. 364.

11. Ibid., p. 412.

12. Warren Bennis in Warren Bennis and Philip Slater, *The Temporary Society* (New York: Harper and Row, 1968).

13. Frederick C. Thayer, *An End to Hierarchy* (New York: Franklin Watts, 1973).

14. Lewis A. Froman, "Organization Theory and the Explanation of Important Characteristics of Congress," *American Political Science Review* 62, no. 2 (June 1968): 518–526.

15. Dwight Waldo, "Public Administration and Culture" in Roscoe Martin, *Public Administration and Democracy* (Syracuse, N.Y.: Syracuse University Press, 1965), p. 59.

16. Polsby, "The Institutionalization of the U.S. House of Representatives."

17. Samuel C. Patterson, "Legislative Research and Legisaltive Reform," *Publius* 4, no. 2 (spring 1974): 115.

18. See Polsby, "The Institutionalization of the U.S. House of Representatives."

19. Stewart L. Udall, *1976: Agenda for Tomorrow* (New York: Harcourt, Brace and World, 1968), p. 150.

20. For example, Senator Henry M. Jackson urged improved committee organization in "Environmental Policy and the Congress," *Public Administration Review* 28, no. 4 (July–August 1968): 303–305.

21. See above chapter 3.

22. See Chris Argyris, *Understanding Organizational Behavior* (London: Tavistock, 1960); Douglas McGregor, *The Human Side of Enterprise* (New York: McGraw-Hill, 1960); and Rensis Likert, *New Patterns of Management* (New York: McGraw-Hill, 1961).

23. See Daniel Katz and Robert L. Kahn, *The Social Psychology of Organization* (New York: Wiley, 1966).

24. See Warren Bennis, *Changing Organizations* (New York: McGraw-Hill, 1966); and Thayer, *An End to Hierarchy*.

25. See Allen Schick, "A Death in the Bureaucracy," *Public Administration Review* 33, no. 2 (March–April 1973): 146–156, and Joseph Wholey et al., *Federal Evaluation Policy* (Washington, D.C.: Urban Institute, 1970). The recently passed Congressional Budget Act undoubtedly will further this interest.

26. Donald G. Herzberg and Alan Rosenthal, eds., *Strengthening the States: Essays on Legislative Reform* (New York: Anchor, 1972), p. vi.

27. Citizens Conference on State Legislatures, *The Sometime Governments* (New York: Bantam, 1971), p. 15.

28. Committee for Economic Development, *Making Congress Effective* (New York: CED, 1970), p. 17.

29. Felix Frankfurter; *Malinski* v. *New York* 324 U.S. 401 (1945). Though the reference was to judicial proceedings, the message is used in broader contexts.

30. Raymond G. Davis, "Strategies for Studying Legis-

lative Staff: An Organization Theory Model," paper presented at the annual meeting of the Southwestern Political Science Association, Dallas, March 1974.

31. Quoted in Arthur Macmahon, "Congressional Oversight of Administration," *Political Science Quarterly* 58, no. 2 (July 1943): 186.

32. Alan P. Balutis, "Legislative Staffing," paper presented at the annual meeting of the Southwestern Political Science Association, Dallas, March 1974.

33. Ralph Braibanti, ed., *Political and Administrative Development* (Durham, N.C.: Duke University Press, 1969), p. 91.

34. Donald R. Matthews, *U.S. Senators and Their World* (New York: Vintage, 1960), p. 97.

35. Roger H. Davidson et al., *Congress in Crisis* (New York: Hawthorne, 1969), p. 175.

36. See Warren Weaver, *Both Your Houses: The Truth About Congress* (New York: Praeger, 1972), p. 165.

37. Ed Crane, "Legislative Service Agencies," in *The Book of the States* (Lexington, Ky.: Council of State Governments, 1971), p. 76.

38. Warren Bennis, in *Changing Organizations,* was one of the first to note this.

39. Thayer, *An End to Hierarchy,* p. vii.

40. Gerald E. Caiden, *The Dynamics of Public Administration* (New York: Holt, Rinehart, and Winston, 1971), p. 20.

41. Albert Lepawsky, *Administration* (New York: Knopf, 1952), p. 268.

42. Froman, "Organization Theory and the Explanation of Important Characteristics of Congress," p. 526; Polsby, "The Institutionalism of the U.S. House of Representatives," p. 168.

43. As for public administrationists, 16 of the 18 noted scholars responding felt the field should assist legislatures.

44. W. F. Willoughby, *Principles of Legislative Organization and Administration* (Washington, D.C.: Brookings Institution, 1934).

45. Marshall E. Dimock and Gladys O. Dimock, *Public Administration,* 3rd ed. (New York: Holt, Rinehart, and Winton, 1964), p. 110. For a more recent analysis, see Karl T. Kurtz, "Legislative Organization and Services," *The Book of the States* (Lexington, Ky.: Council of State Governments, 1974), pp. 53–92.

46. Gladys M. Kammerer, "The Administration of Con-

gress," *Public Administration Review* 9, no. 3 (September 1949) : 175.

47. Warren H. Butler, "Administering Congress," *Public Administration Review* 26, no. 1 (March 1966) : 4.

48. Ibid., p. 8.

49. *The Legislative Administrator* (April 1974) : 5.

50. These demands were recognized and addressed by the recommendations in Alfred de Grazia, ed., *Congress: The First Branch of Government* (Washington: American Enterprise Institute, 1966), p. 492.

51. For a concrete example of recognition of the importance of procedure and organization see National Legislative Conference, *Ways and Means* (Lexington, Ky: Council of State Governments, 1974).

52. See, for example, Richard A. Cooley and Geoffrey Wandesforde-Smith, eds., *Congress and the Environment* (Seattle: University of Washington, 1970), p. 231.

53. For a good discussion of this, see Carolyn L. Kenton, "Modern Legislative Staffing," *State Government* 47, no. 3 (summer 1974) : 165–169.

54. Gladys M. Kammerer, "Legislative Oversight of Administration in Kentucky," *Public Administration Review* 10, no. 3 (summer 1950) : 174.

55. Committee for Economic Development, *Making Congress Effective*, p. 51.

56. John S. Saloma, *Congress and the New Politics* (Boston: Little, Brown, 1969), p. 168.

57. See Hugh A. Bone, "On Understanding Legislatures," *Public Administration Review* 15, no. 2 (spring 1955): 125.

58. Saloma, *Congress and the New Politics*, p. 163.

59. Richard Bolling, "Committees in the House," *Annals of the American Academy* 411 (January 1974) : 2.

60. Bill Brock, "Committees in the Senate," *Annals of the American Academy* 411 (January 1974) : 16.

61. Representative Dave Martin, *Congressional Record*, 93rd Congress, first session, 31 January 1973, H592.

62. Brock, "Committees in the Senate," p. 16.

63. Ibid.

64. Richard Bolling, "Committees in the House," p. 3.

65. De Grazia, *Congress: The First Branch of Government*, p. 479.

66. Committee for Economic Development, *Making Congress Effective*, p. 19.

67. Richard E. Neustadt, "Politicians and Bureaucrats," p. 103.

68. Joseph P. Harris, *Congressional Control of Administration* (Washington, D.C.: Brookings Institution, 1964).

69. Allan Schick, "Review and Evaluation Can Focus Light on Legislative Reform," National Conference of State Legislative Leaders *Annual,* 1971, p. 5.

70. Alexander Smith, "Information and Intelligence for Congress," *Annals of the American Academy* 289 (September 1953): 114.

71. See Charles P. Dechert, "Availability of Information for Congressional Operations" in de Grazia, *Congress: The First Branch of Government,* p. 167 ff.

72. See Kenneth Janda, "Information Systems for Congress," in de Grazia, *Congress: The First Branch of Government,* pp. 415–456.

73. Daniel P. Moynihan, *Hearings: Federal Role in Urban Affairs,* U.S. Senate, 89th Congress, 2nd session, December 1966, p. 2647.

74. Amitai Etzioni, "How May Congress Learn," *Science* (January 1968): 172.

75. Fritz Morstein-Marx, ed., *Elements of Public Administration,* 2nd ed. (Englewood Cliffs, N.J.: Prentice-Hall, 1959), p. 101.

76. James J. Heaphey, "Technical Assistance in the Administration of Legislatures," paper presented at the annual meeting of the American Society for Public Administration, New York, March 1972, p. 2.

77. Alan Rosenthal, "Contemporary Research on State Legislatures" in *Political Science and State and Local Government* (Washington, D.C.: American Political Science Association, 1973), pp. 55–86. See also Patterson, "Legislative Research and Legislative Reform," p. 109.

78. Marilyn Morton, "Short Survey of Research to Date on Local Government Legislative Bodies" (Washington, D.C.: Urban Institute, 1970).

79. Heaphey, "Technical Assistance in the Administration of Legislatures," p. 2.

80. Joint Congressional Committee on the Organization of Congress, *Final Report,* 89th Congress, 2nd session, 1966, report 1414.

81. Stephen P. Gibert, "Congress: The First Branch of Government?" *Public Administration Review* 27, no. 2 (June 1967): 188.

82. See Karl Weick, *The Social Psychology of Organizing* (Reading, Pa.: Addison-Wesley, 1969); Peter M. Blau, *Exchange and Power in Social Life* (New York: Wiley, 1964); D. Katz and R. Kahn, *The Social Psychology of Organization* (New York: Wiley, 1966). All are organization theorists widely studied by public administrationists.

83. Neustadt, "Politicians and Bureaucrats," p. 103.

84. Emmette S. Redford, *Democracy in the Administrative State* (New York: Oxford, 1969), p. 81.

85. Dimock and Dimock, *Public Administration,* 3rd ed., p. 110.

86. Harold Seidman, "New Aspects for Attention," *Public Administration Review* 30, no. 3 (May–June 1970): 273.

87. William M. Capron, "The Impact of Analysis on Bargaining in Government," in Alan A. Altschuler, *The Politics of the Federal Bureaucracy* (New York: Dodd, Mead, 1968), p. 197 ff.

88. V. O. Key, "Legislative Control," in Morstein-Marx, ed., *Elements of Public Administration,* p. 321.

89. Roger H. Davidson, "Congress and the Executive," in de Grazia, *Congress: The First Branch of Government,* p. 413.

9

A Framework for Involvement: The Political Dimension

W. F. Willoughby's books in 1934 focused on "principles" of legislative administration and spoke in terms of "proper" existing procedures.[1] This was during an era when public administration favored a principles approach to administrative questions generally. Since that time the field has recognized that principles are often intellectual tools that are only marginally related to or suited for reality. Particularly with regard to legislatures, diversity and flexibility are so characteristic, and desirably so, that universal principles relevant to real situations are elusive. Rather, the notion of "guidelines" seems more pertinent and useful.

A relationship between public administration and legislatures might include internal action and research. Internal action implies project activity and consulting, and might, for example, involve ASPA committees, professors of public administration, and centers or institutes of public administration. Research might be either general or specific and be conducted by schools and organizations as well as individuals. Each of these general activities can be approached from a clear ideological and practical context. The discussion that follows suggests some guidelines for development of both an ideological perspective and a modus operandi within a broad framework. It emphasizes the need to mingle the organizational with the political dimension of the legislative institution.

IDEOLOGICAL PERSPECTIVE

Involvement of the field of public administration in any area benefits from a clear and realistic ideological vision of the nature of the environment it is entering and of the limits or constraints on the relationship potential. Particularly, differences between a new environment and those with which a relationship already exists should be stressed; the tendency might be to operate as though an unexplored ambience were the same as a more familiar one. Public administration has historically operated chiefly in the milieu of the executive bureaucracy. The legislative environment might, in some critical ways, be strange, require some new premises, and present new forms of relationships. It might also present an opportunity to develop fresh approaches to familiar phenomena.

Nature of the Environment

Though legislatures have a major organizational dimension, they do differ from executive organizations. Three characteristics of the legislative environment are particularly noteworthy. Whereas the executive bureaucracy is functionally an administrative institution, legislatures are political organs. Whereas bureaucracies are typically hierarchical, legislative bodies are often more

[180]

collegial. And third, diversity in goals and structure is normally more extensive in the legislative environment.

The Political Aspect. It is not the basis of the political function of legislatures that needs stress and elaboration in the present context, but rather the implications of that political function for administrative concerns. As far back as Plato and Aristotle this question was recognized. Plato equated management of political organizations with management of any organization, but Aristotle saw a crucial difference and a need to approach administration of political organizations with a recognition of that difference. Whereas typical executive organizations have a rather clearly defined interest that can be assumed, a political organization is marked by a plethora of interests and claims. Management of political organizations, Aristotle noted, is thus a problem of reconciliation —of reconciling, through compromise, various interests. Management of nonpolitical organizations can face similar requirements, but normally to a lesser degree.

The Citizens Conference on State Legislatures crystallized this characteristic in its description of a legislature: "It is both a 'citizen' and a 'professional' legislature; it makes informed decisions but it makes them democratically; it listens to its public, and it leads it." [2] The importance of this awareness was stressed by the director of a state legislative staff: "The failure to distinguish between elected legislators and their total function as compared to appointed executive department officials can create serious distrust between legislators and public administrationists."

In other words, legislative administration operates more within a political framework than within a strict organizational design. Baaklini and Heaphey make the observation with emphasis: "Our point is that when one

[181]

finds a meaningful role for a legislature ... that role is not technological but is political. To overlook this in the search for rationalizing legislative structure, process, and output is a hubris of the expert. ..." [3] This point was forcefully alluded to by one senior legislative staffer who participated in the present study: "The real problem is that administrative theory today concerns a landscape which is quite different from the landscape of the legislative branch. We are told, for example, that the legislature has too many committees, and this I suppose by analogy to ... the executive branch. To me this is not a helpful approach to studying the organization of the legislative branch, but this branch continues to be criticized for not conforming to the norms of a different animal entirely."

Ultimately what needs to be clear in the legislative environment is that, although administrative expertise is important and necessary, politics will, does, and should dominate. As James Robinson pointed out: "You can go just so far with expert knowledge and then it has to be integrated with the policy aspirations and individual philosophies of the individual members." [4] The public administrationist needs to view politics not simply as rational, irrational, or nonrational, but rather as rational in its own terms and as not necessarily inconsistent with efficiency and effectiveness in government. [5] This point was extensively emphasized by legislative participants consulted.

The Organizational Metabolism. Roger H. Davidson et al., in their book on congressional reform, criticize political scientists for holding to an organizational-chart notion of congressional operations. [6] The public administration field, identified as it is with bureaucracy, might tend toward a similar notion. Organizational charts and hierarchical relationships have been fundamental starting points for public administration activity.

Legislatures are in many ways unusual organizations, and they span a spectrum of organizational models. While some are quite oligarchic and rigid, most are collegial to varying degrees, nonhierarchical rather than pyramidal, lateral rather than scaler, consensual more than authoritarian.[7] Public administrationists have relatively little experience with the collegial side of the spectrum, and traditional concepts may thus need adjustment when involved in the legislative environment.

Diversity. Although many differences are evident among administrative agencies, the diversity of legislatures is striking. Not only are there significant variations among national, state, and local legislative bodies, but there is considerable diversity among legislatures at the same level of government, and even within a single legislative body. For example, Cochrane discovered that committee staffs in the U.S. Congress range from the highly professional (as envisioned in the Legislative Reorganization Act) to the highly partisan.[8] Balutis found that in the New York state legislature conditions of staff work vary not only between the two houses but among their committees and even in the same committee from time to time.[9] And the Urban Institute found "a great diversity in the responsibilities, functions, needs, and problems of [local] legislators."[10] Furthermore, there is considerable instability or temporariness in legislative environments. The membership can change rapidly, bringing with it new norms, procedures, and structures.

Thus, insights relevant to one legislature at one particular time may be of dubious relevancy to another legislature or at another time. Public administration procedures, theories, or practices applicable and pertinent to the California senate in 1980 may be inappropriate for the Virginia assembly in 1981 and the Clinton County legislature in 1982; or they may be useful in the Brazilian Congress of 1978. In the words of one legislator: "We must realize and appreciate the differences and individuality of the various legislatures."

Relationship between Politics and Administration

Given the political nature of the legislature, some perspective for relating to that reality is important when considering involvement by public administration. As Norton Long has remarked: "Attempts to solve administrative problems in isolation from the structure of power and purpose in the polity are bound to prove illusory." [11]

Importance of the Relationship. Two points are noteworthy in this regard: (1) without this perspective, efforts of public administrationists are likely to be rebuffed, and (2) without the perspective, administrative efforts are apt to harm rather than improve the legislature. On the first point, "scientific principles," "academic objectivity," and "administrative expertise" are not always unmitigated purposes and values of legislatures. Political excellence is the sine qua non. Neglect of this reality could obstruct any overtures from public administrationists.

Relatedly, were public administration to approach legislatures without an appreciation of and respect for the relationship to politics, the vitality of the legislature, as a political body, might be jeopardized. In Lebanon, where public administration is involved with the legislature, an experience of this type transpired: Administrative reforms implemented with too little regard for the political nature of the parliament disrupted the political climate. According to Baaklini's report: "The special nature of the legislative functions and the nature of the political process in the Chamber were factors not accounted for in the new form." [12] As a result, experts and professional administrators became an empire by themselves and the political functions of the legislature were subverted.

This is not to subscribe to the suggestion that "political rationality" must dominate, nor that "organizational rationality" is irrelevant or dangerous. For, as Baaklini convincingly argues, while political rationality is important, justification for political interests and actions is often couched in terms of organizational rationality.[13] Nor is it accepted here that legislative administration is a political issue first and an organizational matter second. Rather, the point is that the relationship ought not be perceived in dichotomous terms but in symbiotic or process terms; that is, the relationship should be seen as a *relationship*, not as a confrontation. Legislative administration is a political-organizational matter. Institutional excellence—and this is true of executive administration as well—requires both an appropriate political climate and technical proficiency. Most clearly organizational matters can become political issues, just as many clearly political issues have major organizational dimensions.

Relationship Guidelines. Two possible extremes in the relationship of public administration to legislatures can be recognized and avoided. One is the "philosopher king" approach, the other the "rubber stamp" notion. The idea that public administrators should be special people, detached from the struggle for material interests, above the petty concerns that are generic to politics, has surfaced in the past.[14] The dangers of such detachment and independence have been recognized by Baaklini and Heaphey: "Instead of being of service to the political process of the legislature, legislative staff in such a bureaucracy would stifle the political function of the legislature." [15]

Similarly, public administrationists concerned with legislative improvement have been known to preach from pedestals. In an otherwise excellent selection on congressional administration, Gladys M. Kammerer didactically proclaimed: "By simplifying and centralizing its own administrative management, freeing itself from outmoded and undignified patronage demands, and recruiting more competent and more vigorous employees, it [Congress] could set an invaluable example to the nation of the application of the American flair for economy and efficiency it professes to esteem so highly." [16]

On the other hand, it is not suggested that the public administration field play the "rubber stamp" robot passively serving political whims. There is an in-between point where a true relationship forms, where "nonpolitical rationality is intertwined with the values and purposes of the political aspects of legislatures." [17] It is at this point that public administration can be a vital force enabling the legislature to play its role in full measure. Willoughby portrayed the point: "The situation, in a word, is not unlike the relationship that exists between the individual who desires to build a house and his architect. The former determines what he wants, but avails himself of the technical aid and advice of the technician in realizing his desires." [18]

Modus Operandi

Conceptualizing the relationship of public administration to legislatures and actually operating within the relationship are two related but distinct steps. This section discusses some aspects of practical involvement with legislatures and suggests two guidelines: (1) learn the particular environment, and (2) synthesize administration with politics.

Learn the Environment

A legislature is a government institution with tasks to perform and objectives to achieve, and each particular legislature should be learned in terms of its own tasks and objectives rather than approached in preconceived terms or in terms of its relation to the executive. Davidson warns that in the past political scientists have lacked this kind of knowledge and appreciation and have viewed legislative improvement as merely making the Congress more responsive to executive branch proposals.[19]

While each particular legislative body should be learned and appreciated in itself, there are some general characteristics, widely found in legislatures, that can assist in grasping each individual milieu. These are collegiality, diversity, incrementalism, and political presence.

Collegiality. The degree and form of collegial organization varies from legislature to legislature. Depending on the power of the leadership, the party majorities, the influence of key staff personalities, and other factors, actual operation of the legislature can be heavily consensual, somewhat dictatorial, or hierarchical. But seldom does an organizational chart portray actual operations. The director of the Citizens Conference on State Legislatures has remarked that public administration will have to learn how to cope with collegiality if the field is to form a fruitful relationship with legislatures.[20] And one legislative staffer put it: "Clarity of organization, fixed lines of communication, and hierarchical reporting may well be dysfunctional for legislatures, where flexibility and responsiveness are so crucial. Ample attention must be paid to the political dimensions of a legislature's organizational problems—one of the major past faults of public administrators' discussions of legislatures."

Diversity. Specific manifestations of diversity in a legislature need to be known and considered when undertaking involvement. Goal diversification is fundamental in this regard, particularly for public administrationists. As Davidson points out, the conventional notion of reform implies an orderly progression from premises to conclusions to implementations, but the preconditions for such an orderly process—consensus on goals and means/ ends relationships—are seldom found in a legislature: "Although this model may be appropriate for describing one's intellectual processes in a number of problem-solving situations, its requirements are too demanding for application to such large political decision-making structures as legislatures." [21] The extent of goal diversity needs to be learned and accounted for in each particular legislature.

Diversity of perceived problems and needs is an important guide to activity in a particular legislature. A study of the U.S. Congress found that many of the problems articulated by elected members would only marginally be within the competence of administrative reform.[22] These concerned getting reelected, leadership power, caliber of members, and so forth. Another group of complaints related to problems endemic to large, modern bodies—namely, lack of time, complexity of decision making, and policy output. A third group was considered clearly within the domain of administration: committee procedures, staffing, scheduling, and so on. And this last group constituted only 20 percent of the problems mentioned. This type of diversity should be recognized in each specific legislature, and public administration must appreciate that its competency will not apply to all legislative needs and may be applicable to only a small portion of perceived needs. Some legislatures may thus be more "ripe" for a relationship with the field than others.

Staff diversity is another area to be traced and accommodated. One study found significant differences in personal backgrounds and behavioral norms among the members of committee staff, central staff, and leadership staff in the New York state legislature.[23] These differences can be important in each particular case and necessitate adjustment of relationships.

Finally, diversity of interactions should be discovered for each particular legislature. Some legislative bodies have extensive relationships with staff of the executive branch. Some are more tied to political parties than others. Some have important relationships with interest groups. These interactions can be important in forming and guiding the relationship of public administration with legislatures.

Neglect of the diversity phenomenon has been common. Indeed, a 1955 *Public Administration Review* criticism of a major legislative reform report observed disapprovingly: "The report gives the impression that, in terms of re-organization, what is good for Arizona is good for Maine."[24]

When working with legislatures, we public administrationists might do well to remember Kipling: "There are nine and twenty ways of making tribal lays,/And every single one of them is right."[25]

Incrementalism. Incrementalism appears to be a standing operating reality in most legislatures, and an ability to cope with and relate to such a reality has frequently been elusive for political scientists enraptured by idealism.[26] The Hoover Commission, for example, recommended sweeping changes in executive management.

[189]

Legislators face periodic tests by elections and thus live in an insecure atmosphere. Whereas bureaucrats can perhaps less fearfully gamble, legislators can pay a price at the polls. And, as pointed out by a legislative staffer, public administrationists themselves could promise too much from administrative improvement and be quickly discredited.

Public administrationists involved with legislatures can benefit from the insight of Dahl and Lindblom: "Probably the problem of the modern legislature cannot be solved. But it can be reduced...." [27] What is required for an incremental process is a vision of the long-term potential of the legislature combined with a pragmatic sense of what is attainable in the present. Davidson calls it "incremental idealism" and found that, in fact, the best approach to reform in Congress has been through "cautious tinkering with minor cogs in the legislative machinery... much of the development of Congress as an institution is traced through changes that are marginal and gradual in character." [28] Stephen P. Gibert developed a similar argument in noting that the most telling improvements are often those that are quite unexciting. [29]

In some legislatures, particularly in developing countries, incrementalism may not be so important as in others; but where it is, it needs to be recognized, and the relationship of public administration to the body should respect it. One of the few articles in *Public Administration Review* dealing with legislative reform exhibited a distinct lack of appreciation of the incremental notion: Joseph P. Harris, in criticizing the Legislative Reorganization Act of 1946 for not being sufficiently sweeping, cynically remarked: "Citizens alert to the problem will regard the passage of the act in the closing days of Congress... as hardly more than a beginning of the needed reform of Congress, and not a very good beginning at that." [30] The point could have been made that it was, nevertheless, a beginning. George B. Galloway, in reflecting on the same act ten years later, sounded a more tempered tone that can serve as an excellent guide: "As for the future, further steps toward strengthening the internal machinery and methods of our national legislature may be expected as time and opportunity permit and as Congress itself feels the need of improving the legislative process." [31]

Political Presence. The political nature of legislatures was pointed out earlier, but some specification of its operational presence can clarify the kind of awareness suggested for public administrationists. First, though public administration has, at least since Pendleton Herring,[32] recognized the policy-making or "political" role of administrators, writers on legislative staffing frequently express a belief that staff are detached from value judgments.[33] But, as empirical study has found, staff are not merely "neutral agents, devoid of values and providing purely objective data." [34] Rather, "they are, inexorably, important participants in the legislative process in their own right, and their views and activities have important implications for policy making." [35] Again, diversity comes into play, as some legislative staffs are more politically influential than others. On the other hand, particularly in developing countries, some legislative staffs tend to be quite nonpolitical.

Second, the perspective of the participants, of the legislators, needs to be learned and appreciated. Administrative perspective alone can overlook, for example, the validity of mechanisms that disperse and obscure responsibility and thus reduce political pressures on members. Davidson found widespread opposition in Congress to proposals to strip the House Rules Committee of its blocking and delaying power.[36] While this would have been administratively beneficial, politically it was unsound and nonnegotiable.

Similarly, an administrative expert, oblivious to the practitioner's perspective, might recommend electronic voting in the legislature as a time-saver. When this was proposed in the U.S. Congress, many representatives opposed it:

> A number of members pointed out that the 40 minutes or so required for a roll-call vote is hardly wasted time since it permits them to come to the floor from their offices or committee rooms, consult with colleagues who are knowledgeable on the issue, check to see how others are voting, and incidentally engage in a little socializing.[37]

This example highlights a tension between different types of rationality with which public administrationists must deal, particularly in legislatures.

Synthesize Administration with Politics

Politics and administration are often uneasy bedfellows. The compromise aspect of the former can more than occasionally horrify the efficiency elements of the latter, and vice versa. A marriage of the two is in many ways a shotgun affair compelled by mutual exigencies and is surely a union that has to be worked at in order to succeed. Mutual patience, understanding, tolerance, and esteem are desirable. Moreover, a strange type of marriage is necessary: The two must, in a sense, go to bed together without engaging in intimacies. The synthesis must be operational but not transcendent.

It is, again, the nature of the legislative environment that requires and shapes the politics-administration symbiosis. As Heaphey put it: "It is the pervasive use of both political and rational organizational criteria that differ-entiates most legislative bodies from non-legislative in-stitutions." [38] In many cases political criteria can affect the most mundane housekeeping decisions. Public admin-istrationists may thus need to be both "in tune" with the underlying value system of the legislature, and "out of tune" with it to the extent necessary to perceive the area of coincidence with rational-organizational values. As a state legislative staff director cautioned: "There is the danger that public administration with politically anti-septic approaches would be irrelevant to the more politi-cally charged legislature; or, that in trying to account for operation in a more political atmosphere, it would bury its solid administrative knowledge."

For example, an "in tune" perspective might reject some past studies of legislative staffing as being insensi-tive to the political environment. Galloway developed a division between policy making and administrative detail and urged civil service status for staff.[39] Rather than synthesis, he argued for dichotomy between political and organizational roles. Gladys M. Kammerer focused solely on the rational organization of staff and spoke in terms of conflict between political loyalty and technical com-petence.[40] Rather than synthesize political rationality with organizational rationality, her inclination was to sep-arate them. The "in tune" perspective sees legislatures as first and foremost political institutions, and it seeks synthesis rather than separation. A state legislator ex-pressed it as follows: "You cannot satisfy a legislator by giving him only the best professional judgment of how to solve a particular problem. He requires more than that. He needs an understanding of his problems, an apprecia-tion of the public mood, an appreciation of the power implications, and tolerance of his need to modify professional judgment in order to get something worthwhile done."

The "out of tune" co-perspective recognizes the danger of legislative administrationists' becoming independent power centers, usurping legislative roles. As one observer puts it: "Because of the political context of their work, the temptation of a staff member to 'play legislator' is great." [41] An "out of tune" view may be necessary to prevent corruption of the support role and maintain the political function of the legislator. Again, a veteran legislative staffer made the point: "I would perceive only two possible problem areas that could arise in the involvement of the field of public administration with legislatures. One is that the field might try to provide suggestions and recommendations on a theoretical academic level that ignores the pragmatic political world in which legislatures exist. . . . A second potential problem is that because of the intensely political nature of legislatures, should public administration's involvement become one of controversial position-taking, I believe this could serve to prejudice any recommendations concerning legislative improvement."

The symbiosis of politics and administration might be facilitated by development of intellectual sensitivity, of certain emotional behavioral traits, and of a tolerance and appreciation for political rationality.

The public administrationist involved with legislatures can be intellectually sensitive to the political effects of proposed changes, not just to conformity with an orderly theory. Davidson says it well:

> The would-be reformer must first understand the political functions or dysfunctions of existing procedures. Second, he must show either that modifications of current

procedures will serve these functions more faithfully or that the functions themselves are expendable. Third, he ought to be reasonably certain that the proposed reform will yield the desired result X rather than the undesired results Y or Z.[42]

Donald R. Matthews argued, in his study of the U.S. Senate, that every group of people has its own unwritten "rules of the game," its "norms of conduct," its "approved manner of behavior." [43] A study of the New York legislature supported Matthews's view and identified some of the more important staff "norms." Among the most frequently cited behavioral traits in this survey were courtesy, loyalty, and deference.[44] "A cardinal rule of legislative behavior is that political disagreements should not influence personal feelings," it found, because "the man who yesterday was your worst enemy may tomorrow be your best friend." The norm of loyalty to a legislator or to a committee was mentioned most frequently by the legislators Balutis interviewed. And the norm of deference, of being "on tap, not on top," was very strong. Cultivation or appreciation of these behavioral traits might facilitate the politics-administration synthesis.

Finally, an appreciation of political rationality is essential in a marriage of politics and administration. For a legislature, a body that attempts to build consensus out of sharply different interests and perspectives, must frequently act "inefficiently" in order to reduce the conflict level and satisfy needs of individual members. Or, as Dahl and Lindblom put it, "One major limit to effective reorganization of the American Congress to meet its modern tasks is the extent to which bargaining is built into the American political system. . . .[45] A public administrationist who gets involved with legislatures without an awareness and tolerance of this phenomenon might hear the words Speaker Sam Rayburn once uttered to an efficiency-minded reformer: "Joe, I am worried about you. You seem to have an orderly mind—and this is a disorderly body." [46]

In brief, public administration may frequently find an alliance with legislatures frustrating. Legislatures' apparent irrationality, inefficiency, and political pot-pourri might occasionally startle a person with a strong organizational rationality perspective. At those times we public administrationists might remember Churchill's words in paraphrase: Legislatures may well be the worst of systems—except for all the others.

SPECIFIC AVENUES

The foregoing guidelines are intended to be evocative and general. The purpose was not to establish principles and norms, but to suggest a framework within which public administration might approach legislatures. The discussion should thus be viewed not as rigid or comprehensive but as catalytic. Following that general framework some more specific guidelines are indicated in this section focusing on internal action and research.

Four observations are applicable to all areas of possible involvement. First, public administrationists, in approaching legislatures, might heed Professor Mafeje's suggestion that "we are not that different from ordinary human beings who muddle along at the best of times." [47] Public administration works because it is a system of communication about things and their properties among human beings, not because it is a science.

Second, governmental administration, as discussed in the Introduction, is a system, not a branch here and a branch there. Involvement in legislative administration should be approached as complementing, not competing with, executive and judicial administration.

Third, American political scientists study sociopolitical factors of legislatures. They are interested chiefly in inputs to the legislative process—for example, elections, political parties, and sources of motivation. As discussed earlier, public administration should focus on organizational matters within the constraints of those inputs.

Fourth, the basic approach to legislative administration might profitably be what Willoughby calls "the problem standpoint"—that is, a quest to determine the nature of the problems that are presented to a people in creating and operating machinery for the conduct of its political affairs.[48] The need for such an approach has been suggested by the Urban Institute in its study of local legislatures: "Research on . . . local legislative bodies has generally focused on trying to develop models. . . . There has been little research to determine problems of local legislative officials and little effort to develop ways to help them carry out their functions."[49]

Internal Action

When serving as project staff, or particularly as consultants to legislatures, concern for problems of political ideology, confidence, and persuasion is important.

One legislator in New York has remarked that "in spite of all the talk about 'experts,' it's ridiculous to expect committee chairmen to surround themselves with staff people with views contrary to their own."[50] Similarly, public administrationists may be affected by political ideology in certain situations at particular times. Though frequently legislative improvement matters may bridge political ideologies, this cannot be presumed, and a public administrationist needs to be sensitive to the possibility.

Public administrationists also need to be concerned

[197]

about gaining the confidence of legislators. Because of past bad experiences with external critics, legislators have frequently distrusted academicians and observers who have criticized them from ivory towers.[51] Eric Redman, a former congressional assistant, found that legislators had good cause to be leery: "The books I read seemed to describe a wholly different institution from the one I had worked in and had come to know.... It seemed the scholars had been a bit too hasty.... Perhaps, too, the academics had simply swallowed too many White House press releases without the requisite grains of salt." [52] Arthur Maass, a scholar, had previously sounded a similar note: "...exaggeration and misinformation about Congress passes for intelligence." [53] Sensitivity to this record could help public administrationists develop a positive perspective of legislatures.

Third, persuasion is an important element in a political arena. As Davidson reminds us: "Whatever the judgments of professional critics and whatever the attitudes of the general public, questions of congressional reorganization must in the last analysis be confronted within the institution." [54] Public administrationists in legislatures cannot rely on the innate appropriateness of administrative proposals. The legislators who will have to operate with them must be convinced. The political as well as organizational appropriateness must be manifest.

Research

Many of the above observations are relevant to research activity as well; additionally, public administration researchers might consider questions of procedure, methodology, and expectation.

Questions of procedure involve contact with the actors whom the research will affect—namely, the legislators and specifically the legislative leadership. Plausibly, without the proper relationships research will have neither the required access to information nor the chance of having any significant impact. As Davidson asserted: "Reform measures... often flounder because they threaten the existing congressional leadership." [55] Accordingly, convinced that progress does not just happen but is deliberately induced by individuals and groups, the Comparative Development Studies Center (CDSC) at Albany has adopted the procedure of insisting that research projects be consistent with the interests and commitments of legislative leadership.[56] Franklin L. Burdette supported this approach: "Research can properly be geared to public action, but it can lay the groundwork for change only if there are political recognition and acceptances of real advantages to be expected. Genuinely effective insight must go beyond analysis. It must move toward policy decision through responsible and informed use of power." [57]

Methodological guidelines are, of course, subject to individual intent and style. But, again, the successful experience of CDSC merits consideration. It has pursued its research on a "science engage" and comparative basis. Rather than operate from a set of models or preconceptions of what legislatures are or should be, the center undertakes its research on the premise that "the social science of legislatures should be shaped in the context of ongoing practical activities aimed at legislative improvement... and of what people engaged in it believe they are doing." [58] The goal is to provide a setting in which the logic and sentiments of practitioners in specific time and place situations can be interrelated with the logic and sentiments of researchers interested in formulating generalized statements. The approach is intended to avoid the pitfall described by a midwest legislator: "Recommendations from those in the 'ivory towers' often take the form of not being practical because the political atmosphere is not examined closely or because those in the academic field do not examine the day-to-day problems involved in legislative administration." The Albany group has thus stressed a rigorously empirical methodology of research and has found it useful.

Secondly, CDSC has subscribed to Dahl's contention that "as long as the study of public administration is not comparative, claims for 'a science of public administration' sound rather hollow." [59] It has thus adopted a comparative approach utilizing information from a wide variety of cultural, economic, and political types of situations. If some practices work well in the American setting but not in the Brazilian, or are useful in a local legislature but not in a state, researchers should be able to understand why the differences exist.

Finally, the expectations of researchers should not be so high as to induce disillusionment. Administrative reform, while increasingly being held as important, is often given low priority and is susceptible to various fluctuations in the legislative environment. Researchers should thus be prepared for procrastination and rejection.

Again, the guidelines presented in this chapter are intended merely to provide a framework for approaching legislative administration. There is no suspicion that they are comprehensive or pertinent in all cases, but it is suggested that they are useful as a departure point for involvement in this previously neglected area. Specific recommendations for institutional involvement follow in the final chapter.

NOTES FOR CHAPTER 9

1. W. F. Willoughby, *Principles of Legislative Organization and Administration* (Washington, D.C.: Brookings Institution, 1934), p. 4.

2. Citizens Conference on State Legislatures, *The Sometime Governments* (New York: Bantam, 1971), p. 36.

3. Abdo I. Baaklini and James J. Heaphey, "Legislative Institution Building," forthcoming monograph of Sage Publications (Beverly Hills, Calif.), p. 66.

4. James Robinson, quoted in U.S. Congress Joint Committee on the Organization of Congress, *Hearings*, August 2, 1965, p. 799.

5. Baaklini and Heaphey, "Legislative Institution Building," p. 67. See also Karl E. Weick, *The Social Psychology of Organizing* (Reading, Pa.: Addison-Wesley, 1969), for an organization theorist's discussion of this viewpoint.

6. Roger H. Davidson et al., *Congress in Crisis* (New York: Hawthorne, 1969), p. 167.

7. For an incisive discussion of this see James J. Heaphey, "Legislative Staffing: Organizational and Philosophical Considerations" in James J. Heaphey and Alan Balutis, eds., *Legislative Staffing: A Comparative Perspective* (Beverly Hills: Sage Press, 1975.)

8. James D. Cochrane, "Partisan Aspects of Congressional Committee Staffing," *Western Political Quarterly* 17, no. 2 (June 1964): 338–348.

9. Alan P. Balutis, "Professional Staffing in the New York State Legislature" (Ph.D. diss., State University of New York at Albany, 1973), p. 9.

10. Louis Blair and Richard E. Winnie, "The Forgotten

Men of Government: Local Legislators," working paper 201-9, (Washington, D.C.: Urban Institute, 1972), p. i.

11. Norton E. Long, "Power and Administration," *Public Administration Review* 9, no. 4 (December 1949) : 262.

12. Abdo I. Baaklini, "Comparative Legislative Process," paper presented at the annual meeting of the American Society for Public Administration, New York, March 1972, p. 43.

13. Baaklini, "Comparative Legislative Process," pp. 18–19. See also Eduard Schneier, "The Intelligence of Congress," *Annals of the American Academy* 387 (January 1970) : 15–18.

14. Paul H. Appleby, *Big Democracy* (New York: Alfred Knopf, 1945), chapters 3–4, and *Morality and Administration* (Baton Rouge: Louisiana State University, 1952).

15. Baaklini and Heaphey, "Legislative Institution Building," pp. 64–65.

16. Gladys M. Kammerer, "The Administration of Congress," *Public Administration Review* 9, no. 3 (summer 1949) : 181.

17. Baaklini and Heaphey, "Legislative Institution Building," p. 65.

18. W. F. Willoughby, *Principles of Public Administration* (Washington, D.C.: Brookings Institution, 1927), pp. 2–3.

19. Davidson, *Congress in Crisis*, p. 89.

20. Larry Margolis, executive director, CCSL, in personal interview with the author, January 1974.

21. Davidson, *Congress in Crisis*, p. 3.

22. Ibid., pp. 77–78.

23. Balutis, "Professional Staffing in the New York State Legislature," pp. 104–106.

24. Hugh Bone, "On Understanding Legislatures," *Public Administration Review* 15, no. 2 (spring 1955) : 122.

25. Rudyard Kipling, *In the Neolithic Age.*

26. Davidson, *Congress in Crisis*, p. 6, expresses this criticism.

27. Robert A. Dahl and Charles E. Lindblom, *Politics, Economics, and Welfare* (New York: Harper and Row, 1963), p. 322.

28. Davidson, *Congress in Crisis*, p. 166.

29. Stephen P. Gibert, "Congress: The First Branch of Government?" *Public Administration Review* 27, no. 2 (June 1967) : 185.

30. Joseph P. Harris, "The Reorganization of Congress," *Public Administration Review* 6, no. 3 (summer 1946): 268.

31. George B. Galloway, *Congressional Reorganization Revisited* (College Park: University of Maryland, 1956), p. 26.

32. Pendleton Herring, *Public Administration and the Public Interest* (New York: McGraw-Hill, 1936).

33. See Robert T. Golembiewski, "Toward New Organization Theories: A Note on 'Staff,'" *Midwest Journal of Political Science* 5, no. 3. (August 1961): 237–259, for a discussion of this.

34. Dale Vinyard, *Congress* (New York: Scribner, 1968), p. 102.

35. Balutis, "Professional Staffing in the New York State Legislature," p. 251.

36. Davidson, *Congress in Crisis,* p. 194.

37. Ibid., p. 112.

38. James J. Heaphey, "Technical Assistance in the Administration of Legislatures," paper presented at the annual meeting of the American Society for Public Administration, New York, March 1972, p. 21.

39. George B. Galloway, *The Legislative Process in Congress* (New York: Crowell, 1953), p. 415.

40. Gladys M. Kammerer, *The Staffing of the Committees of Congress* (Lexington: University of Kentucky Press, 1949).

41. Balutis, "Professional Staffing in the New York State Legislature," p. 48.

42. Davidson, *Congress in Crisis,* p. 167.

43. Donald R. Matthews, *U.S. Senators and Their World* (New York: Vintage, 1960), p. 92.

44. Balutis, "Professional Staffing in the New York State Legislature," pp. 83–90.

45. Dahl and Lindblom, *Politics, Economics, and Welfare,* p. 322.

46. Quoted in Joseph W. Barr, "The U.S. Congress—A Personal View," address to the American Society for Public Administration, Washington, September 1965.

47. A. Mafeje, "Social Scientists, Witches, and Diviners," address delivered to the Institute of Social Studies, The Hague, June 1973.

48. Willoughby, *Principles of Legislative Organization and Administration,* p. 1.

49. Blair and Winnie, "The Forgotten Men of Government," p. 4.

50. Quoted in Balutis, "Professional Staffing in the New York Legislature," p. 97.

51. See Neil MacNeil, "Congress and its Critics," *New York Herald Tribune,* August 17, 1965.

52. Eric Redman, *The Dance of Legislation* (New York: Simon and Schuster, 1973), pp. 16–17.

53. Arthur Maass, "Congress Has Been Maligned," *Washington Post,* March 3, 1963, p. E-3.

54. Davidson, *Congress in Crisis,* p. 66.

55. Ibid., p. 105.

56. See Heaphey, "Technical Assistance in the Administration of Legislatures," p. 20.

57. Franklin L. Burdette, "Congress, the People, and Administration," *Public Administration Review* 24, no. 4 (December 1964): 265. See also Paul F. Abrams, "Legislative Reform: A Question of Reality," *Publius* 4, no. 2 (spring 1974): 129.

58. Heaphey, "Technical Assistance in the Administration of Legislatures," pp. 5–6.

59. Robert Dahl, "The Science of Public Administration," *Public Administration Review* 7, no. 1 (January 1947): 8.

10

Institutional Launches: Recommendations

The study has discovered a broad range of institutional neglect of legislatures within the public administration field. In addition, it has identified some major areas of legislative administrative need and suggested some guidelines for involvement by public administration in those needs. This final chapter considers possible institutional involvement of the field with legislatures, specifically in terms of the literature, schools, and organizations of public administration.

LITERATURE

The record analysis suggests that the public administration literature has been little touched by legislative thought. Since the literature to a considerable degree shapes the thinking or "self-consciousness" of the field, this may be the area of most necessary, and potentially most fruitful, involvement.

Exploration of Potential

The analysis of textbooks in Chapter 1 can serve a consciousness-raising function, for it appears that much of the neglect may have been subliminal. There is frequent recognition of the importance of legislatures, and the typical stated reason for not including legislatures in the writings is "custom," "tradition," or some similarly unexpounded rationale. The time is appropriate for a modification.

The fundamental need is for an engaged appreciation of a systemic perspective of government. Despite the evident importance of the legislature in the administrative system, management concepts and organization theory have not been explicitly or systematically applied to the study of legislatures. As the examination of the record of the field reveals, public administration literature has exhibited a decidedly executive branch orientation, has tended to treat legislatures as a "rival," and has frequently chimed an antilegislative tone. This tilted perspective has existed in spite of expressed recognition in the literature of the significance of legislative bodies. The past neglect thus appears incongruous. Active attention to legislatures should now follow the already acknowledged recognition of their systemic role.

Specifically, public administration textbooks might include a chapter on legislative administration instead of off-handedly dismissing the subject under the illusion that it is covered in other works of the field. The record has revealed that such a chapter would be all the more appropriate precisely because the subject of legislative administration is not adequately addressed elsewhere. Further, a systemic perspective might be better evidenced throughout the textbooks by ameliorating any slanted references to legislatures and by referring to legislatures in appropriate contexts—for example, mentioning the special problems of legislative staffing in chapters on personnel administration.

Second, periodicals of the field could attempt to publish more articles connected with legislative administration. In the post-Watergate milieu, it may be timely for *Public Administration Review* to offer a symposium on legislative administration. Such a move could serve a major consciousness-raising function and might propel the field into greater involvement.

Third, the general and subfield literature of public administration might incorporate legislative concern. Clearly, for example, organization theory and budgetary literature have much to say and gain from such a perspective. Further, various works that are published outside the field but that address legislative management, such as writings by the Citizens Conference on State Legislatures and the Eagleton Institute and other efforts noted in previous chapters, could be used to advantage within the field and considered as part of the literature.

ORGANIZATIONS

Chapter 4 revealed that the American Society for Public Administration (ASPA) has largely ignored legislatures. Unlike the American Political Science Association, ASPA has never had a committee dealing with legislatures, nor has it shown any significant interest through conferences or studies. Yet every scholar consulted in this study indicated a disposition toward ASPA activity on legislatures, and twenty-two of twenty-three legislative staff members favored formation of an ASPA committee or program on legislatures (see Table 10), as did 94 percent of the legislators responding (see Table 11). Indeed, one respondent, the staff director of a legislative committee, commented: "One finds it hard to believe that such a committee [an ASPA committee on legislatures] is not already in existence."

TABLE 10
RESPONSES OF STAFF

Question: "Would you recommend that the American Society for Public Administration form a permanent committee or program specifically dealing with legislatures?"

	Number	Percentage
Yes	22	96
No	1	4

TABLE 11
RESPONSES OF LEGISLATORS

Question: "Do you think the American Society for Public Administration should have a program and committee specifically dealing with legislatures?"

	Number	Percentage
Yes	44	94
No	3	6

Thus, it is the nearly unanimous recommendation of a cross section of scholars, legislators, and legislative staffers that the American Society for Public Administration undertake some program for legislatures, a recommendation to which both the president and the executive director of the society are receptive.

Many of the respondents recommend formation of a substantial program. The staff director of a state legislature wrote: "ASPA should create a section in legislative service administration and welcome staff people who work for State legislatures and Congress." The director of a state legislative commission suggested a more deliberate approach: "I would recommend a temporary committee of ASPA to deal with legislatures—to examine them, their significance in public administration, and to report on whether there should be such a specific committee or program." The chief of a legislative reference bureau urged that this temporary committee explore staff training, data processing needs, office management, and effective utilization of committee work.

Still others advised that initially legislatures be incorporated into the work of an existing ASPA committee, such as that dealing with public policy. Several practitioners recommended development of an interrelationship between ASPA and the National Conference of State Legislatures (NCSL). Specifically, one respondent suggested that ASPA participate in the annual conference of the NCSL through panels and workshops.

Finally, one scholar expressed impatience: "What I wouldn't recommend is a lot of conferences and talk without really doing something about the nitty-gritty." Instead, he suggests that ASPA, through a foundation grant, sponsor a high-level commission on legislative management needs and publish a monograph demonstrating means for administrative improvement.

In any case, the message supports the logical inference of the preceding chapters—namely, that the American Society for Public Administration institutionally should concern itself with legislative administration. In some form, a committee of the society might focus on legislatures. Special studies might be undertaken and monographs published, and ASPA's national conferences might include a broader range of panels on aspects of legislative administration.

SCHOOLS

A somewhat anomalous finding of the present study is that, though schools of public administration have neglected legislatures in their curricula, an overwhelming number of schools responding to queries expressed the belief that legislative administration should be included in academic programs of the field. As Table 12 indicates, twenty-four of twenty-six schools responded affirmatively when asked whether legislative administration should be part of public administration academic study. All academic research arms responding, most of which currently give no attention to legislatures, indicated that public administration research groups should attend to legislatures. Furthermore, though two of the scholars consulted expressed uncertainty, none opposed the suggestion that public administration curricula include study of legislative organization.

TABLE 12
RESPONSES OF SCHOOLS

Question: "In your opinion should academic programs in public administration include study of legislative administration, organization, and process?"

	Number	Percentage
Yes	24	93
No	2	7

Note: The question was answered by the dean, chairman, or director of the public administration programs listed in Table 4.

Similarly, the great majority of legislators and legislative staff favored public administration programs on legislatures (see Tables 13 and 14). One high-ranking staff person pointedly based his opinion on specific experience that "university graduates with public administration training come better equipped to assist a legislature in its information needs than, for instance, sociologists or political scientists." The principal stated reasons for the few negative views expressed were suspicions that there may not be sufficient numbers of jobs in legislatures to warrant widespread academic training [1] (expressed by two legislators) and belief that a political science course on legislative processes is adequate coverage of legislatures for public administration students (expressed by one school).

TABLE 13
RESPONSES OF LEGISLATORS

Question: "Do you think schools of public administration should offer programs on legislatures thus providing you a source of personnel specifically trained for legislative staff positions?"

	Number	Percentage
Yes	37	79
No	10	21

TABLE 14
RESPONSES OF STAFF

Question: "Would you recommend that schools of public administration provide programs specifically on legislatures?"

	Number	Percentage
Yes	21	91
No	2	9

In view of these findings, supported by the analysis of previous chapters, the recommendation warranted is that at least some academic programs in public administration develop a component in legislatures.

To recommend this is not to suggest something previously unpronounced. When George A. Graham, in 1950, urged that students of public administration turn their attention to legislative processes, he noted: "In looking into the legislative process students of administration today are but returning to a problem which was recognized thirty years ago. They were then as interested in legislation as in administration but getting nowhere in one field they concentrated their efforts in the other.

Now the legislative process can no longer be ignored." [2] But, as the record examination has shown, it continued to be ignored, prompting an echo of Graham's exhortation in John Honey's 1967 report on public administration education: "The realities of governmental operations dictate the pursuit of a much broader outlook and indeed of equating public administration with the total governmental process (executive, legislative, and judicial) in both its career and political manifestations." [3]

Various guides for implementation of this recommendation were offered by the scholars, legislators, and staffers consulted. Chief among these were the following:

1. The number and location of schools developing legislative programs should be deliberated. Specifically, several practitioners cautioned that the number of jobs with legislatures will be limited, even after an anticipated surge in staff size is accounted for. "Nevertheless," remarked one legislator, "there will be a sufficient demand to justify some [academic] efforts. Moreover, executive branch administrators could benefit from legislative curricula." Some school officials suggested that only public administration programs located in or near state capitals should develop a legislative curriculum, for reason of both internship and career accessibility.

2. Any programs developed should be "engage"— that is, thoroughly linked with actual legislative operations. This was the most generally expressed recommendation from all those consulted. Nearly all respondents identified an internship or some similar device for "actual contact" with a legislature. Many respondents urged that legislators and staffers be involved in any program development and utilized as guest lecturers. And several respondents commented that any such program should clearly focus on management concerns, not political sci-

ence types of questions: "The principal focus of public administration in studying the legislature should be with the implications for administrative activity and not with, say, how group memberships on the House Education and Labor Committee influence the policy output of federal aid to education." [4]

3. Recognizing the diversity of legislative organization and procedure, programs should maintain a flexible perspective. Some respondents suggested that each program should be tailored according to the legislative system and needs of the state and localities with which the school has linkage. In the words of a legislative staffer, "No one model program will suit every legislature."

Specific course offerings within an academic legislative curriculum were suggested by many respondents. Table 15 lists all courses mentioned, while Table 16 represents the curriculum of the one legislative administration program that is now operative, namely that of State University of New York at Albany.

Finally, it is recommended that research bureaus connected with public administration schools be responsive to legislative administration needs.

Involvement of the field should be empirical, normative, and theoretical. Present knowledge of legislative organizational phenomena is scanty. Empirical study and description of what exists is thus an obvious activity. Normatively, a plethora of issues result from the organizational-political mix that is peculiar to legislatures. How can the public administration field, accustomed to providing practical solutions based on bureaucratic rationality, adapt its skills to requirements of political rationality? In the realm of theory, how can the field maintain consistency with its experience yet demonstrate its utility to legislatures? The questions needing study concern the

TABLE 15
COURSES RECOMMENDED BY SCHOLARS,
LEGISLATORS, AND LEGISLATIVE STAFF

Introduction to Public Administration
American Politics
Intergovernmental Relations
Administrative Law
Public Relations

Legislative Administration Seminar
Legislative Process
Legislative-Executive Relations
Legislative Research
Bill Drafting
Legislative Auditing
Legislative Staffing

Public Finance
Budgeting
Organization Theory
Personnel Administration
Statistics
Computer Technology
Systems Theory
Communications Systems

possible growth of a legislative bureaucracy leading to the substitution of political control by legislative staff instead of by elected officials.[5]

All of the institutional vehicles can contribute to numerous specific areas germane to legislative improvement. The following examples illustrate the variety of questions to which the public administration field can address itself:

How can the representation function of legislatures be strengthened? That is, how can conflicting groups and interests be organizationally accommodated so as to reach a satisfactory balance between the need for rational policy decisions and the need for democratic decision making?

TABLE 16
LEGISLATIVE ADMINISTRATION CURRICULUM
OF STATE UNIVERSITY OF NEW YORK AT ALBANY

Theories and Processes of Public Administration
Public Administration in the Political Process
National Goals and Public Policy
Methods of Research and Reporting *or*
     Legislative Research
Internship
Seminar in Legislative Administration
State Government

One of the following or other appropriate substitution:
Legal Environment of Public Administration
Regulatory Administration
Administrative Law
Law and Social Change

One of the following or other appropriate substitution:
Government and the Economy
Budgetary Systems
Governmental Finance
State-Local Fiscal Relations

One of the following or other appropriate substitution:
Organization and Management
Program Planning and Evaluation
Productivity Seminar
Methods of Public Policy Analysis
Decision Making in Government and Administration
Organizational Behavior

One of the following or other appropriate substitution:
Legislative Behavior
The Legislative Process

One of the following or other appropriate substitution:
American Political Parties
American Political Behavior
New York State and Local Government

How can the making, review, clarification, and revision of policy through legislation, resolutions, reports,

[215]

and so on be improved? What is the relationship between process and product—that is, between legislative management measures and policy-making effectiveness?

How is the "power of the purse" better exercised? What legislative dimensions did PPBS neglect? How can legislative budget making procedures be improved?

How does legislative oversight improve government operations?

Can constituent services be better managed? Are managerial techniques available for facilitating a legislative ombudsman role?

What are the pluses and minuses of alternative legislative management structures—for example, clerk/secretary, leadership staff, joint staff, and so on?

What are the alternatives for staff patterns and utilization?

How can new concepts in organization theory be adapted and enriched by the legislative environment? What are the ramifications of centralization and decentralization?

How are internships best utilized?

What are the information needs of legislatures and how can they be met by computers?

What are the differences in the managerial needs between state and local legislatures?

The field of public administration has the resources to significantly aid in answering these and other questions that are important to improved legislative functioning. Writers and researchers should address them. Schools should note them. ASPA should be concerned with them.

Summary of Recommendations

The following recommendations stem from this study:

1. Public administration textbooks should include a chapter on legislative administration and generally adopt a more systemic perspective of government administration.

2. Legislative scholars and practitioners should submit more management-oriented articles to the *Public Administration Review*, which, in turn, should solicit and publish more pieces concerned with legislative administration.

3. Authors in the public administration field should consider legislatures as both a source of administrative insight and a subject for analysis. In particular, writers on organization theory, budgeting, and program evaluation should include the legislature in their perspectives.

4. Some schools of public administration, particularly those located near state capitals or local legislature centers, should develop courses and programs geared to the personnel and substantive needs of legislative institutions.

5. Public administration research bureaus should bring their resources to bear on the administrative needs of legislatures as well as of the executive.

6. The American Society for Public Administration should sanction a group to investigate alternative means of formally incorporating the area of legislative administration into ASPA organization.

7. Legislative practitioners should participate more in ASPA, at both the local and national levels. In particular, they should deliver papers at national meetings and join panels on the wide variety of administrative subjects pertinent to legislatures.

8. Legislative practitioners should teach courses in schools of public administration and recruit staff from public administration program graduates.

9. Legislatures should turn to ASPA and public administration research bureaus for assistance on matters of administrative improvement.

10. Foundations should award grants for fellowships in the area of legislative administration and for more research aimed at the organizational improvement of legislative bodies.

CONCLUSION

Today the importance of legislatures is increasingly proclaimed and demonstrated at all levels of government on every continent. This study has discovered that public administrationists for years have on one hand been talking of the significance of legislatures and on the other hand avoided demonstrating that recognition. The literature, the schools, and the organizations of the field have, in effect, treated legislatures as though they were unimportant. It is clear that this anomaly merits a metamorphosis.

Not only is it apparent that legislatures are important in themselves, but particularly it should be recognized that they are a key component of a system—of the government system broadly and of the administrative system specifically. If public administrationists rationally seek efficient and effective administration of government, we can no longer isolate the legislature, treat it as an enemy, and function under the illusion that administration is the executive alone. In this age of detente in foreign affairs, legislators and public administrationists ought to join hands in their common domestic affair— good government administration.

Consultations in the process of this study have revealed not only that the time is ripe for alliance but that few can understand why it has taken so long for such a logical suggestion to materialize. It almost appears as though we public administrationists were mesmerized into accepting the notion that legislative administration was not within our scope; and our typical, unexamined basis for exclusion was a remarkably flimsy following of mere custom. As was mentioned, several of our textbook writers even conceded the logic of including legislatures in public administration study, yet quietly deferred to the custom of exclusion.

As reported, a broad cross section of scholars, legislators, and legislative staff say that public administrationists and legislatures should now join together. The need is manifest, the resources exist; and dispositions are favorable. Instead of being a locus, mired in the executive, public administration should be a focus at the service of the entire governmental system.

Heeding the contributions of our two pathfinders, we public administrationists should now adopt the systemic vision of Willoughby and act on the observation of White that "the field of public administration lies where work is to be done." [6] Surely the legislative work is there.

NOTES FOR CHAPTER 10

1. This point is considered later as reason to limit the number of academic programs. However, the objection does overlook the fact that executive agencies increasingly desire legislative liaison officers, positions for which public administration programs on legislatures might prepare students.

2. George A. Graham, "Trends in Teaching of Public Administration," *Public Administration Review* 10, no. 2 (spring 1950) : 74–75.

3. John C. Honey, "A Report: Higher Education for Public Service," *Public Administration Review* 27, no. 4 (November 1967) : 294.

4. Remarked by a high-ranking legislative staffer and echoed by several school officials.

5. For the first real probe of these questions see Abdo Baaklini, "Public Administration and Legislatures: Theoretical and Practical Caveats," a paper presented at the annual meeting of the American Society for Public Administration, Chicago, April, 1975.

6. Leonard D. White, *Introduction to the Study of Public Administration,* 4th ed. (New York: Macmillan, 1955), p. 2.

Appendix A:
Respondents

Questionnaires appearing in Appendix B were sent to public administration scholars, legislators, and legislative staff. Scholars were selected on the basis of personal prominence, institutional location, and age. Of twenty-five queried, eighteen (72 percent) responded. The eighteen listed below represent both the "old guard" and the "young turks" and are affiliated with most of the major public administration schools. The list includes most of the highly recognized scholars in the field today.

Legislators queried were the speaker of the house or assembly of all states, the leadership of the state senates, and several members of the U.S. Congress. Forty-seven of 125 questionnaires (38 percent) were completed. The list of respondents represents all sections of the country, most of the largest and smallest states, and the U.S. Congress.

Appendix A

Legislative staffers were selected on the basis of age, location, and job. Diversity was sought. The twenty-three of the forty-six who responded (50 percent) represent every section of the country, most of the major staff types (committee heads, research directors, and so on), and both young and older observers.

SCHOLARS

Name	Affiliation
Alan K. Campbell	Syracuse University
Marshall E. Dimock	New York University (Emeritus)
James W. Fesler	Yale University
Richard W. Gable	University of California, Davis
Robert T. Golembiewski	University of Georgia
Luther Gulick	Institute of Public Administration
James J. Heaphey	State University of New York at Albany
Keith M. Henderson	State University College at Buffalo
Albert Lepawsky	University of California, Berkeley
Harvey C. Mansfield	Columbia University
John D. Montgomery	Harvard University
Felix A. Nigro	University of Georgia
Joseph Pois	University of Pittsburgh
Don K. Price	Harvard University
Frank P. Sherwood	American Society for Public Administration
Donald C. Stone	University of Pittsburgh
Dwight Waldo	Syracuse University
Aaron Wildavsky	University of California, Berkeley

LEGISLATORS

Name	Affiliation
Stanley W. Akers	Speaker, Arizona House of Representatives
Charles T. Alfano	Minority Leader, Connecticut Senate
Norman C. Anderson	Speaker, Wisconsin Assembly
David M. Bartley	Speaker, Massachusetts House of Representatives

Richard N. Berry	Majority Leader, Maine Senate
Joseph A. Bevilacqua	Speaker, Rhode Island House of Representatives
W. Robert Blair	Speaker, Illinois General Assembly
Richard Bolling	Chairman, Select Committee on Committees, U.S. House of Representatives
Joseph E. Brennan	Minority Leader, Maine Senate
Kermit O. Burrous	Speaker, Indiana House of Representatives
Anthony O. Calabrese	Minority Leader, Ohio Senate
Francis J. Collins	Speaker, Connecticut House of Representatives
Price Daniel, Jr.	Speaker, Texas House of Representatives
Ernest H. Dean	Minority Leader, Utah Senate
Perry B. Duryea	Speaker, New York Assembly
Richard C. Frame	Floor Leader, Pennsylvania Senate
Harold E. Gerke	Speaker, Montana House of Representatives
Joseph C. Harder	Majority Leader, Kansas Senate
John P. Hawkins	Majority Leader, Rhode Island Senate
Richard D. Hewes	Speaker, Maine House of Representatives
Chester R. Hubbard	Minority Leader, West Virginia Senate
Raymond C. Johnson	Majority Leader, Wisconsin Senate
Thomas H. Kean	Minority Leader, New Jersey Assembly
John F. Kirk	Speaker, Delaware House of Representatives
Harold G. Krieger	Minority Leader, Minnesota Senate
Thomas F. Lamb	Majority Leader, Pennsylvania Senate
A. G. Lancione	Speaker, Ohio House of Representatives
David C. Lane	Minority Leader, Florida Senate
C. Warner Litten	Majority Leader, North Dakota Senate

Appendix A

Lewis H. McManus	Speaker, West Virginia House of Delegates
Ned McWherter	Speaker, Tennessee House of Representatives
Jim Moore	Minority Leader, Montana Senate
James E. O'Neil	Speaker, New Hampshire House of Representatives
John F. Parker	Floor Leader, Massachusetts Senate
Cecil A. Partee	Minority Leader, Illinois Senate
William J. Peeler	Majority Leader, Tennessee Senate
B. G. Perry	President, Mississippi Senate
E. C. Pieplow	Minority Leader, South Dakota Senate
F. A. Porter	Majority Leader, New Hampshire Senate
Archie Pozzi, Jr.	Minority Leader, Nevada Senate
Richard F. Proud	Speaker, Nebraska Legislature
Leonard A. Sawyer	Speaker, Washington House of Representatives
Terrell Sessums	Speaker, Florida House of Representatives
W. Armstrong Smith	Minority Leader, Georgia Senate
Jack Steineger	Minority Leader, Kansas Senate
G. W. Turner	Speaker, Arkansas House of Representatives
Robert Vander Laan	Majority Leader, Michigan Senate

LEGISLATIVE STAFF

Name	Position
Albert J. Abrams	Secretary, New York State Senate
Clyde L. Ball	Legislative Services, North Carolina General Assembly
Bunny Van Brunt	Director, Information Division, Florida Legislature
Morris L. Brusett	Legislative Auditor, Montana State Legislature
Dale Cattanach	Director, Legislative Fiscal Bureau, Wisconsin Legislature
Roger H. Davidson	Select Committee on Committees, U.S. House of Representatives

Appendix A

Name	Position
William L. Day	Research Director, Illinois Legislative Council
Mercer M. Doty	Fiscal Research Director, North Carolina General Assembly
Ronald Duncan	Appropriations Committee, Minnesota House of Representatives
Carl N. Everstine	Director of Legislative Reference, Maryland Legislature
Serge Garrison	Legislative Service Bureau, Iowa Legislature
Mark Heinen	Legislative Council, Arizona Legislature
David A. Johnston	Director, Legislative Service Commission, Ohio Legislature
Joseph F. Kyle	Appropriations Committee Staff Director, Florida House of Representatives
Lyle C. Kyle	Director, Legislative Council, Colorado Legislature
C. Emerson Murray	Legislative Council Director, North Dakota Legislature
Thomas L. Neilson	Committee Staff Director, Florida House of Representatives
David Ogle	Executive Director, Joint Committee on Legislative Management, Connecticut General Assembly
A. Alan Post	Joint Legislative Budget Committee, California Legislature
Bonnie Reese	Executive Secretary, Legislative Council, Wisconsin Legislature
T. Thomas Thatcher	Clerk, Michigan House of Representatives
H. Rupert Theobald	Chief, Legislative Reference Bureau, Wisconsin State Legislature
James M. Tinsley	Deputy Legislative State Auditor, Colorado Legislature

Appendix B:
Questionnaires

To Scholars

1. In 1934 W. F. Willoughby wrote *Principles of Legislative Organization and Administration* in the preface of which he argued that administration is as important to legislatures as it is to the bureaucracy and the judiciary. Was Willoughby right? Should the legislative branch as well as the bureaucracy be a central concern of the public administration field?
2. What factors help explain the apparent past neglect of legislatures by the public administration field (schools, organizations, and literature)?
3. Were the field to turn more attention to legislative administrative needs, what considerations should guide the relationship? Are there any particular dangers? How might ASPA act on the matter? How should academic programs incorporate legislative administration?

To Legislators

1. The field of public administration has a thriving national organization and over 100 schools have programs offering

master's and doctoral degrees in public administration. Do you believe the field could be useful to legislatures in

    a. providing skilled staff   yes _____ no _____

    b. assisting in managerial problems   yes _____ no _____

    c. undertaking specific studies   yes _____ no _____

    d. exploring means of adapting
administrative tools to
political realities   yes _____ no _____

    e. educating bureaucrats on
legislative processes   yes _____ no _____

    f. other (specify)_____

2. In your view has the field of public administration in the past abandoned or neglected legislatures?

                  yes _____ no _____

    If yes, do you have any views on why?

3. In your view would increased attention and availability of the field to legislatures be

    a. welcome   yes _____ no _____

    b. useful   yes _____ no _____

    c. dangerous   yes _____ no _____

    d. extremely helpful   yes _____ no _____

    e. undesirable   yes _____ no _____

4. Do you see any problems, dangers, or obstacles to public administration involvement with legislatures?

                  yes _____ no _____

    If yes, specify if possible.

5. Do you think schools of public administration should offer programs on legislatures thus providing you a source of personnel specifically trained for legislative staff positions?

                  yes _____ no _____

    If yes, do you have any suggestions on what such a program or curriculum should include or how is should be developed?

6. Do you think the American Society for Public Administration should have a program and committee specifically dealing with legislatures and available to requests from legislators?

                  yes _____ no _____

7. Any further comments and viewpoints are appreciated.

Appendix B

To Legislative Staff

1. How do you see the past role of the public administration field (schools, organizations, and scholars and practitioners who identify with public administration) in legislative processes? Did the field abandon legislatures? Has it made any significant efforts or contributions that you know of?
2. What role do you think the public administration field could usefully play in legislative improvement? What particular needs of legislatures might the field be helpful in?
3. Do you see any obstacles, dangers, or problems in public administration involvement with legislatures?
4. Would you recommend that the American Society for Public Administration form a permanent committee or program specifically dealing with legislatures?
5. Would you recommend that schools of public administration provide programs specifically on legislatures?
   Do you have any suggestions on design of such a curriculum?

To Schools

1. Does your public administration program currently include any courses on or attention to legislatures? If yes, please specify.
2. Are there any plans to add a legislative element to your program?
3. In your opinion should programs in public administration include study of legislative administration, organization and processes? Why?
4. If yes, how should legislative studies be incorporated? Would you recommend any specific curriculum courses?

To Research Bureaus

1. Has your unit conducted any projects on or for legislatures?
   yes _____ no _____
2. If yes, please describe.
3. If yes, approximately what percentage of your efforts are devoted to:

Appendix B

    legislatures   _____
    executive bureaucracy   _____
    judiciary   _____

4. Do you think public administration research groups should give attention to legislatures?

Appendix C: National Association of Schools of Public Affairs and Administration

MEMBER INSTITUTIONS
as of January 31, 1974

Alabama
Graduate Program in
  Administrative Science
University of Alabama
Huntsville, Ala. 35807

Bureau of Public
  Administration
University of Alabama
University, Ala.

Arizona
Institute of Public
  Administration
Arizona State University
Tempe, Ariz. 85821

Department of Public
  Administration
College of Business and
  Public Administration

University of Arizona
Tucson, Ariz. 85721

California
Political Science Department
California State
  Polytechnic University
Pomona, Calif. 91768

Public Administration
  Program
Department of Political
  Science
California State University,
  Chico
Chico, Calif. 95926

Public Administration
  Program
California State University
Fullerton, Calif. 92634

[231]

Department of Public
Administration
California State University
Hayward, Calif. 94542

Department of Political
Science
California State University
Los Angeles, Calif. 90032

Center of Public Policy and
Administration
California State University
Long Beach, Calif. 90840

School of Business and Public
Administration
California State University
Sacramento, Calif. 95819

MPA Program
California State University
San Jose, Calif. 95192

Graduate School of Public
Administration
Golden Gate University
San Francisco, Calif. 94105

Institute for Local
Self-Government
Berkeley, Calif. 94705

Public Administration
Program
Pepperdine University
Los Angeles, Calif. 90044

School of Public
Administration and
Urban Studies
San Diego State University
San Diego, Calif. 92115

Urban Management Program

Graduate School of Business
Stanford University
Stanford, Calif. 94305

Graduate School of Public
Policy
University of California
Berkeley, Calif. 94720

Department of Political
Science
University of California,
Davis
Davis, Calif. 95616

MPA Program, Political
Science Department
University of California
Los Angeles, Calif. 90024

Graduate School of
Administration
University of California
Riverside, Calif. 92502

School of Public
Administration
University of Southern
California
Los Angeles, Calif. 90007

Colorado
Graduate School of Public
Affairs
University of Colorado
Boulder, Colo. 80302

Delaware
Political Science and Urban
Affairs
University of Delaware
Newark, Del. 19711

Appendix C

District of Columbia
School of Government and
Public Administration
The American University
Washington, D.C. 20016

Department of Public
Administration
School of Government and
Business Administration
George Washington
University
Washington, D.C. 20006

U.S. Department of
Agriculture Graduate
School
Washington, D.C. 20004

Public Administration
Department
School of Business and
Public Administration
Howard University
Washington, D.C. 20001

Florida
MPA Program, College of
Business and Public
Administration
Florida Atlantic University
Boca Raton, Fla. 33432

Graduate Program in
Public Administration
Department of Government
Florida State University
Tallahassee, Fla. 32306

Graduate Program in Public
Affairs and Administration
Nova University
Fort Lauderdale, Fla. 33314

Pubilc Administration
Clearing Service
University of Florida
Gainesville, Fla. 32601

MPA Program, Faculty of
Political Science
University of West Florida
Pensacola, Fla. 32504

Georgia
Department of Political
Science
Georgia Southern College
Statesboro, Ga. 30458

School of Urban Life
Georgia State University
Atlanta, Ga. 30303

Institute of Government
University of Georgia
Athens, Ga. 30601

Hawaii
College of Continuing
Education
University of Hawaii
Honolulu, Hawaii, 96822

Illinois
College of Urban Sciences
University of Illinois at
Chicago Circle
Chicago, Ill. 60680

Department of Public
Administration
Department of Political
Science
University of Illinois
Urbana, Ill. 61801

[233]

Public Administration and
Public Affairs Program
Center for Governmental
Studies
Northern Illinois University
DeKalb, Ill. 60115

Studies in Public
Management
Northwestern School of
Management
Northwestern University
Evanston, Ill. 60201

Graduate Program of
Public Administration
Roosevelt University
Chicago, Ill. 60605

Department of Political
Studies
Sangamon State University
Springfield, Ill. 62708

Department of Government
Southern Illinois University
Carbondale, Ill. 62708

Indiana
Center for Governmental
Services
Indiana State University
Terre Haute, Ind. 47809

School of Public and
Environmental Affairs
Indiana University
Bloomington, Ind. 47401

Iowa
Programs in Public
Administration

Drake University
Des Moines, Iowa 50311

Kansas
MPA Program, Department
of Political Science
University of
Kansas-Lawrence
Lawrence Kans. 66044

Center for Urban Studies
Wichita State University
Wichita, Kans. 67208

Kentucky
Public Affairs Center
Kentucky State University
Frankfort, Ky. 40601

University Public Affairs
Program
Department of Government
College of Business and
Public Administration
Western Kentucky University
Bowling Green, Ky. 42101

Maryland
Department of Government
and Politics
University of Maryland
College Park, Md. 20742

Massachusetts
Kennedy School of
Government
Harvard University
Cambridge, Mass. 02138

Lincoln Filene Center for
Citizenship and Public

Affairs
Tufts University
Medford, Mass. 02155

Department of Political
  Science
University of Massachusetts
Amherst, Mass. 01002

Michigan
MPA Program, Department
  of Political Science
Michigan State University
East Lansing, Mich. 48823

Institute of Public Policy
  Studies
University of Michigan
Ann Arbor, Mich. 48104

Public Administration
  Program
Department of Political
  Science
Wayne State University
Detroit, Mich. 48202

Minnesota
Urban Studies Institute
Mankato State College
Mankato, Minn. 56001

School of Public Affairs
University of Minnesota
Minneapolis, Minn. 55455

Mississippi
Bureau of Governmental
  Research
Department of Political
  Science
University of Mississippi

University, Miss. 38677

Missouri
Division of Advanced Studies
  in Administration and
  Public Affairs
College of Administration
  and Public Affairs
University of
  Missouri-Columbia
Columbia, Mo. 65201

MPA Program, School of
  Administration
University of
  Missouri-Kansas City
Kansas City, Mo. 64110

Center for Urban Programs
St. Louis University
St. Louis, Mo. 63103

Nebraska
Department of Public
  Administration
University of Nebraska
  at Omaha
Omaha, Nebr. 68101

New Jersey
Public Administration
  Institute
College of Business
Fairleigh Dickinson
  University
Rutherford, N.J. 07070

Woodrow Wilson School
Princeton University
Princeton, N.J. 08540

[235]

Public Service Institute
of New Jersey
Princeton, N.J. 08540

New Mexico
Division of Public
Administration
University of New Mexico
Albuquerque, N.M. 87105

New York
School of Business and
Public Administration
Bernard M. Baruch College
City University of New York
New York, N.Y. 10010

Department of Urban Affairs
Hunter College
City University of New York
New York, N.Y. 10021

Graduate Studies
John Jay College of
Criminal Justice
City University of New York
New York, N.Y. 10010

Public Policy and
Administration Program
Cornell University
Ithaca, N.Y. 14850

Institute for Public
Administration
New York, N.Y. 10036

Center for New York City
Affairs
New School for Social
Research
New York, N.Y. 10011

Graduate School of Public

Administration
New York University
New York, N.Y. 10003

Program in Public
Management
Rensselaer Polytechnic
Institute
Troy, N.Y. 12181

Public Administration
Program
Russell Sage College
Albany, N.Y. 12208

Graduate School of Public
Affairs
State University of New York
at Albany
Albany, N.Y. 12203

Public Policy Analysis and
Administration
Department of Political
Science
State University of New York
at Binghamton
Binghamton, N.Y. 13901

Maxwell School of Citizenship
and Public Affairs
Syracuse University
Syracuse, N.Y. 13210

North Carolina
Institute of Policy Sciences
and Public Affairs
Duke University
Durham, N.C.

MPA Program, Department
of Political Science
University of North Carolina
Chapel Hill, N.C. 27514

Ohio
Graduate Program in Public
Management Science
Case Western Reserve
University
Cleveland, Ohio 44106

Graduate Program in
Public Administration
University of Cincinnati
Cincinnati, Ohio 45221

Public Administration
Program
Department of Political
Science
University of Dayton
Dayton, Ohio 45469

Division of Public
Administration
Ohio State University
Columbus, Ohio 43210

Oklahoma
Graduate Program in
Public Administration
University of Oklahoma
Norman, Okla. 73069

Oregon
Division of Public
Administration and
International Development
University of Oregon
Eugene, Ore. 97403

Graduate School of
Administration
Willamette University
Salem, Ore. 97301

Pennsylvania
School of Urban and Public

Affairs
Carnegie-Mellon University
Pittsburgh, Pa. 15213

Institute of Urban
Management
College of Business
Administration
Drexel University
Philadelphia, Pa.

Division of Business and
Public Administration
Pennsylvania State
University
Middletown, Pa. 17057
Capitol Campus

Institute of Public
Administration
Pennsylvania State
University
University Park, Pa. 16802

MPA Program
University of Pennsylvania
Philadelphia, Pa.

Graduate School of Public
and International Affairs
University of Pittsburgh
Pittsburgh, Pa. 15260

Department of Social Sciences
Shippensburg State College
Shippensburg, Pa. 17257

South Carolina
Department of Government
and International Studies
University of South Carolina
Columbia, S.C.

South Dakota
Department of Government

University of South Dakota
Vermillion, S.D. 57069

Tennessee
Department of Political
  Science
East Tennessee State
  University
Johnson City, Tenn. 37601

Institute of Governmental
  Studies and Research
Memphis State University
Memphis, Tenn. 38111

Bureau of Public
  Administration
University of Tennessee
Knoxville, Tenn. 37916

Texas
MPA Program, Political
  Science Department
East Texas State University
Commerce, Tex. 75428

Graduate Program in Public
  Administration
Southern Methodist
  University
Dallas, Tex. 75222

Department of Political
  Science
Southwest Texas State
  University
San Marcos, Tex. 78666

Graduate Program in Public
  Administration
Texas Christian University
Fort Worth, Tex. 76129

Center for Public Service
Texas Tech University
Lubbock, Tex. 79409

Institute of Urban Studies
University of Texas
Arlington, Tex. 76010

LBJ School of Public Affairs
University of Texas
Austin, Tex. 78712

Utah
Institute of Government
  Service
Brigham Young University
Provo, Utah 84601

Virginia
Urban Affairs Program
Virginia Polytechnic
  Institute and State
  University
Blacksburg, Va.

Department of Government
and Foreign Affairs
University of Virginia
Charlottesville, Va. 22901

Federal Executive Institute
Charlottesville, Va.

Washington
School of Business
  Administration
Pacific Lutheran University
Tacoma, Wash. 98447

Graduate School of Public
  Affairs
University of Washington
Seattle, Wash. 98195

West Virginia
MPA Program
West Virginia University
Morgantown, W.Va.

Wisconsin
Public Policy and
   Administration
University of Wisconsin
Madison, Wis. 53706

Canada
Department de science
   politique

Université du Québec
   à Montreal
Montreal 101, P.Q. Canada

School of Public
   Administration
Queen's University
Kingston, Ontario, Canada

Foreign
Graduate Management
   Program
The American University
   in Cairo
Cairo, Egypt

Bibliography

Books

Allen, W. H. *Efficient Democracy*. New York: Dodd, Mead, 1907.

Altshuler, Alan A. *The Politics of the Federal Bureaucracy*. New York: Dodd, Mead, 1968.

Anderson, William, and Gaus, John M. *Research in Public Administration*. Chicago: Public Administration Service, 1945.

Appleby, Paul H. *Big Democracy*. New York: Russell and Russell, 1970.

————. *Morality and Administration*. Baton Rouge: Louisiana State University Press, 1952.

Argyris, Chris. *Personality and Organization*. New York: Harper, 1957.

Baaklini, Abdo I. *Legislatures and Political Development: Lebanon 1840-1970* Durham, N.C.: Duke University Press, forthcoming.

Bailey, Stephen. *Congress Makes a Law*. New York: Columbia University Press, 1950.

Barnard, Chester I. *The Functions of the Executive*. Boston: Harvard University Press, 1938.

Bibliography

Bartholomew, Paul C. *Public Administration*. Totowa, N.J.: Littlefield, 1972.

Bendix, Reinhard. *Max Weber: An Intellectual Portrait*. New York: Bantam, 1967.

Bennis, Warren, *Changing Organizations*. New York: McGraw-Hill, 1966

Bennis, Warren, and Slater, Philip. *The Temporary Society*. New York: Harper and Row, 1968.

Bradford, Gamaliel. *The Lessons of Popular Government*. New York: Macmillan, 1899.

Braibanti, Ralph, ed. *Political and Administrative Development*. Durham, N.C.: Duke University Press, 1969.

Buechner, John C. *Public Administration*. Belmont, Calif.: Dickenson, 1968.

Burns, James M. *Presidential Government*. Boston: Houghton Mifflin, 1965.

Caiden, Gerald. *Administrative Reform*. Chicago: Aldine, 1969.
_____. *The Dynamics of Public Administration*. New York: Holt, Rinehart and Winston, 1971.

Charlesworth, James, ed. *Theory and Practice of Public Administration*. Philadelphia: American Academy, 1968.

Chartock, Alan S., and Berking, Max. *Strengthening the Wisconsin Legislature*. New Brunswick, N.J.: Rutgers University Press, 1970.

Citizens Conference on State Legislatures. *The Sometime Governments*. New York: Bantam, 1971.

Committee for Economic Development. *Making Congress More Effective*. New York: CED, 1970.

Corson, John J., and Harris, Joseph D. *Public Administration in Modern Society*. New York: McGraw-Hill, 1963.

Crick, Bernard. *The American Science of Politics*. Berkeley: University of California Press, 1964.

Culver, Dorothy C. *Legislative Reorganization*. Berkeley, Calif.: Bureau of Public Administration, 1941.

Dahl, Robert A., and Lindblom, Charles E. *Politics, Economics, and Welfare*. New York: Harper and Row, 1953.

Davidson, Roger H.; Kovenock, David M.; and O'Leary, Michael K. *Congress in Crisis*. New York: Hawthorne, 1969.

De Grazia, Alfred, ed. *Congress: The First Branch of Govern-*

ment. Washington, D.C.: American Enterprise Institute, 1966.

Dimock, Marshall E. *Congressional Investigating Committees*. Baltimore: Johns Hopkins University Press, 1929.

Dimock, Marshall E., and Dimock, Gladys O. *Public Administration*. New York: Holt, Rinehart and Winston, 1953.

Downs, Anthony. *Inside Bureaucracy*. Boston: Little, Brown, 1967.

Dunham, Philip, and Fahey, Robert J. *Congress Needs Help*. New York: Random House, 1966.

Fisher, Joel, et al. *The Legislative Process in California*. Washington, D.C.: American Political Science Association, 1973.

Freeman, J. Leiper. *The Political Process: Executive Bureau–Legislative Committee Relations*. New York: Random House, 1965.

Galloway, George B. *Congress at the Crossroads*. New York: Crowell, 1946.

_____. *Congressional Reorganization Revisited*. College Park: University of Maryland Press, 1956.

_____. *The Legislative Process in Congress*. New York: Crowell, 1953.

Gaus, John; White, Leonard D.; and Dimock, Marshall E. *The Frontiers of Public Administration*. New York: Russell, 1936.

Gawthrop, Lewis G. *Administrative Politics and Social Change*. New York: St. Martin's, 1971.

Golembiewski, Robert T.; Gibson, Frank; and Cornog, Geoffrey Y. *Public Administration*. Chicago: Rand McNally, 1966.

Graham, George A. *Education for Public Administration*. Chicago: Public Administration Service, 1941.

Graves, W. Brooke. *Public Administration in a Democratic Society*. Boston: Heath, 1950.

Gross, Bertram M. *The Legislative Struggle*. New York: McGraw-Hill, 1953.

_____. *The Managing of Organizations*. New York: Free Press, 1964.

Gulick, Luther, and Urwick, L., eds. *Papers on the Science of Administration*. New York: Kelley, 1937.

Bibliography

Haines, C. G., and Dimock, M. E., eds. *Essays on the Law and Practice of Governmental Administration.* Baltimore: Johns Hopkins University Press, 1935.

Harris, Joseph D. *Congressional Control of Administration.* Washington, D.C.: Brookings Institution, 1964.

Heady, Ferrel. *Public Administration: A Comparative Perspective.* Englewood Cliffs, N.J.: Prentice-Hall, 1966.

Heaphey, James J., ed. *Legislative Security.* Albany: State University of New York, 1972.

Heaphey, James J., and Baaklini, Abdo I. *Legislative Institution Building.* Beverly Hills, Calif.: Sage, forthcoming.

Heard, Alexander, ed. *State Legislatures in American Politics.* Englewood Cliffs, N.J.: Prentice-Hall, 1966.

Henderson, Keith, *The Emerging Synthesis in American Public Administration.* New York: Asia House, 1966.

Heller, Robert. *Strengthening the Congress.* Washington, D.C.: National Planning Association, 1946.

Herring, E. Pendleton. *Presidential Leadership.* New York: McGraw-Hill, 1940.

_____. *Public Administration and the Public Interest.* New York: McGraw-Hill, 1936.

Herzberg, Donald G., and Rosenthal, Alan, eds. *Strengthening the States: Essays on Legislative Reform.* New York: Doubleday, 1971.

Herzberg, Donald G., and Unruh, Jesse. *Essays on the State Legislative Process.* New York: Holt, Rinehart, and Winston, 1970.

Hollis, Christopher. *Can Parliament Survive?* London: Hollis and Carter, 1949.

Huitt, Ralph K., and Peabody, Robert L., eds. *Congress: Two Decades of Analysis.* New York: Harper and Row, 1969.

Hyneman, Charles. *Bureaucracy in a Democracy.* New York: Harper, 1950.

Institute of Government. *Strengthening the Georgia General Assembly.* Athens, Ga.: University of Georgia Press, 1970.

Jewell, Malcolm E. *The State Legislature. New York:* Random House, 1969.

Jewell, Malcolm E., and Patterson, Samuel C. *The Legislative Process in the United States.* New York: Random House, 1966.

Kammerer, Gladys. *The Staffing of the Committees of Con-*

[244]

gress. Lexington: Kentucky University Press, 1949.

Katz, Daniel, and Kahn, Robert L. *The Social Psychology of Organization.* New York: Wiley, 1966.

Keefe, William J., and Ogul, Morris S. *The American Legislative Process.* Englewood Cliffs, N.J.: Prentice-Hall, 1964.

Kornberg, Allen, and Musolf, Lloyd, eds. *Legislatures in Developmental Perspective.* Durham, N.C.: Duke University Press, 1970.

La Palombara, Joseph, ed. *Bureaucracy and Political Development.* Princeton: Princeton University Press, 1963.

Lee, Eugene C. *The Presiding Officer and Rules Committee in Legislatures of the U.S.* Berkeley, Calif.: Bureau of Public Administration, 1952.

Leighton, Alexander. *The Governing of Men.* Princeton: Princeton University Press, 1945.

Lepawsky, Albert. *Administration.* New York: Knopf, 1952.

Likert, Rensis. *New Patterns of Management.* New York: McGraw-Hill, 1961.

Lowenberg, Gerhard, ed. *Modern Parliaments: Change or Decline.* Chicago: Aldine Atherton, 1971.

McCurdy, Howard E. *Public Administration: A Bibliography.* Washington, D.C.: American University Press, 1973.

McGregor, Douglas. *The Human Side of Enterprise.* New York: McGraw-Hill, 1960.

March, James G. *Handbook of Organizations.* Chicago: Rand McNally, 1965.

March, James G., and Simon, Herbert A. *Organizations.* New York: Wiley, 1958.

Marini, Frank, ed. *Toward a New Public Administration.* Scranton, Pa.: Chandler, 1971.

Matthews, Donald R. *U.S. Senators and Their World.* New York: Vintage, 1960.

Mayo, Elton. *Human Problems of Industrial Civilization.* New York: Viking, 1933.

Millett, John D. *Management in the Public Service.* New York: McGraw-Hill, 1954.

Morstein-Marx, Fritz, ed. *Elements of Public Administration.* Englewood Cliffs, N.J.: Prentice-Hall, 1959.

Mosher, Frederick. *Democracy and the Public Service.* New York: Oxford, 1968.

Bibliography

Mosher, William E., and Kingsley, J. Donald. *Public Personnel Administration*. New York: Harper, 1936.

New Horizons in Public Administration. Montgomery: University of Alabama Press, 1945.

Nigro, Felix A. *Modern Public Administration*. New York: Harper and Row, 1965.

Normanton, E. L. *The Accountability and Audit of Governments*. Manchester, England: University of Manchester Press, 1966.

Ogle, David B. *Strengthening the Connecticut Legislature*. New Brunswick, N.J.: Rutgers University Press, 1970.

Ostrom, Vincent. *The Intellectual Crisis in American Public Administration*. Birmingham: University of Alabama Press, 1973.

Pfiffner, John M., and Presthus, Robert. *Public Administration*. New York: Ronald, 1967.

Reagan, Michael D. *The Administration of Public Policy*. Glenview, Ill.: Scott, Foresman, 1969.

Redford, Emmette S. *Democracy in the Administrative State*. New York: Oxford, 1969.

Redman, Eric. *The Dance of Legislation*. New York: Simon and Schuster, 1973.

Rehfuss, John. *Public Administration as Political Process*. New York: Scribner, 1973.

Rosenthal, Alan. *The Improvement of State Legislatures*. Rutgers, N.Y.: Eagleton Institute, 1971.

Saloma, John S. *Congress and the New Politics*. Boston: Little, Brown, 1969.

Schlesinger, Arthur M. *The Imperial Presidency*. Boston: Houghton Mifflin, 1973.

Selznick, Philip. *Leadership in Administration*. New York: Row, Peterson, 1957.

————. *TVA and the Grass Roots*. Berkeley: University of California Press, 1949.

Sharkansky, Ira. *Public Administration*. Chicago: Markham, 1970.

Siffin, William J. *The Legislative Council in the American States*. Bloomington: Indiana University Press, 1959.

Simon, Herbert. *Administrative Behavior*. New York: Macmillan, 1946.

Simon, Herbert; Smithburg, D. W.; and Thompson, V. A.

Public Administration. New York: Knopf, 1950.

Smith, C. Lynwood. *Strengthening the Florida Legislature.* New Brunswick, N.J.: Rutgers University Press, 1970.

Stahl, O. Glenn. *Public Personnel Administration.* New York: Harper and Row, 1962.

Stein, Harold. *Public Administration and Policy Development.* New York: Harcourt, Brace, 1952.

Swerdlow, Irving, ed. *Development Administration.* Syracuse, N.Y.: Syracuse University Press, 1963.

Tantillo, Charles. *Strengthening the Rhode Island Legislature.* New Brunswick, N.J.: Rutgers University Press, 1968.

Taylor, Frederick W. *The Principles of Scientific Management.* New York: Harper and Row, 1911.

Tead, Ordway. *The Art of Administration.* New York: McGraw-Hill, 1951

Thayer, Frederick C. *An End to Hierarchy.* New York: Franklin Watts, 1973.

Thomas, James D. *The Alabama Legislature.* University of Alabama: Bureau of Public Administration, 1974.

Truman, D. B., ed. *Congress and America's Future.* Englewood Cliffs, N.J.: Prentice-Hall, 1965.

Tugwell, Rexford, and Cronin, Thomas. *The Presidency Reappraised.* New York: Praeger, 1974.

Uveges, Joseph A. *Dimensions of Public Administration.* Boston: Holbrook, 1971.

Vinyard, Dale. *Congress.* New York: Scribner, 1968.

Waldo, Dwight. *The Administrative State.* New York: Ronald, 1948.

———. *Public Administration in a Time of Turbulence.* Scranton Pa.: Chandler, 1971.

———. *The Study of Public Administration.* Garden City, N.Y.: Doubleday, 1955.

Walker, Harvey. *Public Administration in the United States.* New York: Farrar and Rinehart, 1937.

Weaver, Warren. *Both Your Houses.* New York: Praeger, 1972.

Weick, Karl. *The Social Psychology of Organizations.* Reading, Pa.: Addison-Wesley, 1969.

Weidner, Edward W. *Technical Assistance in Public Administration Overseas.* Chicago: Public Administration Service, 1964.

Bibliography

White, Leonard D. *Introduction to the Study of Public Administration*. New York: Macmillan, 1926.

Wholey, Joseph S., et al. *Federal Evaluation Policy*. Washington, D.C.: Urban Institute, 1970.

Wildavsky, Aaron. *The Politics of the Budgetary Process*. Boston: Little, Brown, 1964.

Willoughby, William F. *Principles of Legislative Organization and Administration*. Washington, D.C.: Brookings Institution, 1934.

————. *Principles of Public Administration*. Washington, D.C.: Brookings Institution, 1927.

Wise, Sidney. *The Legislative Process in Pennsylvania*. Washington, D.C.: American Political Science Association, 1971.

Wolin, Sheldon. *Politics and Vision*. Boston: Little, Brown, 1960.

Young, Roland. *This Is Congress*. New York: McGraw-Hill, 1943.

Zeller, Belle, ed. *American State Legislatures*. New York: Crowell, 1954.

ARTICLES

Appleby, Paul. "Making Sense Out of Things in General." *Public Administration Review* 22, no. 4 (December 1962): 178–179.

Bennett, David. "From Teapot Dome to Watergate." *Syracuse Alumni Review* (spring 1974): 3–5.

Bolling, Richard. "Committees in the House." *Annals of the American Academy* 411 (January 1974): 1–4.

Bone, Hugh A. "On Understanding Legislatures." *Public Administration Review* 15, no. 2 (spring 1955): 121–126.

Brock, Bill. "Committees in the Senate." *Annals of the American Academy* 411 (January 1974): 15–18.

Burdette, Franklin L. "Congress, the People, and Administration." *Public Administration Review* 29, no. 4 (fall 1964): 259–264.

Butler, Warren. "Administering Congress: The Role of Staff." *Public Administration Review* 26, no. 1 (January 1966): 3–13.

Bibliography

Casselman, Robert C. "Massachusetts Revisited." *Public Administration Review* 33, no. 2 (March–April 1973): 129–135.

Cochrane, James D. "Partisan Aspects of Congressional Committee Staffing." *Western Political Quarterly* 17, no. 2 (June 1964): 338–348.

Crane, Edgar. "Legislative Service Agencies." In *The Book of the States*. Lexington: Council of State Governments, 1971, pp. 75–79.

Dahl, Robert. "The Science of Public Administration." *Public Administration Review* 7, no. 1 (January 1947): 1–10.

Engelbert, Ernest A. "The Content of PAR, 1940–1952." *Public Administration Review* 13, no. 4 (autumn 1953): 257–261.

Engelbert, Ernest, and Wernimont, Kenneth. "Administrative Aspects of the Federal-State Legislative Relationship." *Public Administration Review* 2, no. 2 (spring 1942): 126–138.

Etzioni, Amitai. "How Congress May Learn." *Science* (January 1968): 170–172.

Fainsod, Merle. "The Presidency and Congress." *Public Administration Review* 11, no. 2 (spring 1951): 119–123.

Froman, Lewis A. "Organization Theory and the Explanation of Important Characteristics of Congress." *American Political Science Review* 62, no. 2 (June 1968): 518–526.

Gaus, John M. "Trends in the Theory of Public Administration." *Public Administration Review* 10, no. 3 (Summer 1950): 161–168.

Gibert, Stephen P. "Congress: The First Branch of Government." *Public Administration Review* 27, no. 2 (June 1967): 178–189.

Glaser, Comstock. "Managing Committee Work in a Large Organization." *Public Administration Review* 1, no. 3 (spring 1941): 249–256.

Golembiewski, Robert T. "Toward New Organization Theories: A Note on 'Staff.'" *Midwest Journal of Political Science* 5, no. 3 (August 1961): 237–259.

Graham, George A. "Trends in Teaching Public Administration." *Public Administration Review* 10, no. 3 (spring 1950): 69–77.

Bibliography

Harris, Joseph P. "Needed Reforms in the Federal Budget System." *Public Administration Review* 12, no. 4 (autumn 1952): 242–250.

————. "The Reorganization of Congress." *Public Administration Review* 6, no. 3 (summer 1946): 267–282.

Heaphey, James J. "Legislative Staffing: Organizational and Philosophical Considerations." In James J. Heaphey and Alan Balutis, eds. *Legislative Staffing: A Comparative Perspective*. Beverly Hills, Calif. Sage Press, 1975.

Hilling, Helen C. "Public Administration: Study, Practice, Profession." *Public Administration Review* 26, no. 4 (December 1966): 319–326.

Honey, John C. "A Report: Higher Education in the Public Service." *Public Administration Review* 27, no. 4 (November 1967): 294–321.

————. "Research in Public Administration." *Public Administration Review* 17, no. 4 (autumn 1957): 238–241.

Hubbell, Robert L. "Techniques for Making Committees Effective." *Public Administration Review* 6, no. 4 (autumn 1946): 348–353.

Illchman, Warren F. "Rising Expectations and the Revolution in Development Administration." *Public Administration Review* 25, no. 4 (December 1965): 314–328.

Jackson, Henry M. "Environmental Policy and the Congress." *Public Administration Review* 28, no. 4 (July–August 1968): 303–305.

Kammerer, Gladys M. "Legislative Oversight of Administration in Kentucky." *Public Administration Review* 10, no. 3 (summer 1950): 169–175.

————. "The Administration of Congress." *Public Administration Review* 9, no. 3 (summer 1949): 175–182.

Kenton, Carolyn L. "Modern Legislative Staffing." *State Government* 47, no. 3 (spring 1974): 169.

Kerr, James R. "Congress and Space: Overview or Oversight?" *Public Administration Review* 25, no. 3 (September 1960): 185–192.

Koehler, Curtis T. "Policy Development and Legislative Oversight in Council Manager Cities." *Public Administration Review* 33, no. 5 (September–October 1973): 433–442.

[250]

Bibliography

Kurtz, Karl T. "Legislative Organization and Services." *Book of the States*. Lexington, Ky.: Council of State Governments, 1974: 53–92.

Lawton, Frederick J. "Legislative-Executive Relationships in Budgeting." *Public Administration Review* 13, no. 3 (summer 1953): 169–176.

Long, Norton. "Bureaucracy and Constitutionalism." *American Political Science Review* 46, no. 3 (September 1952): 808–818.

————. "Power and Administration." *Public Administration Review* 9, no. 4 (December 1949): 260–270.

Lowell, A. L. "Expert Administrators in Popular Government." *American Political Science Review* 8, no. 1 (February 1913): 45–62.

Lyden, Fremont J. "Congressional Decision Making and PPB." *Public Administration Review* 30, no. 2 (March–April 1970): 167–168.

MacMahon, Arthur. "Congressional Oversight of Administration." *Political Science Quarterly* 58, no. 2 (July 1943): 184–189.

Mansfield, Harvey C. "The Legislative Veto." *Public Administration Review* 1, no. 3 (spring 1941): 281–285.

Millett, John, and Rogers, Lindsay. "The Legislative Veto." *Public Administration Review* 1, no. 2 (winter 1941): 175–189.

Mosher, W. E. "The Making of a Public Servant." *National Municipal Review* 28, no. 2 (June 1939): 416–419.

Olson, David M. "Studies in American Legislative Process." *Public Administration Review* 28, no. 3 (May–June 1968): 280–286.

Patterson, Kenneth D. "Legislative Budget Review." *Public Administration Review* 24, no. 1 (January 1969): 7–12.

Patterson, Samuel C. "Legislative Research and Legislative Reform." *Publius* 4, no. 2 (spring 1974): 112–117.

————. "The Professional Staffs of Congressional Committees." *Administrative Science Quarterly* 15, no. 1 (March 1970): 22–38.

Pipe, G. Russell. "Congressional Liaison." *Public Administration Review* 26, no. 1 (January 1966): 14–19.

Bibliography

Polsby, Nelson N. "A Note on the President's Modest Proposal." *Public Administration Review* 26, no. 3 (September 1966): 156–159.

_____. "The Institutionalization of the U.S. House of Representatives." *American Political Science Review* 62, no. 1 (March 1968): 144–168.

Riggs, Fred W. "Relearning an Old Lesson." *Public Administration Review* 25, no. 1 (March 1965): 70–79.

Roback, Herbert. "Congress in Transition." *ASPA News and Views* 24, no. 2 (February 1974): 3–5.

Rosenthal, Alan. "Contemporary Research on State Legislatures." *Political Science and State and Local Government.* Washington, D.C.: American Political Science Association, 1973, pp. 55–86.

Sayre, Wallace S. "Premises of Public Administration: Past and Emerging." *Public Administration Review* 18, no. 2 (spring 1958): 101–105.

_____. "Trends of a Decade in Administrative Values." *Public Administration Review* 11, no. 1 (winter 1951): 1–7.

Schaeffer, Wendall G. "Management in the Judiciary." *Public Administration Review* 13, no. 2 (spring 1953): 89–93.

Scher, Seymour. "Conditions for Legislative Control." *Journal of Politics* 25, no. 3 (August 1963): 526–531.

Schick, Allen. "A Death in the Bureaucracy." *Public Administration Review* 33, no. 2 (March–April 1973): 146–156.

_____. "Review and Evaluation Can Focus Light on Legislative Reform." National Conference of State Legislative Leaders *Annual,* 1971.

Schneier, Edward. "The Intelligence of Congress." *Annals of the American Academy* 387 (January 1970): 15–18.

Schten, Edward V. "Administration and Legislative Research." *Public Administration Review* 23, no. 2 (June 1963): 81–87.

Seidman, Harold. "New Aspects for Attention." *Public Administration Review* 30, no. 3 (May–June): 272–274.

Smith, Alexander. "Information and Intelligence for Congress." *Annals of the American Academy* 289 (September 1953): 112–116.

Bibliography

Smith, Harold D. "The Budget as an Instrument of Legislative Control." *Public Administration Review* 4, no. 3 (summer 1944): 181–188.

Strang, Michael L. "The Case for the Citizen Legislator." *State Government* 47, no. 3 (spring 1974): 135 ff.

Sundquist, James L. "Reflections on Watergate: Lessons for Public Administration." *Public Administration Review* 34, no. 5 (September–October 1974): 453–461.

Waldo, Dwight. "The Administrative State Revisited." *Public Administration Review* 25, no. 1 (March 1965): 21–30.

_____. "Developments in Public Administration" *Annals of the American Academy* 404 (November 1972): 217–245. 217–245.

_____. "Public Administration and Culture." In Roscoe Martin, *Public Administration and Democracy*. Syracuse, N.Y.: Syracuse University Press, 1965.

_____. "Scope of the Theory of Public Administration." In James Charlesworth, *Theory and Practice of Public Administration*. Philadelphia: American Academy, 1968.

Wilson, Woodrow. "The Study of Administration." *Political Science Quarterly* 2, no. 2 (June 1887): 197–222.

Worthley, John A. "Legislatures and Political Development: The Congress of Micronesia." *Western Political Quarterly* 27, no. 4 (December, 1973): 675–685.

Young, Roland. "Legislative Reform." *Public Administration Review* 8, no. 2 (spring 1948): 141–146.

PROFESSIONAL PAPERS, DISSERTATIONS, AND DOCUMENTS

Baaklini, Abdo I. "Legislative Staffing Patterns in Developing Countries." Paper presented at the annual meeting of the American Society for Public Administration, Los Angeles, April 1973.

_____. "Legislatures and Public Administration: Theoretical and Practical Caveats." Paper presented at the annual meeting of the American Society for Public Administration, Chicago, April 1975.

_____. "Legislatures in Developing Countries: Myths and Realities." Paper presented at the annual meeting of the

Bibliography

Society for International Development, San Jose, Costa Rica, 1973.

Balk, Walter, "Decision Constructs and the Politics of Productivity." Paper presented at the annual meeting of the New York Political Science Association, Albany, March 1973.

Balutis, Alan P. "Professional Staffing in the New York State Legislature." Doctoral dissertation, State University of New York at Albany, 1973.

Brown, Brack. "Lessons from Foreign Administrative Experience." Paper presented at the annual meeting of the American Society for Public Administration, Syracuse, New York, May 1974.

Citizens Conference on State Legislatures. Annual Reports, 1968–1974.

Davis, Raymond G. "Strategies for Studying Legislative Staff: An Organization Theory Model." Paper presented at the annual meeting of the Southwestern Political Science Association, Dallas, March 1974.

Heaphey, James J. "Technical Assistance in the Administration of Legislatures." Paper presented at the annual meeting of the American Society for Public Administration, New York, March 1972.

Joint Congressional Committee on the Organization of Congress. Report 1414. Final Report. 89th Congress, 1966.

New York State Joint Legislative Committee on Legislative Methods, Practices, Procedures, and Expenditures. *Legislative Document No. 31.* Albany: Williams Press, 1946.

Ohio Legislative Service Commission. *Legislative Services, Facilities, and Procedures.* Staff Research Report No. 81, December 1966.

Pereira, Eduardo. "Legislative Reform in Brazil." Paper presented at the annual meeting of the Society for International Development, San Jose, Costa Rica, February 1973.

Poschman, Gene S. "The Images of Organization, Pluralism, and Community in American Social Science Literature on the Legislature." Doctoral dissertation, University of California at Berkeley, 1970.

Soares, Rosinethe M. "Legislative Reform in Brazil." Paper presented at the annual meeting of the National Legislative Conference, Chicago, August 1973.

Bibliography

Urban Institute. "The Forgotten Men of Government: Local Legislatures." Working paper, Washington, 1972.

U.S. Congress. *Panel Discussions Before the Select Committee on Committees*. Washington, D.C.: U.S. Government Printing Office, 1973.

Name Index

Subject Index

About the Author

John A. Worthley is presently research associate, Comparative Development Studies Center, and deputy director, New York State Legislative Internship Program, Albany, New York. In the former position, the author's research projects were aimed at the legislative improvement of the Congress of Brazil, the New York State Senate, and the Clinton (New York) County Legislature. He is now involved with the recruitment, selection, supervision, and evaluation of interns for the state senate. As a naval officer, he wrote and revised U.S. Navy correspondence courses on management and administration. As Chief Executive Officer of Military Sealift Command in the Far East, his responsibilities included the fiscal administration of a million dollar budget, the administration of contracts and activity in ocean transportation between the Department of Defense and civilian shipping companies, supervision of numerous support personnel, public relations, and logistics planning.

He has taught undergraduate courses in organizational theory and comparative administration at SUNY at Albany, as well as preparing a systematic evaluation of their graduate curriculum. He was also involved in similar work at the University of Guam. He received his A.B. (Political Science) from College of the Holy Cross, Worcester, Massachusetts; M.A. (International Relations) from the University of Virginia, Charlottesville; and Ph.D. (Public Administration) from the State University of New York, Albany.

The author has had articles published in *Public Administration Review*, *Public Administration* (Ireland), *Western Political Quarterly*, and *Current Municipal Problems*.